EDWARDIAN ENGLAND
A.D. 1901–1910

EDWARDIAN ENGLAND

A.D. 1901–1910

A SERIES OF LECTURES DELIVERED AT KING'S COLLEGE,
UNIVERSITY OF LONDON, DURING THE SESSION 1932–3

Edited by

F. J. C. Hearnshaw, M.A., LL.D.

*Fellow of King's College and Professor of Medieval History in
the University of London*

Essay Index Reprint Series

Originally published by:
ERNEST BENN LIMITED

BOOKS FOR LIBRARIES PRESS, INC.
Freeport, New York

First Published 1933
Reprinted 1968

LIBRARY OF CONGRESS CATALOG CARD NUMBER:
68-22097

PRINTED IN THE UNITED STATES OF AMERICA

PREFACE

For eight consecutive years the public lectures arranged by the History Department of King's College dealt with social and political ideas, covering the whole period from the early Middle Ages to the Victorian Era, and treating of thinkers so far removed from one another in outlook as well as time as St. Augustine and Herbert Spencer. When, however, with the death of Spencer in 1903, the Edwardian Age was reached it was felt that it would be difficult to continue the series. To do so would necessarily involve the treatment of writers still alive, some of whom might feel disposed to attend the lectures and express dissent from the interpretations of their expositors. It was, therefore, decided to discontinue the series on social and political ideas and to offer a course on the Edwardian Age broader and more comprehensive in scope. The present volume is the result. It is hoped that as many aspects of the important decade under review have been dealt with as could be expected in a course of ten lectures.

Most of the lectures have been written by members of the staff of King's College. Three, however, have been contributed by distinguished visitors, and the College is exceedingly grateful to the Dean of Exeter (formerly Dean of King's College), Professor Lascelles Abercrombie, and Professor H. Levy for their generous and invaluable aid.

The attempt to interpret a period so recent as the Edwardian decade has presented peculiar difficulty. The materials necessary for a final judgment are not always available, nor is it easy to approach such as are accessible with the detachment desirable in a historian. Hence it will be found that the opinions of the various lecturers do not always coincide. No effort whatever has been made to secure harmony except in bare statements of fact.

5

At first it was intended to append a book-list to each lecture. The difficulty, however, of compiling satisfactory lists of reasonable compass proved to be insuperable. Much of the source-material for the reign of King Edward VII has still to be sought in newspapers, magazines, and unpublished collections of letters. Among printed books, however, the following have proved to be particularly valuable :—Sir Sidney Lee's *King Edward VII*, M. E. Halévy's Epilogue (1895–1914) to his monumental *History of the English People in the Nineteenth Century*, Mr. R. H. Gretton's *Modern History of the English People*, the *British Documents on the Origins of the War*, Vols. i–vii, and *Die Grosse Politik*, especially Vols. xx, xxv, xxvi.

F. J. C. HEARNSHAW.

KING'S COLLEGE.
14th February, 1933.

CONTENTS

I

The Edwardian Decade

[1901–1910]

The Edwardian era opens with the death of Queen Victoria and closes with the outbreak of the Great War. For though Edward VII died in 1910, the England over which he reigned continued without change till the call to arms turned the world upside down. Close to us in time as is the opening decade of the twentieth century, we stand already upon the further shore, and look back with a certain cool detachment on an age that has passed away.

No one would seriously claim that King Edward meant so much to his people as his mother had meant to generations of Victorians. That she reigned for sixty-four years and he for nine was not the sole nor indeed the principal cause. There was a deeper reason : both as a ruler and as a human being he was of smaller stature. At his accession to the throne in his sixtieth year he was generally regarded, at home and abroad, as rather a light weight. Allowances were freely made for his unfortunate training, and the Queen's stubborn refusal to take him into partnership met the censure it deserved. But temperament cuts deeper than circumstance, and the new ruler was neither universally respected nor deeply beloved. The tireless industry, the dignity and the massive austerity of Victoria had set a standard which her son seemed unlikely to maintain. Despite his good abilities, his social gifts and his kindly heart, there was a shaking of heads when the longest reign in English history came to a close. Would he, or would he not, prove himself worthy of his glorious heritage ?

That he rose to the occasion is the verdict of his official biographer, a judgment confirmed on the whole by his people and the world. Had Lord Esher received the mandate, as

9

he desired, we should possess a portrait as well as a record. Sir Sidney Lee did his best with an unfamiliar theme, and his volumes, though lacking colour and distinction, are indispensable. They must be supplemented, however, by the more intimate testimony of friends such as Lord Redes-dale and Baron Eckardstein, and a mass of evidence, both personal and political, is still to come. In the fulness of time we must hope for a companion to the masterpiece of Lytton Strachey.

The new ruler possessed two dominating interests, society and foreign affairs. Since the death of the Prince Consort the Queen had withdrawn behind her widow's veil, and the social life of the upper classes had revolved round Sandring-ham and Marlborough House. The Court now awoke from its winter sleep, for the King loved happy faces and good cheer, and the gracious charm of Queen Alexandra won every heart. No British sovereign since Elizabeth paid so many visits to the great country houses, and none was more assiduous at the race-course. Pleasure-hunting, however, no longer interfered with the conscientious discharge of his duties. Every move in the diplomatic game was followed with eager interest, and his Continental journeys assumed a new political significance. The belief, still widely held abroad, that he fashioned British policy is a legend ; but he was by no means a mere fly on the wheel. He read the more important dispatches with care, and his knowledge of the men who were making history all over the world surpassed that of any of his ministers. His share in facilitating the reconciliation with France in 1903 was a memorable achievement. His touch, however, was not always equally sure ; and the suspicions aroused by his travels, however unfounded, suggest that a constitutional monarch is better at home.

In domestic politics the King showed scarcely more interest than in the government of the Church, and he was speedily bored by attempted explanations of legislative schemes. He shared the dislike of Liberalism prevalent among the

upper classes, and the Radicalism represented by Mr. Lloyd
George filled him with alarm. He could never understand
the feeling of repugnance aroused by his meetings with the
Tsar in 1908 and 1909, and he equally failed to realize the
angry impatience which culminated in the Veto Bill of 1911.
Yet, though a Conservative, he was never a Die-hard, and
his personal relations to the statesmen of his time were
unaffected by his party sympathies. The Order of Merit,
which he founded, was carefully and impartially bestowed.
Arthur Balfour was too highbrow for his taste, and he was
far more at ease in the company of Campbell-Bannerman,
the shrewdest and most genial of men. Next to the Premier
his favourites in the Liberal team were Lord Carrington,
the friend of his childhood, Haldane, who could get on with
everybody, and John Burns, in his own line a racy *raconteur*.
Asquith was never a *persona grata*, and Grey inspired more
confidence than affection. None of these men felt the slightest
interest in sport or cared for the so-called smart set, and the
King's closest friends were outside politics. That he played
his royal part so well was in some degree due to the unselfish
sagacity of his private secretary, Lord Knollys. Though a
less imposing and less memorable figure than his mother,
the prestige of the British monarchy was undimmed when
the succession passed from King Edward to his son.

By far the most important event of the Edwardian era was
the abandonment of our policy of isolation, and it deserves
to be treated in some detail. Since the fall of Napoleon we
had kept our hands free, determining our attitude to every
question as it arose in the light of our national interests.
The strongest navy in the world guaranteed the security of
our coasts, and the rivalries of the Powers ruled out the danger
of irresistible coalitions. Even when the South African war
revealed that we had scarcely a friend in the world, Salisbury
saw no reason to alter the course of the ship. When Chamberlain and Lansdowne pointed to the perils of isolation and
favoured a working partnership with Germany, the veteran

Premier replied that in his judgment the risks of such an association outweighed its advantages. But Salisbury was the last Foreign Secretary of the old school, and a younger generation was ready for a change.

The substitution of Continentalism for isolation was the result of circumstances rather than of deliberate choice. Since the completion of the Trans-Siberian line and the seizure of Port Arthur in 1898, a collision between Russia and Japan was in the logic of events, and when the former cast covetous eyes on Corea the conflict was within sight. A month or two after the accession of Edward VII Japan broached the project of an alliance, and in January, 1902, a treaty was signed. Its specific object was to keep the ring in the event of a Russo-Japanese war, Great Britain undertaking to intervene if her ally found herself at grips with more than a single foe. The benefit to ourselves was to be sought in averting the military and commercial domination of the Far East by a Power with whom, ever since the Crimean war, we had been on the worst possible terms. The Prime Minister, now a tired old man on the eve of resignation, accepted the departure without enthusiasm ; but despite a few warning voices in the press, the partnership with Japan was welcomed as strengthening our position in Asia by the winning of a powerful friend.

In the summer of 1903 a second approach was made to us from a quarter nearer home. With the conclusion of the struggle in South Africa warmer breezes began to blow between Paris and London. The Dreyfus case was settled, the memory of Fashoda was growing dim, and Chamberlain's eyes were no longer riveted on Berlin. King Edward's sojourn in Paris in the spring of 1903 broke the ice, and when President Loubet returned the visit he was accompanied by Delcassé. As the object of the Japanese advances had been to save Corea from the claws of the Russian bear, so the purpose of the French Foreign Minister was to secure a free hand for his country in Morocco. There was at that stage

no thought on either side of a diplomatic partnership covering
the whole field of international affairs. The negotiations,
however, were soon ranging over the entire colonial empires
of the two Powers. The core of the agreement signed in
April, 1904, was the recognition by France of our position
in Egypt and our promise of diplomatic support for French
ambitions in Morocco. Critics in both countries argued
that their own negotiators had got the worst of the bargain ;
but to most observers the scales seemed to hang fairly level
in the air. The relief to British statesmen at cleaning the
scribbled slate was immense, and warnings as to the long-
range implications even of a limited partnership were uttered
by Rosebery alone.

The rapprochement with France would have been
welcomed in any case, for the friction had been an intolerable
nuisance since our occupation of Egypt in 1882. But it
was doubly desirable in view of our steadily worsening
relations with Berlin. Chamberlain's independent discussions
of an alliance in 1898 and 1899, and Lansdowne's official
negotiations of 1901, had revealed the impossibility of
bridging the gulf. In view of the unsleeping hostility of
France and Russia many Englishmen at the turn of the
century would have been glad of a powerful friend in the
interest of the Balance of Power. Bülow and Holstein,
however, fearing that an alliance with Great Britain would
involve a break and possibly a war with Russia, desired to
spread the risk by inviting us to join the Triple Alliance.
Such a scheme of unlimited liability made no appeal, and
from the end of 1901, when discussions came to a close, the
two countries drifted rapidly apart. The co-operation of the
Governments in the coercion of Venezuela was widely
resented, and Lansdowne's desire to share in the making of
the Bagdad railway was frustrated by an outcry in the press.
Meanwhile Germany was building up a formidable fleet.
We may date the beginning of our apprehensions, not from
the passing of the navy laws of 1898 and 1900, but from the

visit of King Edward and Lord Selborne to Kiel in 1904. The launching of the Dreadnought in 1905 opened a new and dramatic phase of the struggle. The rivalry in the North Sea only became a nightmare in 1908 ; but it played its part in the determination of British policy during the Moroccan crisis of 1905–6.

Delcassé's plan of turning Morocco into a second Tunis required for its success the preliminary assent of the Powers chiefly concerned. He proceeded to win Italy by recognizing her claim to Tripoli, Great Britain by accepting our occupation of Egypt, and Spain by a secret treaty of conditional partition. He made no corresponding attempt to buy off the opposition of Germany, on the ground that she was not a Mediterranean Power. Yet Germany was a signatory of the Treaty of Madrid, she had concluded a commercial treaty with Morocco, and her nationals were busy with plans for the development of its mineral resources. Of still greater importance was the elementary fact that she was a formidable neighbour, equally solicitous of her dignity as a Great Power and of the prospects of her overseas trade. Delcassé's omission to secure the good will of Berlin by the same process of bargain as that by which he had secured the assent of Rome, London, and Madrid, destroys his title to be a statesman of the first rank. He was playing with fire at a time when, as his colleagues were forced to remind him, France was in no condition to face a German attack.

Delcassé's cardinal mistake turned our treaty assurance of diplomatic support into a risky obligation. Germany had as good a legal right to be consulted about the status of Morocco as ourselves, and at the opening of 1905, when the French campaign of penetration was being launched, in strident tones she called a halt. Lansdowne's desire for close consultation was misinterpreted by Delcassé into a promise of armed support, on the strength of which he proposed to decline the summons to a conference. He was thrown over by the Rouvier Cabinet, and the danger of war passed away.

But the brief crisis had taught both France and Germany to believe that we should take an active part in a struggle, and indeed Lansdowne informed the German Ambassador of his personal opinion that in the event of a conflict about Morocco we should intervene. The Treaty of 1904 removed the grounds of enmity between England and France. The crisis of 1905 created the *Entente Cordiale* and inaugurated a working partnership which extended far beyond the meridian of Tangier and Fez.

When Grey succeeded Lansdowne as Foreign Secretary at the close of 1905 we were already deeply pledged to France; and now that the Moroccan question was to be fought out at the Algeciras Conference the French asked for assurances of military support. We refused. But Grey reiterated Lansdowne's personal warning to the German Ambassador, while British and French military and naval experts were authorized to work out plans for co-operation if the British Government ever decided to join in a Franco-German war. This momentous departure has been sharply criticized; but one step led to another and, in January, 1906, it was difficult if not impossible to draw back. The implications of the Treaty of 1904 were becoming apparent. We had gained a powerful friend, but we had at the same time entangled ourselves in her age-long feud with her neighbour beyond the Rhine. When the Conference of Algeciras ended, though the expert conversations were unknown even to the majority of the Cabinet, it looked as if we were already, in everything but name, the allies of France.

Our moral support of Japan during the desperate conflict in the Far East filled Russia with anger; the firing on our fishermen in the North Sea brought the two countries to the verge of war; and the Pact of Björkö registered the high-watermark of the Tsar's Anglophobia. But with the signing of the Treaty of Portsmouth the atmosphere quickly changed. The Björkö Pact was cancelled; Russia co-operated with us at Algeciras in eager support of France; and with the substitution of Izvolski for Lamsdorff as Foreign Minister a sharp turn was given to the helm. Already in the autumn of 1903 the Russian Ambassador had broached the subject of a rapprochement to Lansdowne, and had met with a sympathetic response. The task was inherited by Grey, who carried it through with conviction and zeal.

Anglo-Russian friction in the Far East had been eliminated by the victories of Japan, and the problem of the Near East was multilateral. Our negotiations were, therefore, confined to the Middle East, and after prolonged discussions the Anglo-Russian Convention was signed in August, 1907. For Russia the main object was to procure a free hand in northern Persia, for Great Britain to obtain security for the Indian frontier. British concessions in Persia were accordingly balanced against Russian sacrifices in Tibet and Afghanistan. The settlement, which was denounced by Curzon as a humiliating surrender, was defended by Grey and Morley as the utmost that could be obtained. The importance of the Treaty, however, lay far less in its details than in the fact of its conclusion. With Russia as with France the cleaning of the slate was followed by co-operation over the whole diplomatic field, beginning with Macedonia, for whose unhappy inhabitants Lansdowne and Grey had laboured as disinterestedly as for the victims of King Leopold's Congo misrule. The visit of King Edward to Reval in June, 1908, completed what the Convention had begun. The hostility of half a century rolled away, and the Triple Entente faced the Triple Alliance on the chessboard of Europe. Henceforth Great Britain, for good or evil, was a Continental Power.

The meeting at Reval, where Macedonian reform was a leading topic of discussion, gave the signal for the Young Turk revolt, which in turn induced Aehrenthal to annex Bosnia and Herzegovina in October, 1908. That Izvolski had consented in principle, in return for a free hand in the Straits, was a secret, and loud was the outcry in Downing Street and Balmoral at the breach of the Treaty of Berlin.

But while the Kaiser stood in shining armour behind his Austrian ally, Russia was still too debilitated by the Japanese War for more than a platonic response to the appeal of her Serbian protégé. Moreover, Izvolski was muzzled by the guilty secret which Aehrenthal, if provoked too far, was determined to reveal. For six months the Bosnian crisis kept Europe on the rack ; but there could only be one end to a dispute in which the Central Powers were ready to fight and the Triple Entente was not. The capitulation of Russia to a diplomatic ultimatum from Berlin in March, 1909, seemed a triumph for Aehrenthal ; but her dramatic humiliation rankled in Slav hearts, and common resentment of his action tightened the bonds between Great Britain and her friends. Henceforth the Triple Entente was a close working partnership, though Russian policy in Persia was impossible for us to approve.

Our quarrel with Austria was soon over, but meanwhile the Anglo-German antagonism steadily increased. The lull of nearly two years which followed the Conference of Algeciras ended in 1908, which revealed the disastrous effects of the Tirpitz policy. The letter to Lord Tweedmouth let loose a tempest of vituperation, and Sir Charles Hardinge's historic conversation with the Kaiser at Cronberg in August proved that an agreed limitation of shipbuilding was unacceptable at Berlin. September brought the Casablanca crisis, and November the *Daily Telegraph* interview. A momentary *détente* occurred at the opening of 1909 with the King's visit to Berlin and the Moroccan Agreement between Germany and France. But the false rumour of secret acceleration of the German navy programme led to a panic which was reflected in the laying down of eight Dreadnoughts in a single year ; and the drastic step by which the Bosnian crisis was ended intensified Grey's distaste for the forcible methods of the Wilhelmstrasse.

When Bethmann succeeded Bülow in June, 1909, he at once endeavoured to bridge the yawning gulf. His sincerity

B

was beyond cavil, but the task was hopeless from the first. Negotiations lasting nearly three years established the fact that Germany declined to diminish her naval programme and that Great Britain refused to tie her hands or alienate her friends by a formula of neutrality. When the King died the Triple Entente was firmly established, and our estrangement from Germany was complete. Our old rivals had been turned into friends, and our old friends had become potential foes. Was our position weaker or stronger in 1910 than in 1901 ? Was Continentalism a wiser policy than isolation ? We may answer these difficult questions as we will. In the critical year 1908 Lord Roberts solemnly appealed to his countrymen to adopt compulsory service as the only means of preserving our heritage against a German attack. His prescription was rejected not only by the Government but by the leaders of the Opposition, but his campaign helped to keep the European situation before the public eye. We were aware that peace was at the mercy of a hazard, and that at any moment the dreaded avalanche might descend upon our heads. Armaments were piling up, and at the Second Hague Conference in 1907 the vital question was ruled out in advance. It was in vain that Norman Angell, in the most widely read book of the Edwardian era, argued that under modern conditions war did not pay. The conception of unfettered national sovereignty and of force as an instrument of policy was too firmly entrenched to be dislodged by anything short of a cataclysm. An unorganized world drifted steadily towards its doom. As the skies darkened, it was some consolation to remember the growing cordiality of our relations with the United States, due in large measure to our great ambassadors Pauncefote and Bryce.

The Edwardian era witnessed momentous changes within the Empire no less than in the field of foreign affairs. The South African war was ended on terms which the Dutch farmers could accept without dishonour, and in a few years the Transvaal and Orange River Colony were granted autonomy. The courageous generosity of the act struck the imagination of the world, and the far-sighted statesmanship of Campbell-Bannerman and his colleagues was vindicated in 1914. The two Dutch communities quickly joined Cape Colony and Natal in a united South Africa, with a constitution hammered out by themselves. Under the guidance of Botha and Smuts the new Dominion became a pillar of the British Empire, and the South African question, which had embittered our politics for a generation, passed into history.

The second outstanding event in our Imperial history was the advance towards Indian self-government. For seven years Curzon had laboured with matchless devotion for the country that he loved ; but he was the last of the Viceroys of the old school. His successor, Minto, a man of smaller calibre but more elastic mind, realized that India was growing up, and that the old methods of paternal autocracy were out of date. The same discovery was made in Whitehall when John Morley entered on his memorable quinquennium at the India Office in 1905. The Morley-Minto reforms, in the shaping of which Gokhale, the wisest of Indian statesmen, took an active part, reached the Statute-book in 1908. Their main feature was the expansion of the Provincial Councils ; but the most significant departure was the appointment of Indians on the Viceroy's executive and on the Council of the Secretary of State. Apprehensions that they might betray the *arcana imperii* were brushed aside, and the experiment proved a conspicuous success. It was particularly important thus to display our confidence in Indian statesmen at a time when sharp repressive measures were being employed in combating revolutionary unrest. The Conservative Viceroy and the Liberal Minister worked in perfect harmony, and their joint achievement launched the greatest of our Dependencies on the road that winds slowly upwards towards Dominion status. In Egypt the nationalist ferment that had accumulated during Cromer's long dictatorship

burst forth on the eve of his departure, and proved once
again that material prosperity is no preservative against
political discontent.

In the field of domestic politics the opening decade of
the century witnessed both virulent controversy and valuable
reforms.   The greatest achievements of the Conservative
administration were Balfour's Education Act of 1902, which
abolished the School Boards and placed denominational
schools on the rates ; Wyndham's Land Purchase Act of
1903, which completed the transformation of the tenantry
of Ireland into peasant proprietors ; and the Committee
of Imperial Defence. The outstanding reforms of the Liberal
Ministry, which took office at the end of 1905, were Haldane's
creation of a General Staff, an Expeditionary Force and a
Territorial Army, and the inauguration of Old Age Pensions
in 1908. Less spectacular but no less useful were the creation
of Trade Boards for sweated industries, the legislation for
the care of children, and the establishment of Labour
Exchanges ; and Mr. Birrell's Catholic University solved
a problem which had baffled his predecessors in the Irish
Office.   Fisher's epoch-making reforms at the Admiralty,
which included the concentration and the modernization
of the fleet, received unstinted support from his political
chiefs, who belonged to both the historic parties in the state.

Though excellent constructive work was accomplished
by both sides in turn, the surface of the waters was ruffled
by frequent storms. No sooner had the passions of the South
African War died down than the raising of the Protectionist
banner by Chamberlain rent his party in twain. Votes for
Women provided a still more explosive issue, for both parties
were divided on the demand put forth by the constitutionalists
under Mrs. Fawcett and the militants of the Pankhurst school.
A third problem, which, like the others, only found its solution
after the death of the King, arose with the Liberal victory
of 1906.   During the Gladstone-Rosebery Administration
of 1892–5 the House of Lords had been on reasonably strong

ground in playing havoc with the measures of a fragile government. But though they were now confronted with the largest
majority won by any party since the Reform Bill, they
proceeded to act in exactly the same way. The Education
Bill, the principal measure of 1906, was wrecked; the
Licensing Bill, the principal measure of 1908, was rejected;
and, to crown all, the Lloyd George Budget of 1909, with its
taxes on the unearned increment of land, was thrown out.
The challenge was immediately taken up. The election of
January, 1910, secured the passage of the Budget; and the
December election of the same year procured authority to
limit the veto of the Upper House in ordinary legislation
and to forbid its interference with measures of finance. The
Parliament Act was a milestone in our constitutional history
and a fresh symbol of the march of democratic ideas.

While passions ran high between the two historic parties
of the state, a third party was gradually forcing its way
towards the centre of the political stage. The election of thirty
Labour members in 1906 was the second stage of a process
which began with the arrival of Keir Hardie at Westminster
in 1892. Among the leading figures in the influential little
group were Keir Hardie, Ramsay MacDonald, Philip
Snowden, Arthur Henderson, David Shackleton, and George
Barnes, who quickly won and kept the ear of the House.
It was the political flowering of the Trade Union Movement,
and in those early days it was almost entirely a movement of
the manual workers. But it contained a few Intellectuals,
such as Ramsay MacDonald, who preached a gospel of
evolutionary Socialism, and Snowden, who made our flesh
creep with visions of income tax at five shillings in the pound.
Nine times out of ten the Labour members voted in the
Government lobby, and they were generally regarded as the
left wing of the progressive army rather than as serious
competitors for the control of the state. The Liberal party
was shedding its Victorian individualism, and the co-operation
of the Labour group quickened the pace of social reform.

In their preference for direct over indirect taxation they were at one.

As the tide of democracy advanced the Press became a factor of ever greater significance in our national life. Stead's best days were over, but Fleet Street was dazzled by the rapidity of Northcliffe's ascent, and in 1908 the founder of the *Daily Mail* secured the controlling influence in *The Times*. Scarcely less sensational was the rise of Arthur Pearson, who enlisted the *Daily Express* in the service of Tariff Reform. The Liberal gospel was preached with apostolic fervour in the *Daily News* with George Cadbury as proprietor and A. G. Gardiner in the editorial chair. The *Daily Chronicle* under Robert Donald was a shade less radical ; Alfred Spender spoke for the right wing of the party in the balanced leaders of the *Westminster Gazette* ; and many Liberals found their spiritual home in the *Manchester Guardian*, the distinguished organ of C. P. Scott. The Chamberlain brand of democratic Imperialism was voiced by Mr. Garvin in *The Observer* and the *Pall Mall Gazette*. St. Loe Strachey steered an independent course in *The Spectator*, challenging his own party on Protection and chastising the Socialist taint in Liberal bills. Massingham, perhaps the most brilliant journalist of his time, made *The Nation* the organ of Gladstonian Liberalism abroad and Lloyd George Radicalism at home. No editor in England could boast such a staff as that which he gathered round him, and which included Brailsford and Masterman, Leonard Hobhouse, John Hobson and Henry Nevinson.

In the Edwardian era the wealth and the well-being of the British Isles rapidly increased. Unemployment was relatively small, and every class shared in the growing prosperity of the world. The Tariff Reform campaign was a failure for the simple reason that there seemed to be no need for a change. Wages rose, savings accumulated, hours decreased, the national health improved. The work of the County Councils began to tell. A minimum standard for every citizen was the goal of the best minds of all parties and every school of thought. The recognition of social solidarity which had begun to dawn in the later decades of the Victorian era grew apace. Life became richer in amenities, more decent, more humane. Applying the maxim of Robert Lowe, " We must educate our masters," we multiplied scholarships and founded new Universities in Sheffield and Bristol, Liverpool and Leeds. The academic curriculum was widened by the recognition of new studies and the endowment of new chairs. Colonial, American, and German students trooped to Oxford under the will of the romantic Empire-builder Cecil Rhodes. In secondary education we still lagged behind Germany ; but we had little cause to be ashamed of our elementary schools.

We were moving in the right direction, but there were plenty of dark shadows in the sky. Agriculture had failed to keep pace with industry, and we became ever more dependent on foreign sources for our supplies of food. Human beings still rotted in the slums, which Garden Cities and Town Planning, two excellent innovations, were powerless to remove. Millions of lives were dwarfed and stunted by lack of opportunity and lack of means. I well remember the interest excited by Seebohm Rowntree's study of industrial conditions in York, by Chiozza Money's *Riches and Poverty*, by Charles Masterman's *The Condition of England*, and by the Anti-sweating Exhibition of 1906. We had thought too exclusively of production, too little of distribution. Such challenges to complacency, following on the grim revelations of Charles Booth, reminded us that we were only just beginning to build Jerusalem in England's green and pleasant land.

The opening decade of the new century witnessed changes in the realm of thought not less momentous than among the busy haunts of men. The influence of the·Churches began to decline, church-going ceased to be a social convention, belief in the miraculous wilted away, and widening horizons undermined the authority of the creeds. But the old mechanistic interpretations of life and the universe were also losing their hold. The human spirit was feeling its way towards a larger synthesis, among the ministry and the laity alike. The success of the *Hibbert Journal*, under the skilful guidance of Dr. Jacks, revealed a widespread interest in the study of religions. We all read William James's *Varieties of Religious Experience*, and Oliver Lodge's reconciliations of religion and science brought comfort to many troubled souls. Fundamentalism in England died with Spurgeon, and young men were occasionally ordained who rejected the Virgin birth. The Anglican Church was fortunate in possessing an archbishop so cautious and wide-minded as Davidson, a moderator rather than a leader, who realized that the Establishment could survive by comprehensiveness alone. Very different was the policy of Pius X, the saintly peasant in the Vatican, who drove the Catholic Modernists bag and baggage out of the Church. Loisy became a Professor at the Collège de France, and Father Tyrrell's brilliant career was cut short by his early death. His friend and counsellor Baron von Hügel, the greatest Catholic thinker of his time, once remarked to me with a smile that he too would have got into trouble had he been a priest.

In the domain of philosophy we can affix no single label to the Edwardian era. The empiricism of the mid-Victorians had been driven out of the Universities in the closing decades of the nineteenth century by Green and the Cairds, Bradley and Bosanquet, McTaggart and James Ward. But Hegelian idealism had now to fight for its life as rival teachers began to raise their heads. The New Realism of Bertrand Russell, the Pragmatism and Pluralism of William James, the *élan vital* of Bergson, however widely they differed from each other, agreed in rejecting the intellectualism of their predecessors. The most arresting study of the things which are unseen was made in Frederick Myers' majestic volumes on *Human Personality and its Survival*. In a neighbouring section of the vast field of the moral sciences Freud's researches in psychology opened up new lines of thought for students all over the world. Graham Wallas's penetrating dissection of *Human Nature in Politics* gave an impetus to social psychology ; and Leonard Hobhouse, one of the most universal thinkers of his age, described Mind and Morals in Evolution.

The greatest triumphs of science at the opening of the century were achieved in the realm of chemistry and physics. Mme Curie isolated the element of radium. The pioneering work of J. J. Thomson was carried forward by Rutherford, who taught us that the atom was itself a tiny solar system, with electrons flying round a central nucleus, the number varying with every element. In Germany still more startling discoveries were afoot ; for the quantum theory dates from 1901 and the beginnings of relativity go back to 1905, though the work of Planck and Einstein was little known till after the war. A new chapter in biological studies was opened when Bateson and Punnett disinterred the discoveries of Mendel, and built their researches into heredity on the foundations he had laid. In the region of applied science the motor revolutionized transport, the submarine turned the conditions of naval warfare upside down, the range of wireless telegraphy was enlarged, and the conquest of the air was begun. Since the coming of railways and steamships two generations before, no such dramatic advance had occurred in harnessing the forces of nature to the service of man. The cinema provided a new instrument of education and entertainment. Our knowledge of the earth on which we live was enriched by Peary's conquest of the North Pole and Amundsen's of the South, and by the Younghusband expedition to Lhassa, the Forbidden City on the highlands of Tibet.

The literature of a decade could hardly be expected to compare in quantity with that of the whole Victorian era, and in poetry at any rate we must confess to a qualitative decline. Swinburne lived on at Putney, an extinct volcano ; Francis Thompson was a mental and physical wreck ; Kipling lost the thrilling inspiration of his youth ; Sir William Watson and Stephen Phillips ceased to charm ; Alfred Austin as Poet Laureate was a bad joke ; and Robert Bridges, his successor in that dignifi d office, seemed rather an expert in philology than a foun.ain of melodious verse. Perhaps Yeats alone maintained the promise of his youth. In drama and fiction, on the other hand, work of a high order was produced. Hardy's *Dynasts*, though too long for the stage, is a masterpiece in execution and design, accurate in its rendering of the Napoleonic epic and impressive in its philosophic depth. In a lighter vein the plays of Bernard Shaw, with their scintillating dialogue and their paradoxical thrusts, took the world by storm. His career as a playwright dates from the nineteenth century ; but it was with *Man and Superman* and *John Bull's Other Island* that he began to win recognition as the greatest of our playwrights since Sheridan. Most of his pieces had a message or a purpose ; but he was more of a satirist and less of a preacher than Galsworthy, whose *Silver Box*, *Justice*, and *Strife* were eloquent pleas for the under-dog. Barrie was at the height of his powers, and *Peter Pan* went straight to the heart of the nation. At the Abbey Theatre in Dublin a rich feast was spread, with Synge's *Playboy of the Western World* as its choicest dish.

With Galsworthy and Arnold Bennett, Conrad and Wells the art of fiction displayed something of the inspiration of the palmy Victorian days. In its broad sweep, its rich humanity and its penetrating insight the chronicles of the Forsyte family claim the first place. *Tono Bungay* and the *New Macchiavelli* were the greatest imaginative creations of Wells' astonishing career. In his *Old Wives' Tale* Arnold Bennett produced a novel likely to endure, and his trilogy of the Five Towns depicted the drab life of the lower middle classes of industrial England with the pitiless realism of a Dutch interior. In *Typhoon* and *Nostromo* Conrad continued his loving interpretation of the sea. Kipling recaptured something of his early appeal in *Kim*. Samuel Butler's *The Way of all Flesh*, that savage satire on family life, though published in 1904, belongs to the Victorian epoch, for it had been written twenty years before. William de Morgan, potter and artist, astonished his friends by turning to fiction in old age and producing *Joseph Vance* and its successors.

Edwardian England contributed little of primary importance to the world's treasure-house of art. In painting Sargent drew steadily ahead of his competitors, and the landscapes of his closing years were not unworthy of the portraits of his prime. The most popular architect of the time was Aston Webb, to whom we owe imposing structures in South Kensington and The Mall. *The Dream of Gerontius*, followed by *The Apostles*, placed Elgar at the head of British composers, and Stanford and Hubert Parry were not very far behind. Coleridge-Taylor never repeated the success of *Hiawatha*, though he tried his hand again and again. A new source of delight was opened up by the Promenade Concerts under the inspiring leadership of Sir Henry Wood.

The advance of scholarship is happily less dependent on individual genius than literature or art. The foundation of the British Academy in 1902, in large measure due to the determination of Balfour and Haldane, provided a recognized centre for learning, like the Royal Society for science and the Royal Academy for art. Steady progress continued to be made in the reconstruction and interpretation of the life of mankind by the anthropologist, the archæologist and the historian. The most dramatic enrichment of our knowledge of the ancient world was due to Sir Arthur Evans, whose unwearying labours disinterred the various phases of Minoan civilization at Cnossus in Crete. No single historical work equalled in importance and utility the *Cambridge Modern History*, Lord Acton's posthumous child, which was adopted and brought up by Sir Adolphus Ward. Among the more memorable individual achievements of British scholarship we may recall Sir James Frazer's *Totemism*, a worthy sequel to the *Golden Bough* ; George Trevelyan's superb Garibaldian epic ; *The History of Local Government* by Sidney and Beatrice Webb ; and Lord Cromer's authoritative treatise on Modern Egypt. The death of Maitland, the greatest of our legal historians, was an irreparable blow to medieval studies. In the sphere of political biography, in which our country excels, Morley's *Gladstone* and Winston Churchill's brilliant tribute to his father claim first place.

Let me attempt a few closing reflections on the Edwardian decade. In comparison with the spacious Victorian days we note a waning of authority, both as a steadying and a fettering influence. The crown, the aristocracy, the churches, even the bourgeoisie, counted for less. Society widened its bounds. Conventions and tabus began to lose their hold. There was less reverence and also less solemn hypocrisy. Young women found opportunities of self-realization such as they had never known before, and corresponding facilities for going astray. The chaperon vanished like a ghost at sunrise. Parents learned to drive the family cart with a lighter rein. Prudery diminished without moral standards becoming perceptibly relaxed. Drunkenness continued its slow decline. In social intercourse there was less starch, less boredom, less pretence. The *tempo* of life quickened, though there was as much of restlessness as of *joie de vivre*. Not every one knew how to use his or her new-found liberties. The hunt for pleasure or distraction found fresh outlets in the week-end habit, in the growth of night-clubs, in the craving for bridge. To superficial observers it seemed as if Edwardian England cared more for sport than for the graver aspects of life, as if she was becoming forgetful of her duties and unmindful of her risks. Such critics were looking through the wrong end of the telescope, for despite our frivolities we remained sound in wind and limb. When the call came in 1914 it was answered by an alert and united nation, ready for the supreme sacrifice in defence of principles dearer than life itself.

G. P. GOOCH.

II

King Edward VII

I

The monarchy has played very different parts during successive periods of English history. In Anglo-Saxon times it was the nucleus round which the numerous and various tribes of Teutonic settlers in southern Britain attained to some sort of constitutional unity. But the Anglo-Saxon monarchy remained weak, reaching the nadir of its impotence under Edward the Confessor. The Norman conquest effected a striking change : William I was as strong as his saintly predecessor had been feeble, and within a very few years from his coming he centralized the administration, asserting the royal authority over both feudal nobles and ultramontane clergy. For some six hundred years (1066–1642) the monarchy maintained itself as the centre and mainspring of government. The king ruled as well as reigned. He was the source of legislation ; the head of the executive ; the fountain of justice ; the well of honour ; the representative both of national sovereignty and of divine majesty. He was invested with an impressive panoply of royal prerogatives ; he was set apart from his subjects and protected by a formidable code of treason laws ; he was exalted and dignified by the ritual of an increasingly gorgeous ceremonial.

The early English monarchy attained its apogee under the two great Tudors, Henry VIII and his daughter Elizabeth. Their ill-starred successors, the Scottish Stuarts, misunderstanding the English people, failing to comprehend the nature of the English constitution, and filled with illusions respecting the English Church, rapidly precipitated a rebellion and a revolution. For fifty years (1642–92) the balance of power in

the administration of the country oscillated violently from
side to side, from monarchy to oligarchy and back again ;
but finally, under William III, the centre of gravity shifted
from the Crown to the landed aristocracy, who constituted
the House of Lords and dominated the House of Commons.
From 1692 to 1832 was the period of the rule of the Whig
nobility—the " Venetian Oligarchy ", later held up to execration in the great novels of Benjamin Disraeli. It is notable,
however, that even in this period of aristocratic sovereignty
the royal prerogatives were not in theory diminished. The
king's powers remained intact ; but the channels through
which they could be exercised were restricted. The king
was more and more compelled—mainly by reason of his
financial necessities—to act through responsible ministers,
into whose hands more and more of effective authority passed.
Nevertheless, an active and resolute monarch remained a
potent person in the constitution. William III, for example,
energetically conducted and controlled the foreign policy
of England during the decade 1692–1702. So, too, during
the double-decade 1760–80, in domestic affairs, was the
will of George III of dominant influence and importance.
After 1780, however, the royal power steadily declined. The
insanity of George III, the infamy of George IV, the infantile
imbecility of William IV, combined to bring the kingship
into hatred or contempt. Republicanism, stimulated by the
teaching and example of France, became prevalent ; and in
1837 it seemed very doubtful whether the institution of
monarchy would continue to be maintained at all in Great
Britain and Ireland. The coronation of Queen Victoria was
almost apologetic in its simplicity. Confident predictions
were made that never again would Westminster Abbey see
the ceremony repeated.

The long and glorious reign of Victoria, however, witnessed
a remarkable rehabilitation of the monarchy. On the one hand,
the young queen, under the influence of her masterful uncle,
Leopold, king of the Belgians, showed a strong determination

to exercise to the full all the effective prerogatives that remained to her. On the other hand, she won the respect of her ministers by her devotion to duty and by the soundness of her judgment ; while at the same time she also speedily established herself in the affections of her people by the simplicity and purity of her character, by her wealth of sympathy, and by her natural kindliness and goodness. Her personal influence grew as her reign progressed, until, at the close of the nineteenth century, she stood eminent above all possible rivals in the reverence of her subjects, the loyalty of the peoples of her widespread dominions, and the respect of the nations of the world.

Queen Victoria lived and reigned during a period of unprecedented social and political change. Five years before her accession the first Reform Act had broken the power of the " Venetian Oligarchy " that had governed England since the revolution of 1688. During the reign two further franchise laws—Disraeli's of 1867 and Gladstone's of 1884—definitely transferred state-sovereignty from the nobility to the democracy. Thus the queen was faced by the novel and difficult task of demonstrating to the world that a monarchy, distinctly more than merely titular, is compatible with constitutional government, and that a king or queen can be an invaluable adjunct to a system in which the ultimate control rests with the many-headed multitude. She performed her task to perfection, and passed on to her son and heir, King Edward VII, a splendid heritage of dignity and influence.

II

Albert Edward, Prince of Wales, was in his sixtieth year when his mother's death, on 22nd January, 1901, placed the crown upon his head. Never before had an heir-apparent in England had to wait so long for his succession. Rarely, moreover, had anyone been compelled to endure so severe an apprenticeship to his prospective profession. Almost from the moment of his birth (November 9th, 1841) he had been treated by his parents as a public institution, and made the subject of endless conferences and memoranda. In particular the prince consort, most conscientious and humourless of men, together with the Prince's *fidus Achates*, Stockmar, most pedantic and impracticable of academic bores, had burdened his early existence with educational and disciplinary programmes of the most portentous ponderousness. For the whole of his sixty years, indeed, he had been subjected to restrictions and disabilities which, had he been less dutiful and amiable, would have goaded him to violent rebellion. The story of these sixty years is a deplorable record of mistaken pedagogy, misapplied authority, and misdirected suspicion. From the point of view of the victimized prince— who remained " Bertie " to the end—it is a lamentable tale of repressed energies, thwarted desires, crushed talents, frustrated ambitions, prohibited opportunities. Had his powers in their prime been allowed full fruition in their proper spheres, he might, during the last quarter of the nineteenth century, have modified for permanent good the whole subsequent course of English, Irish, and Indian history. As it was they found a less propitious outlet in such places as Tranby Croft and Epsom Downs. These sixty years of apprenticeship, however, lie outside the scope of this lecture. Hence they must not be treated in detail. Nevertheless, they may not be wholly ignored. For the greatness of King Edward's all-too-brief reign cannot be fully appreciated unless it is displayed against the dark background of his previous protracted servitude.

These sixty years of the prince's servitude are divisible into three equal periods, the punctuating events being the death of the prince consort in 1861, of Disraeli in 1881, and of the queen in 1901. The first was the period of severe tutelage ; the second, of severe repression ; the third, of severe maternal disapproval.

1st Period, 1841-61

When, on 25th January, 1842, the prince was baptized by Archbishop Howley, the queen remarked in her diary " Little Albert behaved so well ". This was one of the rare occasions, if not actually the last occasion, on which Her Majesty felt it possible to express unqualified approbation of her son's conduct. From that time onward, stern discipline on the one side, instinctive resistance and resentment on the other, caused ever-increasing friction and unhappiness. A less judicious and more oppressive system of education than that applied to the infant prince it would be scarcely possible to conceive. Based on the erroneous Lockian psychology, which regarded the human mind as a *tabula rasa* whereon any desired characters could be impressed, it aimed at converting its victim into an encyclopædia that should epitomize the learning of the age, and a paragon that should serve as a model of religion and virtue to the rising generation. Stockmar's ideal, derived from the well-meaning King Leopold of Belgium, was the negative one of preventing Albert Edward from following the undutiful and baneful course pursued by the previous possessor of the title " Prince of Wales ", namely, the profligate, partisan, and prodigal last of the four Georges. Hence the young prince, segregated from boys of his own age, was beset with elderly governesses, venerable clergymen, superior officers, erudite professors, and other fully-developed products of Hanoverian civilization. Never left alone, never suffered to go his own way, he was stuffed with miscellaneous information in which he had not the slightest interest ; compelled to do things that he intensely disliked ; debarred from all games such as cricket and football ; prevented from seeing anyone not specially selected for him as suitable. Even on his seventeenth birthday (1858), when he was gazetted as an honorary colonel and made a Knight of the Garter, he received a memorandum, signed by both the queen and the prince consort, one section of which ran :—

"You are placed under the supervision and guidance of a
governor selected from among the members of the aristocracy
and the superior officers of the army. . . . The equeries
will take and receive their orders from the Governor.
You will never leave the house without reporting
yourself, and he will settle who is to accompany you, and will
give general directions as to the disposition of the day."

He was sent for brief uncoördinated spells of study to
the universities of Edinburgh (1859), Oxford (1860), and
Cambridge (1861) ; but in none of them was he allowed to
mingle with the undergraduates or to participate in the life
of the place. He was kept aloof in donnish isolation, and
constantly crammed by specialists with useful (i.e. for him
useless) information. Some slight relief did he secure from
the dull monotony of incessant tuition when he was sent
—although, of course, with the full complement of governors
and equeries—during successive vacations, to Rome, in
order to study archæology (1859) ; to Canada and the
United States, in order to perform his first public functions
(1860) ; and to Ireland, in order to undergo military training
(1861). His first taste of diluted liberty was exhilarating ;
his first draught of social popularity intoxicating ; his first
experience of falling in love embarrassing and alarming.
He realized that he was a person of some importance when
he witnessed the American republicans struggling to secure
as relics the fowl-bones that he left on his plate, the cigar-
ends that he threw away, and the water in which he had
washed.

But always on his return from the qualified freedom of
the vacations he was driven back to the coercion and restraint
of tutors and lecturers. In his twentieth year he began
spasmodically to rebel, and occasional terrific outbursts of
passion signalized the fact that suppressed individuality
was getting beyond control. It was in order to deal with
such an emotional eruption in the autumn of 1861 that the
prince consort, when seriously unwell, made the journey to
Cambridge which led to his untimely death, at the age of
42, on 14th December of that year.

2nd Period, 1861–81

The fact that Queen Victoria must have held her eldest son in some measure responsible for the premature and lamentable death of the prince consort may perhaps in part account for the severe disfavour with which she regarded him and his doings for the remainder of her life. But, apart from that, the queen shared her deceased husband's profound dissatisfaction with the fruits of the young prince's long-continued and intensive education. He knew little of the contents of books ; when he attempted to write he displayed an infantile literary incapacity. Of the knowledge that the prince had gained by intercourse with men, and of his growing power of felicitous speech the queen took little count. She came to the conclusion that her eldest son, by reason of his lack of learning, his tendency to injudicious talk, his apparent want of seriousness, and his general untrustworthiness, was unfit to take any place in the public service. Sub-consciously, moreover, she was probably jealous of a possible rival in the popular regard, and also fearful lest Albert Edward should follow the example of the eighteenth century princes and become an intolerable nuisance to his parent. The English constitution is defective in that it makes no provision either for the political training or for the permanent employment of the heir-apparent. And when an heir-apparent has to wait sixty years for his succession to his inheritance this defect is a grave one. Queen Victoria had a golden opportunity, after the death of the prince consort, to take her eldest son into partnership, to train him in affairs of state, and to get him to relieve her of many of the ceremonial burdens of monarchy. She threw away the opportunity, to her own loss, to the country's disadvantage, and to the prince's own serious injury. For he ardently desired something systematic to do. It was all very well to open bazaars, to lay foundation stones, to distribute prizes, to attend banquets, and the like. But these functions did not provide a full-time occupation for an energetic and

capable man. Minister after minister listened sympathetically
to the prince's appeal for work. Minister after minister made
tentative suggestions to the unsmiling and irresponsive
queen. Would it not be a useful training for the prince, said
one, if he were to serve a short apprenticeship in each of
the great governmental departments in turn ? Would not
a seat on the Local Government Board, said another, give
him an invaluable insight into the condition of England ?
Would not membership of the Indian Council, said a third,
bring him into close bond with the greatest of the
dependencies of the Crown ? To every suggestion the queen
said No. But the project that was most strongly pressed upon
her was that of associating her son with Ireland. Ireland
was restless, but enthusiastically loyal. Whenever the prince
visited the island he was received with wild demonstrations
of friendship and devotion. Would not the bonds of allegiance
be permanently strengthened if a royal residence were
established in the country, and if the prince were appointed
viceroy ? The project seems first to have been mooted by
Disraeli in 1868. Gladstone took it up and urged it in 1871.
But the man who made it peculiarly the object of his desire
was the noble and devoted Earl Spencer whose painful task
it was to govern Ireland at the time of the Phœnix Park
murders and the first Home Rule agitation. His heart was
almost broken when the queen rejected the proposal with
indignant emphasis.

The prince, then, now become a man, had to find such
occupation as he could in social functions, in foreign travel,
in visits to India and other overseas dominions of the crown,
in sports, in amusements, in freemasonry, and in philanthropy.
He widened the boundaries of society, bringing within its
pale Jewish financiers, commercial magnates, theatrical and
operatic stars, eminent lawyers and doctors, who hitherto
had been regarded as outside the inner circle of the elect.
He visited all the courts of Europe and acquired an unequalled
knowledge of the monarchs and ministers of the Continent.

Long before he came to the throne he excelled all other British statesmen in the intimacy of his familiarity with the problems of world-politics. His grasp of international affairs was immensely facilitated by his wide acquaintance with foreign languages : German was the language of his infancy and he spoke it with the ease of a native ; French he learned at an early age and he became a past-master in its grace and subtlety ; of Italian and Spanish he gained a good working knowledge. He was, in short, admirably equipped for travel and diplomacy, and he was aided in such tasks as came his way by his perfect manners, his innate tact, and his genuine geniality. At home, he threw himself with ardour into such duties as the jealous suspicion of his mother allowed him to assume. He showed peculiar interest in the housing of the working-classes, in the provision of pure water for cities, in the operation of the poor-law, in the relation of capital to labour, in the safeguarding of British industry, in the organization of international exhibitions, in the Sunday opening of museums and picture-galleries and (*mirabile dictu*) in the passage of the bill legalizing marriage with a deceased wife's sister ! In 1861 Marlborough House, Pall Mall, was prepared for him as a London residence ; in 1862 he bought Sandringham out of the accumulated funds of the duchy of Cornwall ; in 1863 he married the Princess Alexandra of Denmark.

The prince's political proclivities were determined in the main by three cardinal events of his early years—namely, by (1) the Crimean War ; (2) the long ascendancy of Palmerston ; (3) the prince's own marriage with the Danish princess. The Crimean War made him pronouncedly pro-French and anti-Russian : a visit which he paid with his parents to the brilliant court of Napoleon III in Paris, during the summer of 1855, left an indelible impression of grandeur and grace upon his boyish mind. From Palmerston —prime minister almost continuously from 1855 to 1865— he learned the principles of constitutional government and of religious toleration ; learned, too, the importance of maintaining the national prestige, and the duty of protecting the native inhabitants of Britain's overseas dominions. His marriage with the Danish princess made him vehemently anti-Prussian in the Prusso-Danish war of 1864, and caused him to remain definitely and outspokenly anti-Prussian during the wars of 1866 and 1870—the wars which resulted in the extrusion of Austria from the Germanic Confederation, the overthrow of Napoleonic France, and the founding of the German Empire. Of Bismarck, in particular, he shared with his wife, a profound dread and loathing. His love of France and his friendship with French statesmen enabled him from time to time to render valuable service to the British foreign office : in 1878, for example, when friction between the governments of England and France concerning the Treaty of Berlin was intense, he earned the formal and generous thanks of Lord Salisbury for his lubricating talks with Gambetta.

3rd Period, 1881–1901

At the time of the Treaty of Berlin Disraeli (who had recently been made Earl of Beaconsfield) was prime minister. He was friendly with the prince, recognized his powers, and was anxious to gratify his desire for permanent and useful employment. But he was first and foremost the queen's man, and he was not prepared to forfeit the royal favour by unduly pressing the prince's cause. Disraeli's retirement in 1880 and death a year later opened the way for the return of Gladstone and the Radicals, and their coming into office considerably increased the importance and influence of the prince. For one thing the prince was on exceptionally intimate terms with Gladstone, and so long as Gladstone's expanding liberalism remained within Palmerstonian limits the two men had many common political interests. The prince's first governess, moreover, Lady Lyttelton, had been connected by family ties with the Gladstones, and early social intercourse had laid a solid foundation of good understanding. Further, the prince was on terms of close friendship with Lord Rosebery and Sir Charles Dilke, two colleagues of Gladstone, whose interests, like those of the prince himself, lay in the sphere of foreign affairs. From these—although the queen prohibited his access to foreign office papers— he learned much concerning the course of British diplomacy. The lessons of the period were not lost upon him, and when at its close he mounted the throne, he did so with a well-defined and thoroughly matured foreign policy.

The last two decades of Victoria's reign were filled with international and imperial excursions and alarms. During Gladstone's ministry (1880–5) in particular, in addition to grave trouble with the Afghans, the Boers, the Irish, and the Dervishes, there was serious friction with the French concerning Egypt, Morocco, Newfoundland, Mauritius, and Siam; with Germany concerning her sudden occupation of four regions in Africa; and with Russia concerning her encroachments in the Middle East. It was evident that Britain stood in dangerous isolation in the midst of a militant, an envious, and an unfriendly world. Lord Salisbury, who succeeded Gladstone in 1885, and controlled British affairs for almost the whole remainder of the queen's reign, perceived the peril, and did what he could to remove it by pursuing a policy of conciliation and concession. But his efforts to terminate Britain's " splendid isolation " were unsuccessful. During the Boer War, indeed, at the end of Victoria's reign (1899–1902), there was at one time a grave possibility that Germany, France, and Russia would combine to impose upon Britain a pacification that would have been fatal to her imperial sovereignty. The projector of this anti-British combination was the young German Kaiser William II, who from the time of his accession (1888) showed a strong anti-British bias (due to reaction from the pronounced Anglophile propensities of his detested parents), and a peculiar animosity towards his uncle, Albert Edward, prince of Wales (due to the prince's defence of his sister, the kaiser's persecuted mother, and to his resentment at the kaiser's insolent speeches and atrocious bad manners). Thus when Albert Edward became King Edward VII he was clearly convinced that Britain's dangerous isolation must be ended, and he was sharply suspicious that friendship and alliance would have to be sought almost anywhere rather than in the parvenu and blustering German Empire. Nevertheless, as we shall see, for several years after his accession, he lived and laboured in hope.

III

The all-too-brief reign of Edward VII can, like the period of his principality, be divided into three parts. The first is the two years of his settlement on the throne (1901–3); the second is the lustrum of his apogee (1903–8), commencing with his cardinal visit to Paris, and terminating with his critical interview with the tsar at Reval; the third is the two years of anxiety and decline that marked the termination of his reign and life (1908–10).

The materials for the life of the king in relation to his time are abundant, although not yet complete. Most of the external facts are collected and tabulated in the semi-official pages of Sir Sidney Lee's two-volumed biography. Lee's somewhat arid and unsympathetic tabulations are supplemented by the far more intimate and humane reminiscences of Lords Redesdale and Esher, Baron Eckardstein, Sir Lionel Cust, and Mr. Legge. What we still lack are the memoirs of several of his close personal friends, and above all a full collection of his letters. He wrote voluminously to selected correspondents. One correspondent alone is supposed to possess nearly 3,000 of his epistles; but access to them has been persistently refused. It is improbable, however, that when the letters of the king are published they will have the interest or importance of Queen

Victoria's letters. For Edward was not a good letter-writer. Like many polyglot persons, he conspicuously lacked the literary gift. Even in the days of his youthful servitude the epistles which, under tutorial compulsion, he sent to his parents from the scenes of his travels filled them with profound disappointment. And such letters of his later life as have been printed, e.g. by Lieut.-Col. J. P. C. Sewell, add little either to the world's knowledge or to the king's reputation. The king, moreover, cannot be said to have been fortunate in his biographer. In 1912 Sir Sidney Lee, as editor of the *Dictionary of National Biography*, unhappily decided himself to write the article on Edward VII for the supplementary volume about to be issued. He had no personal acquaintance with the king ; he had no access to special documents ; he had little familiarity with the history of the Edwardian period, since he specialized in the Shakespearian age ; he lacked sympathy with his subject. The result was a sketch bald in outline, and in substance distinctly prejudicial to the king's fame. The king's friends and relatives, justly indignant at the distorted picture presented by the national biographer, invited him to inspect the archives of Windsor Castle and Buckingham Palace. He did so, and he found there abundant cause to revise his estimates of the king's influence, his diligence, his devotion to duty, and his political capacity. Having professed his penitence and his conversion, he was (to his dismay) asked to show the fruits of repentance by writing the king's semi-official and full-length biography. He could not very well refuse. But his heart was not in the task. His main energies continued to be devoted to Shakespeare, and only the tail-ends of exhausting days were assigned to the Edwardian memoir. The result was that its compilation dragged on for the whole of the remaining fourteen years of Sir Sidney Lee's life. He published the first volume in 1925 ; the second was unfinished at the time of his death (March, 1926), and it had to be completed by other hands

(1927). No wonder that it lacks vitality. The doings of the king are tabulated, with a devastating disregard of chronological sequence, under topical headings. The classified catalogue of deeds is there ; the dry bones of a biography. But the spirit of life does not move among them : the form of the man does not emerge. The great shade of King Edward still awaits its Lytton Strachey to recall it to earth out of the void. Nevertheless, enough has been revealed to show that when the predestined biographer arrives, the figure that he will represent to the students of the Edwardian age will be one of considerable magnitude.

IV

1st. *The Period of the Settlement*, 1901-3

The speech which King Edward made at the privy council immediately after his accession clearly indicated to the assembled magnates of the realm that they were in the presence of no *roi fainéant*. The speech had not been written, and the king spoke without notes. He began with a filial tribute to his mother, whom he had much cause to respect, but little to love. He continued by asserting his determination to be a constitutional sovereign, and he laid as strong a stress upon the noun as upon the adjective. He announced that he would be known by the name of " Edward ", assigning the adequate, if not really most potent, reason that he wished his father's name of " Albert " to remain in solitary eminence. He quite properly had no desire that either the Albert Memorial or the Albert Hall should be associated with anyone except the good prince to whom they had been dedicated. He ended by appealing to both parliament and nation to support him in the arduous duties which then devolved upon him. The speech made a profound impression both upon those who heard it, and upon those who read the summary account of it which was published in the Press.

The king's inaugural speech was speedily followed by

decisive action. The four tasks which first claimed the royal attention were (1) the rejuvenation of the court and of London Society ; (2) the reorganization of the great governmental departments, and especially of the war office, the admiralty, and the foreign office ; (3) the termination of the protracted and dangerous Boer war ; (4) an attempt to effect a rapproachement with Germany.

The court, under the aged and melancholy queen, had become a centre of depression and gloom. It was dominated by dowagers in mourning, and by relics of the long-deceased prince consort. The royal residences, and in particular Buckingham Palace and Windsor Castle, were dingy with mid-Victorian decorations, and congested with furniture of obsolete hideousness. The king effected a speedy and thorough purge both in personnel and properties, and in place of the deadly " drawing-rooms " whose solemn dullness had darkened countless Victorian afternoons, he instituted balls and concerts, dinner-parties and evening receptions, wherein youth and gaiety were enabled to display their fascinations. One royal residence, Osborne House, the private property of Queen Victoria—a house which King Edward intensely disliked because of its architectural ugliness and because of its associations with John Brown—he got rid of altogether. Leaving the old queen's private apartments as a memorial and museum, he bestowed the remainder of the mansion upon the nation to serve in part as a hospital for invalid officers and in part as a college for naval cadets.

The stagnation that had characterized the late Victorian court had had its counterpart in the lethargy that had overspread the great governmental departments. They were largely controlled by survivals from the decades of Gladstone and Disraeli, estimable but ineffective antiquities to whom the king gave the collective name of " old women ". The perils through which the country had passed in the early period of the Boer War had revealed dangerous defects

in the administration of the army, the navy, and the foreign
office. King Edward, acting through the proper constitutional channels, took an energetic lead in the reformation
of the military, naval, and diplomatic services.

Meantime, the Boer War itself dragged its weary length
along. The Boers were beaten, of course, but they refused
to acknowledge it. Hence by the methods of guerrilla warfare
they prolonged a contest which was fraught with a distinct
menace to the general peace of the world. True, the fear
of a triple alliance directed against Great Britain had passed
away. But anti-British feeling, stirred up by able Boer
emissaries, still burned high, and the king realized that at
any moment it might cause a conflagration. A letter which
he received from the Tsar Nicholas II in June, 1901, was
ominous of danger. He replied to the tsar (19th June, 1901)
in a masterly, conclusive, and crushing rejoinder, the materials
for which were furnished by Lord Salisbury. But he realized
that the country could never be secure until peace was
restored. Hence he vigorously exerted his influence to
advance and facilitate the negotiations that culminated in
the exceedingly moderate and conciliatory treaty of
Vereeniging (31st May, 1902).

All through the period of the Boer war there could be no
doubt respecting the general unfriendliness of both Russia
and France towards Great Britain. Not only was the Press
openly on the side of the Afrikanders, but in many parts
of the world Russian and French interests patently clashed
with those of Britain. In particular, Russia and Britain
were in strong antagonism in both Middle and Far East ;
while France and Britain were in formidable rivalry in Egypt
and the Soudan. It seemed beyond the bounds of political
possibility that good relations should be restored in these
quarters. Hence it was to Germany that, at the beginning
of his reign, King Edward looked in the hope of friendship
and alliance. There were, of course, difficulties in the way.
The king and the kaiser had long been personally antipathetic

to one another ; but the kaiser's presence at Queen Victoria's funeral ; his obvious reverence for his grandmother's memory, and the cordiality of his words during his visit to England, had seemed to restore domestic harmony. For several years, moreover, the powerful Joseph Chamberlain—the colonial secretary whose influence in both cabinet and country exceeded that of his nominal chief, Lord Salisbury— had been labouring for an Anglo-German entente.[1] The kaiser had appeared to respond favourably to Chamberlain's advances, although not quite in the way that Chamberlain had hoped : for he wanted to attach Britain as, like Italy, a subordinate and submissive member of the Triple Alliance, thus converting it into a quadruple alliance. But during the course of 1901 the mirage of an Anglo-German entente faded away. The German Press displayed a persistent unfriendliness to Britain, in particular condemning the " barbarity " with which the Boers were being subjugated. The German Navy League continued its demand for bigger and better battleships, and the imperial government responded with ever-increasing programmes of construction. Friction arose between London and Berlin as to the policy to be pursued in respect of the Boxer rising in China. Finally, the kaiser roused the intense resentment of the king by sending him a hectoring letter in which he spoke of the British ministers as " unmitigated noodles ". The kaiser seems to have been proud of the phrase, for he had used it a short time previously in conversation with Sir Frank Lascelles, the British ambassador in Berlin. It is always dangerous for a foreigner to try to pick up and employ the slang of a country other than his own ; for its exact connotation is almost sure to elude him. Now the expression " unmitigated noodles " is in England, as is well known, a term of affection genially employed by modern children

---

[1] Cf. Chamberlain's speech at Leicester in November, 1899 : " The natural alliance is between ourselves and the German Empire . . . both interest and racial sentiment unite the two peoples," etc., etc.

to describe their venerated parents, or by devoted students to characterize their respected teachers ; but it is not used at all in the language of international diplomacy in reference to ministers of the rank and calibre of Lord Salisbury and Lord Lansdowne. The king sent for the secretary of the German Embassy and gave him a lesson in comparative philology which, when conveyed to Berlin, must have enlightened, if not soothed, the kaiser (14th April, 1901). It was just at this time, moreover, that the German Press became most lyrical in its expressions of horror at the " barbarities " of the British in South Africa. On 25th October, 1901, Mr. Chamberlain signalized his abandonment of all hope of an Anglo-German entente by comparing, in a speech at Edinburgh, the mild " barbarities " of the British in South Africa with the notorious " atrocities " per-petrated by the Prussians in the Franco-German and earlier wars. The Germans, led by Count Bülow in the Reichstag, replied to Chamberlain's historic résumé with howls of execration, and it became abundantly clear that any sort of Anglo-German rapprochement was out of the question. The king's recognition of this painful fact was indicated at an official dinner given at Marlborough House on 8th February, 1902. On the one hand, the king himself told Baron Eckardstein that he regretted his inability to attach any weight to the kaiser's assurances of friendship. On the other hand, he provided facilities for a long and confidential conversation on high politics which Mr. Chamberlain had with the French ambassador, within sight of Eckardstein. This date may be regarded as the critical point at which British policy veered decisively from the direction of Germany into the direction of France. The year 1902 also saw the conclusion of the Anglo-Japanese alliance ; but in the achievement of this pact the king played little or no part. On one occasion, indeed (23rd August, 1901), the kaiser showed himself to be better acquainted than the king with the progress of the Anglo-Japanese negotiations.

v

2nd. *The Apogee of the Reign*, 1903–8

The year 1903 saw King Edward firmly established on
his throne ; in occupation of his rejuvenated palaces ; in
undisputed leadership of society ; and in close touch with
all departments of government. On 9th August, 1902, he
had been crowned in much magnificence.[1] The previous
month Lord Salisbury had brought to a close his long tenure
of high office,[2] and had been succeeded as prime minister
by his nephew, Mr. A. J. Balfour. Between the king and
his new prime minister there was little in common. On
the one hand, the king had no acquaintance with that world
of speculation and surmise in which Mr. Balfour lived and
moved and had his being ; was bewildered by that atmosphere
of philosophic doubt which Mr. Balfour constantly carried
about with him ; was frankly bemused by his disquisitions
and arguments. " He is always so vague that probably
he is wrong," was one of the royal comments on a Balfourian
oration. On the other hand, Mr. Balfour unquestionably
depreciated and under-estimated the king's qualities. He
did not recognize the value of his intimate personal knowledge
of continental statesmen and internal politics ; did not
realize the intuitive soundness of his judgment ; did not
perceive his flair for diplomacy. Certainly, at no period
of his reign did the king have to struggle so strenuously
to retain those vestiges of the royal prerogative that he had
inherited from Queen Victoria as he had during the three
and a half years of Mr. Balfour's ministry. When, in
December, 1905, Mr. Balfour gave place to Sir Henry

[1] The coronation, originally fixed for 26th June, had been postponed
because of a sudden and severe illness of the king.

[2] Lord Salisbury had been minister for foreign affairs, 1878–80 ; prime
minister and foreign secretary 1885–6, 1886–92, and again 1894 onward.
In 1900 he had transferred the foreign office to Lord Lansdowne. He
ceased to be prime minister on 11th July, 1902, and he died on 22nd August
1903.

Campbell-Bannerman things became much easier. The
king and the genial knight were able to converse on terms of
mutual comprehension and reciprocal confidence. Under
Campbell-Bannerman the royal influence operated bene-
ficently through countless constitutional channels.

The four principal tasks to which the king was called to
apply himself during this central and most fruitful five
years of his reign were first, the termination of Britain's
isolation in Europe ; secondly, the reorganization of the
army and navy ; thirdly, the maintenance of international
peace ; and, fourthly, the furtherance of domestic harmony.

(1) Early in 1903 the king commenced that series of visits
to foreign courts which formed so marked a feature of his
reign. His charming geniality, his polished manners, his
unfailing tact, his transparent honesty and freedom from
guile, his obvious desire to foster peace and goodwill among
the nations made him everywhere a welcome visitor. He
usually took with him a high official from the foreign office,
and when he talked politics with continental potentates
he did so along lines laid down beforehand by his minister
for foreign affairs, whether Lord Lansdowne or Sir Edward
Grey. There can be no doubt that the king's visits immensely
smoothed the paths of official diplomacy. On the other
hand, they gravely exasperated and perturbed the kaiser,
who in vain tried to neutralize them by counter-visits.
He had better have stayed at home. The contrast between
his own craft and pomposity and his uncle's easy bonhomie
was most conspicuous. Respecting this very tour of 1903
an Italian journalist, comparing King Edward's visit to
Rome with that of Kaiser William which immediately
followed it, spoke of the king as the sun spreading genial
light and warmth all around, but of the kaiser as a cuttle-
fish polluting and darkening his vicinity. Not Rome,
however, but Paris was the grand objective of this 1903
tour. The relations between England and France were
still somewhat strained, although strenuous effort had been

made on both sides to ease them. Lord Lansdowne was
frankly apprehensive lest the king should suffer indignity
in Paris, and it was with much hesitation that he yielded
to his desire to go thither. The king reached Paris on
1st May and he stayed there until the 4th. His reception
by the populace at first was worse than cool : the cries that
assailed his ears as he drove through the streets were
" Vivent les Boers . . . Vive Marchand . . . Vive Fashoda ".
But within the four days of his visit a complete transformation
took place. His geniality, his strong will to friendship,
his graceful acts and his felicitous words, won all hearts,
and as he rode away the air was rent with the multitudinous
cry " Vive notre roi ". Rarely has a monarch achieved in
so brief a time so complete and spectacular a triumph.
In the atmosphere of goodwill created by this visit it was a
comparatively simple task for Lord Lansdowne and
M. Delcassé to conclude the three treaties of 1904 that marked
the formation of the Anglo-French *entente cordiale*.

Three years later, when Lord Lansdowne had given
place to Sir Edward Grey, the still more difficult problem
of a rapprochement with Russia came up for consideration.
Distrust and dread of Russia were ingrained in British
politics. They formed part of the great tradition handed
down from Canning to Palmerston, and from Palmerston
to Disraeli ; and of that tradition King Edward himself
was undoubtedly the heir. And certainly nothing that
had transpired in his lifetime had tended to weaken the
force of the tradition. In the Near, the Middle, and the
Far East Russia and Britain had been in constant and ominous
antagonism. The two empires had been on the verge of
war in 1878, in 1885, and again in 1898. Once more, in
1904, during King Edward's own reign, when Russia was
at war with Britain's new ally, Japan, and when British
public opinion was highly inflamed against the tsar, an
armed conflict came well within sight when a Russian fleet
on its way from the Baltic to the straits of Tsushima fired on

and sank some British trawlers in the North Sea. There was a vehement demand in the British press not only for apology and compensation, but also for the exemplary punishment of the Russian admiral. Russia, when she discovered the appalling mistake that she had made, was prepared for abject apology and ample compensation. But she was not prepared for more. And if the demand for the punishment of the admiral had been made it would have been refused. What then? King Edward saw the peril of the situation. " Are we prepared to go to war ? " he wrote to Lord Lansdowne, and later (after he had read the newspapers) he telegraphed to him, " Strongly deprecate pressing for punishment of admiral. Russia could not accept such a humiliation," and this telegram he followed up by a second letter in which he said, " War between Russia and Great Britain would be so serious a calamity that we can hardly think of its possibility." So the demand for the punishment of the admiral was not made, and the episode was closed by Russia's expression of profound regret, and by her payment of £65,000. There can be little doubt that King Edward's personal influence helped to save the country from a disastrous embroilment.

The conclusion of the Russo-Japanese war (1905) eased the tension between Russia and Britain. One result of the war, moreover, was the removal of that dread of Muscovite magnitude and might which, like a nightmare, had disturbed Britain's repose for more than a century. The decisive victory of the minute Japanese state over her colossal antagonist did much to restore a mental balance that had been upset by the statistics of the Russian population and by the study of Russian geography on maps drawn according to Mercator's projection. Just at this time, also, Germany, encouraged by the temporary disablement of Russia, became exceptionally aggressive and offensive : it was on 31st March, 1905, that the kaiser paid his deliberately provocative visit to Tangier, thus directly challenging the French suzerainty over Morocco. On hearing of it, King Edward wrote to Lord Lansdowne and described the incident as " the most mischievous and uncalled for event which the German emperor had ever been engaged in since he came to the throne ". He then went on to characterize the kaiser as " a political *enfant terrible* " in whose assurances " one can have no faith ". He concluded that " his own pleasure seems to wish to set every country by the ears " and that " these annual cruises are deeply to be deplored " as " mischief is their only object ".

The kaiser's wanton meddling in Morocco instantly brought France and Britain together on the one hand, and France and Russia on the other. It was clearly evident that Germany with her enormous army and her swelling navy, under the control of Moltkian militarists and Bismarckian real-politicians, was out for world-dominance. The three powers primarily threatened—France, Russia, and Britain— inevitably drew together. Before the Algeciras Conference, which met in January, 1906, to unravel the tangle of Tangier, the king said to the French ambassador in London : " Tell us what you wish on each point, and we will support you without restriction or reserve." The tsar, too, loyally supported his French ally. In these circumstances of common danger and mutual aid Britain and Russia forgot their ancient animosities and sought a basis of co-operation. They felt the cohesive power of a new antagonism : they were driven into harmony by fear. The king did much to facilitate an understanding. He had confidential con- versations with M. Izvolski, the Russian minister for foreign affairs, with whom he became extremely friendly ; in London he cultivated the society of the urbane and courtly Russian ambassador, Baron Benckendorff, and he encouraged his prolonged negotiations with Sir Edward Grey. In short, he played a conspicuous part in those delicate and protracted discussions which in the end resulted in the settlement of the old Anglo-Russian disputes respecting Persia,

Afghanistan, China, and Tibet, and in the establishment of the Anglo-Russian entente (September, 1907). The seal to the new Anglo-Russian friendship was set by the king's visit to the tsar at Reval in June, 1908. The utmost cordiality prevailed. M. Stolypin, the tsar's chief minister, who had several interviews with the king, spoke of him afterwards with enthusiasm as " an artist in international politics whom Europe regards as its first statesman ".

Unquestionably the formation of the Triple Entente was not only one of the main achievements of King Edward's reign, but also an achievement in which he himself played a prominent part. Its formation seemed at the time, in view of the German menace, essential to both the security of Britain and the peace of the world. How posterity will regard it we cannot foresee. For it undoubtedly had some unexpected and unfortunate reactions. The Anglo-French entente of 1904 sent the kaiser to Tangier in 1905 ; the Anglo-Russian entente of 1907 precipitated the Turkish revolution, the Bulgarian pronunciamento, and the Austro-Hungarian coup of 1908, and so set in motion the train of events that ended in the great war of 1914.

(2) From 1905 onward King Edward distinctly envisaged the possibility, if not the probability, of a war with Germany. Even apart from his incalculable and exasperating nephew, the military controllers of Germany policy—and in particular Holstein of the foreign office and Tirpitz of the admiralty—were pursuing a policy of provocation which could hardly have any other end than an armed conflict. In these circumstances King Edward felt it imperative that the army and the navy should be in the highest state of readiness and efficiency that the lethargic condition of public opinion would sanction and the parsimony of parliament permit. The South African war (1895–1902) had revealed the gravest defects in the British military administration, and a royal commission, appointed soon after the close of the war, recommended drastic reforms. Mr. Brodrick, the king's first war-secretary,

seemed to think that all that was necessary for the regeneration of the army was a new hat which should render the
soldier indistinguishable from a postman. His successor,
Mr. Arnold-Forster (1903-5), took a wider view, and he found
a keenly interested and expertly skilled adviser in the king
as he proceeded to institute a defence committee of the
cabinet; to set up an army council; to supersede the
obsolete commander-in-chief by an inspector-general with
a competent staff; to revolutionize the system of enlistment;
to decentralize the administration of the army, and to introduce far-reaching economies. But the war-minister who
won the king's most enthusiastic approval and most ardent
support was Mr. R. B. (later Lord) Haldane. Haldane's
great innovation, of course, was the territorial force which
took the place of the antiquated militia and the obsolete
volunteers as the second line of British defence. The
scheme was (within the limits imposed by an unawakened
democracy) a fine one; but it involved a considerable initial
expense, and on that ground it was strenuously opposed
by Mr. Lloyd George and other pacifists in the Cabinet,
who wished to use the money to provide the " rare and
refreshing fruits " of social reform. The king, to whom
Mr. Haldane appealed, exerted all his vast influence on
behalf of the scheme, and when the measure had become
law (July, 1907), he did what no one else could have done to
make its operation successful. He summoned all the lord-
lieutenants of the counties of Great Britain to a meeting
in Buckingham Palace, and in a powerful and impressive
speech urged upon them the duty of making the scheme
effective. A little later he issued the command, which
was within his competence, that no one should in future
be appointed a deputy-lieutenant unless he had served for
at least ten years in either the regular or the territorial army.

Not less zealous and decisive was the support which the
king gave to Sir John (later Lord) Fisher in his reconstruction
and reorganization of the navy. To Fisher, of course, was

primarily due the introduction of the Dreadnought type of battleship, whose creation restored for a time Britain's indisputable ascendancy at sea. But Fisher's most controversial innovation was the transference of the main might of the British navy from the Mediterranean to the North Sea (1907). This move, patent to the eyes of the world, was a clear recognition of the fact, hitherto discreetly veiled, that Britain's chief potential enemy was the German Empire. On that point Fisher had no illusions and few reticences. "Our only probable enemy," he wrote in October, 1906, "is Germany. Germany keeps her *whole* fleet always concentrated within a few hours of England. We must, therefore, keep a fleet twice as powerful concentrated within a few hours of Germany." Again in a confidential communication to the king he expressed his firm conviction that Germany was bent on an early war. "The German Empire," he added, "is the one Power in political organization and in fighting efficiency where one man—the kaiser—can press the button and be confident of hurling the whole force of the empire, instantly, irresistibly, and without warning on its enemy." The only safeguard against an overwhelming attack was, he urged, the presence of an invincible fleet in the North Sea. Both the king and his son (now King George V) entirely agreed with Fisher's diagnosis of the situation, and they were able to give him invaluable support in the carrying out of his revolutionary reforms.

(3) Although King Edward distinctly foresaw the possibility of war, and although he gave long and anxious thought to the military and naval defence of his empire, his dominating concern was the maintenance of international peace. One of the biographies, indeed, written shortly after his death,[1] not inaptly called him "Edward the Peacemaker". Even when he fostered the territorial associations and fathered the dreadnoughts, he did so because he was sure

[1] By Mr. W. H. Wilkins, 1911.

that the best and indeed the only way to keep Germany
quiet was to make the task of invading Britain too doubtful
and dangerous for her to attempt. He recognized fully
that the supreme British interest was peace, and he laboured
by correspondence and by personal visits to soothe dissensions
that might lead to conflict, and to solve problems that
threatened to lead to complications. This is no place in
which to enter into details of his diplomatic toils. Students
of the reign must refer to Sir Sidney Lee's biography,
and to official publications, for particulars as to how he eased
the painful separation of Norway from Sweden in 1905;
how he helped to secure the transference of Crete from
Turkish suzerainty to Greek control in 1906–8; and how
he strove in 1908 by means of intimate and earnest conversations with the German and Austrian kaisers to keep
the Balkan revolution from imperilling the peace of the world.
With the Austrian kaiser he got on well, although in the end
the old man deceived him; but with the German kaiser
nothing could be done. Interchanges of visits led to misunderstanding rather than to reconciliation. The two men,
uncle and nephew, constantly got on to one another's nerves.
And each of them expressed too freely and too frequently
his detestation and distrust of the other. Reported remarks
could not be silenced or recalled. "Thank God, he's gone,"
said the king, with an audible groan of relief, as he saw the
kaiser depart from Sandringham after an irritating visit
in 1902. "He's a Satan, you can hardly believe what
a Satan he is," blurted out the kaiser, under the combined
influence of dyspepsia and alcohol, in the presence of 300
guests at a banquet in 1907. Rumours of remarks such as
these, crossing and recrossing the North Sea, tended still
further to estrange the already alien courts of London
and Berlin.

(4) The gradual and ominous increase of Anglo-German
unfriendliness during the years 1903–8 was unfortunately
accompanied by an alarming growth of social unrest and

political dissension at home. The coming into power of the Liberals in 1906, after twenty years of almost unbroken exclusion from office, was followed by a spate of revolutionary legislation. Much as the king liked personally the Liberal prime minister, Sir Henry Campbell-Bannerman, he found himself in sharp disagreement with most of the measures that he brought forward. He disliked his Trades Disputes Act; he disliked his Education Bill; he disliked his revival of the Irish Home Rule agitation; he disliked his proposals for Welsh Disestablishment; he disliked his attacks upon the House of Lords. But he clearly recognized that he must restrict his expression of his dislikes to private conversations with his prime minister, and that he must not attempt to determine otherwise than through the cabinet the course of the government's policy. His main overt function was to act as mediator between the contending factions and parties. In particular he arranged for meetings between the prime minister and the archbishop of Canterbury in the hope that they could arrive at some solution of the problem of the teaching of religion in schools. Similarly he called a conference of the Irish leaders to Buckingham Palace in order to see if there were any possibility of compromising the Home Rule issue. Again he actually formulated a scheme of House of Lords reform with a view to the more equitable balancing of the parties in the peerage.

It cannot be said that the king's noble efforts at mediation in home affairs were very successful. Political passions raged too high in that time of incessant British strikes and of impending Irish civil war, for the voice of reason or moderation to be heard. The king was intensely disappointed to find that, potent though he was in international affairs, he seemed to have no power to mollify or assuage enflamed ecclesiastics, or die-hard lords, or militant trade unionists, or belligerent suffragettes, or wild Irish nationalists, or embittered Ulster unionists, or Welsh emancipationists, or

ardent tariff reformers, or any other of the violent groups
into which the peoples of the United Kingdom seemed to
be disintegrating.   There can be no doubt that the anxieties
and annoyances arising from the dissensions of domestic
politics accelerated the decline that marked the two closing
years of his reign.

VI

3rd.   The Period of Decline, 1908-10

Every February from 1905 onward King Edward suffered
from an attack of acute bronchitis which severely taxed
his strength and gravely depressed his spirits.   For several
years his recovery, under the skilled attention of Sir Felix
Semon and Sir Francis Laking, was rapid and fairly complete ;
but in February, 1907, the two physicians were sufficiently
alarmed to draw up a state paper in which they expressed
grave apprehensions concerning the king's future powers of
recuperation.   The violent and continuous coughing caused
by his malady put a heavy strain on his blood-vessels and
his heart.   Every spring his medical advisers hurried him
away from the fogs and smoke of London to the purer and
milder air of the Mediterranean or of Biarritz.   As one attack
succeeded another, and as his speed of recovery diminished,
his natural gaiety declined, and he became a prey to prolonged fits of melancholy.   He thought and talked of
abdication.   He took a gloomy view of politics and of the
prospects of the monarchy.   " My son may reign, but my
grandson never will," was one of the utterances of his
migraine.

He was away at Biarritz in April, 1908, when Sir Henry
Campbell-Bannerman, already on the verge of the grave,
resigned his ministry.[1]   The king then made what was
regarded by those who did not know the state of his health

---

[1] Sir Henry Campbell-Bannerman resigned on 1st April and died on
22nd April, 1908.

as one of the few tactical errors of his reign, when, instead
of returning to England to speed the departing and institute
the coming cabinet, he summoned Mr. Asquith to the South
of France. It is undoubtedly a pity that he did not come
back, even at some inconvenience; for his inaction caused
the enemy to jibe. Three months later he made another
and more serious mistake—a mistake which in his better
days he would instinctively have avoided. He withheld
invitations to a garden-party at Windsor from three members
of parliament who had grossly offended him by remarks on
his recent visit to the tsar at Reval. Their offence had
indeed been colossal; the king's anger was natural; it
would indeed have been difficult for him to shake hands
with them. But all the same it was incumbent upon him
to do the unpleasant thing (as he did many other unpleasant
things); for no one knew better than he how easy it would
be for perverted animosity to represent the royal wrath as
an attempt to interfere with parliamentary freedom of speech
and to influence the course of politics.

As the king's health and spirits declined, the course of
politics, both domestic and foreign, became more and more
perturbed. Affairs in the Near East—Turkey, Bulgaria,
Serbia, Greece, Bosnia, Herzegovinia, Montenegro, Crete—
grew increasingly involved. The Great Powers—Russia
and Austria, France and Germany—came to be implicated,
and a world-conflagration seemed to be imminent. At
home, great industrial strikes, under the fostering encouragement of the Trades Disputes Act of 1906, became every year
more numerous, more violent, more pronouncedly revolutionary in aim. The suffragettes, favoured by the immunities
of their sex, displayed a progressive recklessness and
irrationality; a destructive and abusive Bedlam seemed
let loose. Mr. Lloyd George, who had forced himself upon
Mr. Asquith as his chancellor of the exchequer, regardless
of the traditions of his office, brought in (1909) a predatory
and vindictive budget calculated to injure his political

enemies and benefit his political friends rather than to serve
the interests of the nation or the state. He accompanied
it by blatant and blustering speeches which intensely
aggravated the irritation that his actual proposals caused.
The house of lords decided to go to the extreme constitutional
length of rejecting the budget. The king was much
perturbed. He tried to mediate. On the one hand, he
appealed to Mr. Asquith to restrain the provocative eloquence
of his Welsh insubordinate ; on the other hand, he implored
the lords, through Lord Lansdowne and others, not to commit
the fatal blunder of rejecting a money bill. His efforts were
wholly futile. The chancellor continued to fulminate.
The lords perpetrated the irremediable mistake of throwing
out the budget. The consequences, which the king
prophesied but did not live to see, were a Liberal victory at
the polls in December, 1910, and the Parliament Act of
1911. To add to the tribulation of the time, the demand
of the Southern Irish for self-government and for the
coercion of Northern Ireland, led the unhappy Emerald
Island to the verge of civil war.

It was then, amid circumstances of exceptional anxiety,
that in March, 1910, King Edward went to pay his annual
visit to Biarritz. He was extremely ill on his arrival, but
his doctors did not communicate their anxieties to the public.
He rallied and returned to England on 27th April. On
Sunday, 1st May, however, he caught a fresh chill at
Sandringham, and he came back to Buckingham Palace
next day only to die. Desperately ill though he was, he would
not surrender. More than once he said : " I will not give
in : I will work to the end." The end was not long delayed.
The tired heart could hold out no longer. Although on
the very last day of his life, Friday, 6th May, 1910, he got up,
dressed, and transacted business, in the late afternoon he
had to be put to bed. He sank into unconsciousness and
at 11.45 p.m. he passed peacefully away.

VII

Not even at the death of Queen Victoria had so wide and profound an outburst of public grief been seen as that which followed the passing of Edward VII, nine years later. The queen had been a revered but remote figure ; her son and successor had moved freely and genially among his subjects, known to multitudes and beloved by nearly all. He had long been recognized as a great ruler, an expert in the business of constitutional kingship. His intense patriotism ; his large humanity ; his cosmopolitan sympathy ; his sincere devotion to the cause of peace, had inspired profound admiration and affection in the breasts of his people. " Mon métier à moi est d'être Roi," he had once remarked to two importunate envoys who had vainly tried to get him to condone the murder of King Alexander of Serbia. For this business of kingship few men have ever been better equipped. He had more than made good the defects and irrelevances of his pedantic and inappropriate education. He had an admirable technical apparatus in his easy command of foreign languages, in his ingrained habits of punctuality and orderliness, in his power of direct and lucid speech. He had, moreover, an unequalled knowledge of all the leading countries and statesmen of the Continent. His acquaintance too, with the problems of international politics was intimate and profound ; his extensive travels had made him unquestionably the most eminent citizen of the twentieth-century world. Then again, he had acquired an exceptional skill in the art of managing men ; he possessed a marvellous charm of manner, combined with an impressive regality that made any undue familiarity impossible. Well said Lord Morley : " He managed to combine royal dignity with bonhomie, and strict regard for form with entire absence of spurious pomp." He showed, too, an instinctive sound judgment of men and things. He had a profound and natural wisdom. What could be better than the words,

added in his own writing, to the draft of an indirect communication to Mr. Winston Churchill, when Mr. Churchill
was an under-secretary in Sir Henry Campbell-Bannerman's
government ? " His Majesty is glad to see that you are
becoming a reliable minister, and above all a serious
politician." I have already spoken of his conspicuous good
manners, of his unfailing tact, of his cordiality and kindliness.
He has been described as " the first amiable king since
Charles II ". And his good manners were not, like those of
Charles II, merely external trappings concealing a cold and
treacherous heart. King Edward established his permanent
dominion over those who got to know him intimately by
the sterling integrity of his nature ; by his patent honesty,
by his trustfulness, by his openness and candour, by his
freedom from craft and guile. None except the unbalanced
Kaiser William and his German band suspected the king
of any secret or sinister designs. It was, indeed, the very
clarity and publicity of his purposes that bewildered and
deceived the Teutonic intriguers. Another characteristic
of the king was his bravery. Courage, of course, was a
tradition of the Hanoverian house ; the worst of the Georges
had not lacked that regal virtue. Not only, however, was
King Edward naturally fearless, he cultivated the habit of
imperturbability. He recognized the incompatibility ,of
princedom with panic, and realized that, come what might,
a king should never manifest alarm. He always remained
cool and resourceful from the day when, in his infancy
(October, 1847), his pony ran away in Windsor Park, to the
day, more than half a century later (April, 1900), when the
miscreant Sipido tried to assassinate him in the railway
station of Brussels. Scarcely less courage did he show
in the social sphere when he broke the Victorian taboos
and made his friends where merit or money called. And
another attractive feature of his character was his fidelity
to his friends. He never forgot them or failed them, and
those who were privileged to be taken into the inner circle

of his regard came to love him with an affection that rose almost to the height of adoration.

That Edward VII was a great king there can be no doubt. He left a permanent impress upon his age. His reign was all too short. Not that it should have been continued longer, but that it should have been begun earlier. Queen Victoria should have retired sometime—almost any time— between 1861 and 1887. When King Edward came to the throne he was already past the prime of his powers. After 1908 he rapidly and visibly decayed, and he could never have recovered his hold. He felt the world slipping away from him, and he was *felix opportunitate mortis.* He was spared the vexations of the Parliament Act, the tragedy of the great war, and the complications of the consequent peace. He could not materially have modified the fated course of events, and his impotence would have plunged him into profound dejection. It was well that he died in 1910. He died before his decline had become too conspicuous, and he has left a name which will stand for many generations as a synonym for all that is best in constitutional kingship.

F. J. C. HEARNSHAW.

III

Religion

The subject with which I have somewhat rashly undertaken to deal has peculiar difficulties. I imagine that in
all its aspects the reign of Edward VII fails to constitute
a rounded epoch, and the death of the monarch gives no
real historical resting place where we can say, here something
has been concluded. Everything goes forward to that
genuine gulf, the outbreak of the Great War, which marks
a real division between an old world and a new. This is
certainly true of the religious development of our nation.
At the beginning, we may discern forces and tendencies,
which were in being during the later years of Victoria,
producing their appropriate results. They remain in force
during the reign of Edward and, in most cases, persist
beyond it, so that their character and importance can only
be understood by looking at that which comes after. There
is, however, a further difficulty which must be faced by one
who takes in hand to describe religion in this or any other
period. " True religion and undefiled before God and the
Father," we are told by an apostolic writer, is " to visit
the fatherless and widow in their affliction and to keep one-
self unspotted from the world." This is not, of course,
intended as a definition of religion but as a statement of
the true expression of spiritual religion. It is obviously
beyond the power of any historian to estimate with accuracy
the progress of mercy and pity in human hearts, and still
more impossible to penetrate the secret places of the spirit
where the battle with " the world's slow stain " proceeds.
We shall be concerned with phenomena which are, in some
degree, superficial. We shall be thinking of the vicissitudes
of organized religion and the progress or decline of the

Church ; we shall also have to say something of the changes in religious thought and the development of theology. These are intimately connected with religion, they are its products and its integument : but they are not religion. It is well to remind ourselves of this at the outset, for many of the facts which we shall recount are far from encouraging. It may be, indeed I think it is, true that the spirit of religion was being renewed even while its outer man was visibly decaying : the spirit of brotherliness and mercy was growing even in the decline of dogma.

I shall divide my discourse into two parts. We will first try to deal, very sketchily, with the external facts, the " ecclesiastical history " of the period, and then we will say something of the religious thought of the time, its " history of dogma ". There is, of course, a grave danger in this division, since we cannot divorce thought and act in this absolute way. The history of institutions reflects the thoughts of the leading minds of the period. But perhaps the danger is not so serious in this instance as in others, because one of the remarkable features of this period of Church history is that the questions discussed with great heat in ecclesiastical politics had little connection with the living issues in the intellectual sphere.

If we try to get a picture of the religious world in England at the opening of Edward's reign we have the impression that, in many aspects, new lines of movement are opening. There is change in the air. In January, 1902, the Pope appointed a Commission on Biblical Studies, which, it was expected by many, would result in a liberalizing of the Roman Catholic doctrine of Scripture and make things easier for the " Modernists ", who were already feeling the yoke of orthodoxy intolerable. It was thought by some that a useful step might be taken towards reunion as a result. All these hopes were destined to be frustrated, and the Roman Church remains to-day officially as " fundamentalist " on the subject of Scripture as the inhabitants of Tennessee.

An event of great importance, not only to the Church of England but to religion in England as a whole, took place at the same time—the appointment of Charles Gore to the Bishopric of Worcester. Gore had already made a great name as the leader of a modern catholic party in the Church of England. In *Lux Mundi* he had definitely broken with the narrow conservatism of the older Tractarians and High Churchmen. He had claimed the right to accept the assured results of Biblical criticism, and had contended that such acceptance was in no way contradictory to a sane catholicism. But his liberalism was not confined to theology. His conception of the meaning of the Incarnation compelled him to consider human society as the sphere for the exemplification of Christian principles. From his position in Westminster Abbey he had awakened men's consciences with regard to social evils and had stimulated reflection on the problem of the relation of the Christian faith to the new learning in history and science. It was not to be expected that such a man would be allowed to ascend the episcopal bench without opposition. Objection was taken at the legal "confirmation" of his election on two grounds—his Romanizing tendencies and his heretical views on Scripture. These objections were not heard by the Court of Arches. An appeal caused the consecration of the bishop-elect to be postponed, but it was finally decided that objections concerning doctrine were out of order at the ceremony of confirmation and he was consecrated on 23rd February, 1902.

When the century and reign opened, a subject was occupying the minds of religious persons, at least of ecclesiastics, which, from our present standpoint, appears remote—the marriage of a deceased wife's sister. The religious issues involved were, it must be confessed, obscure, in spite of the voluminous explanations given, but the Upper House of the Convocation of Canterbury was in 1902 unanimous in condemnation of a proposed act to permit such unions. But other and deeper anxieties weighed upon the minds of religious

E

leaders. The supply of candidates for the ministry was reported to be gravely insufficient ; and various suggestions were made to improve the situation. A sign of the times was the publication in the *Guardian* of a letter from the Rev. Hubert Handley arguing that our antiquated theology repelled thoughtful men, who would have been otherwise valuable recruits, from seeking ordination. This decline in the number of candidates for the ministry does not appear to have affected the Nonconformist Churches at this time, though there were complaints that the quality of candidates had deteriorated. Two notable figures among Nonconformist divines passed from the stage at the opening of our period— the Rev. Hugh Price Hughes and Dr. Joseph Parker. Both represented the type of powerful personality and evangelistic preacher which was the strength of the old dissenting ministry. The latter had fulfilled a ministry of nearly thirty years at the City Temple which had exerted a remarkable influence. Dr. Parker, who had on the whole avoided the questions raised by the higher criticism of the Bible and modern knowledge, was succeeded by the Rev. R. J. Campbell, who was to bring these matters forcibly before the public in his *New Theology* before he found his spiritual home in the Church of England. Perhaps we may regard the contrast between Dr. Parker and his successor as a sign that great mental and spiritual changes were really taking place beneath the almost unruffled surface.

The Church of England was distracted by controversies which, as we have seen, were reflected in the protest against the election of Dr. Gore as bishop. The opposition to " ritualism " and the alleged Romanizing tendencies of the Anglo-Catholic party was still fierce. Men of good will had, however, begun the attempt to reach understanding by conferences, and in the first years of the reign a round table meeting assembled at Fulham under the presidency of Dr. Wace, the Principal of this College, on the subject of Confession and Absolution. The report of the conference showed that much could be done by way of frank discussion of opposite views. We may see in this, and other similar conferences, a real contribution made in the Edwardian decade to unity in the Church, and they may be justly recognized as the predecessors of the Commission on the Doctrine of the Church which is now sitting and which will, in my opinion, be one of the most valuable means of drawing Church people together and explaining the Christian faith to the modern world.

At the same time another notable figure in religious life passed away, Robert Dolling. It is well to dwell upon his name, because he recalls the real force which was in the successors of the Oxford movement. The Ritualists survived the storm of Protestant clamour and legal attack partly, no doubt, because they had able scholars to defend their views, but still more because they could point to effective work and saintly lives among the poorest classes. The whole of Dolling's life as a priest was spent in three obscure slum parishes. At his death people asked themselves whether it was the best use to make of such powers and such devotion, whether in fact the Church, by neglecting such men, was not failing to take the fullest advantage of its resources.

The religious world was, in truth, moving towards tolerance, and a notable example of the abandonment of supposed safeguards of orthodoxy, which had in practice become hindrances, occurred in this place. In June, 1902, the Council of King's College abolished the test which had hitherto been imposed on all members of the staff of the College. Henceforth it was resolved that only teachers of Theology should be required to be members of the Church of England. This wise and courageous action of the Council has proved to be a lasting benefit to the College and also to the cause of religion. It deserves to be chronicled among the events of ecclesiastical history.

But unfortunately the spirit of tolerance and mutual understanding had first to encounter a terrible obstacle. The history of religion is overshadowed during the whole of this period by the bitter controversy which arose over education. It does not belong to my province to consider the subject in detail, since another lecturer has the question of education assigned to him, but we cannot understand the religious situation unless we have some grasp of the principles which divided earnest and sincere religious people. It is difficult even at this day to speak frankly and at the same time avoid reawakening discussions which we would willingly forget.

The Education Bill of Mr. Balfour's government was an attempt to deal with the problem of the voluntary or " provided " schools. Most of these were Church of England or Roman Catholic. The advance of educational demands made it impossible that these schools should be still conducted on a purely voluntary basis, and it was proposed that they should be assisted out of the rates, in return for which assistance a share, though not a predominant share, should be given to the public authority in the government of the schools. The bill, which appeared in April, 1902, was at first received even by Liberal newspapers with mild approval ; but it was not long before the rumbling of a great storm was heard. The redoubtable Dr. Clifford and Dr. Guiness-Rogers lifted up voices of indignation and described it as " the accursed bill ", " the new church rate ". The controversy which began in these terms did not become more equable as time passed. A large meeting at Leeds inaugurated a popular agitation which was formidable though not without its humorous elements. Among them we may surely reckon the hymn sung at the Leeds meeting, composed by the Rev. J. Hirst Holliwell, which contained the moving lines,
　　" Priest and traitor sought to bring
　　The people's schools to nought."
We need not follow the course of this miserable controversy between Christians. There can be no doubt that it caused great harm to the cause of religion, and I cannot refrain from adding that, in my opinion, the development of " passive resistance " when the Act had been passed was a deplorable

episode. The motives of the leaders were unquestionably
of the highest, and I do not doubt that they followed their
conscience, but the spectacle of Christian ministers leading
a resistance to the law was fraught with consequences which
went far beyond the particular dispute.

When the Balfour government fell and Sir Henry Campbell-
Bannerman succeeded, it was the turn of the Church to lift
up voices of indignant protest against the attempt, as it was
regarded, in Mr. Augustine Birrell's Bill to destroy Church
schools. The House of Lords, however, " filled up the cup,"
or " vindicated its place in the constitution," however you
like to put it, by rejecting the Bill. Dr. Temple, the Archbishop of Canterbury at the opening of the reign, collapsed
during a speech on the Balfour Education Bill in the House
of Lords and died shortly afterwards. Dr. Randall Davidson,
who succeeded him, was untiring in his efforts to seek
understanding and compromise with the Nonconformists.

It would be a mistake to suppose that this religious quarrel
was a dispute about nothing. Real principles were involved
which went deeper than the particular points in question.
On the one side, there was a genuine desire that the education
of the people should be unfettered by dogmatic religion
and that there should be no domination by the Church.
It seemed that the principles of freedom for teachers and
democratic control were at stake. On the other side,
there was the conviction that life, and therefore
education, should be based upon the Christian faith, and
that this faith was essentially supernatural. There was
also the claim that the parent had the right to obtain
the kind of education which he desired for his children.
If I confess that my sympathies are on the Church side of
this controversy it may be due to the fact that my first
appearance in print was a little bolt against undenominational
religion in the schools. The syllogism which I produced
then still seems to me worthy of attention. " The Bible
and the Bible only is the religion of Protestants ; but the
Bible and the Bible only is that which it is proposed should

alone be taught in schools assisted by the rates. Therefore
it is proposed to subsidize at the public expense only one
kind of religion—the religion of Protestants." We may
hope, perhaps, that this kind of argument, however conclusive, has ceased to be of importance and confidently assert
that Churchmen and Nonconformists are not likely to fight
each other again with such bitterness. We have other and
sterner work to do against a common foe, who, as we all see
clearly now, will, unless we stand together, overwhelm us all.

We may turn to chronicle some more cheerful events in
the religious life of the nation. In 1904 the Bishopric of
Birmingham was founded and Dr. Gore, who had been the
moving spirit in this, left his ancient see to occupy the new
episcopal throne, beginning a fruitful and memorable period
of work in the city. The Pan-Anglican Congress assembled
on June 15th, 1908, and was representative of the whole
Anglican Church throughout the world. The object of the
Congress, as stated by the Archbishop of Canterbury, was
to discuss the means of making the living message of Jesus
Christ tell more fruitfully in the world. Addresses were
given by many distinguished authors and philosophers as
well as theologians, and there can be no doubt that the
Congress helped to bring out the world-wide mission of
the Anglican Church and to arouse a stronger missionary
spirit. The Congress concluded with a great missionary
meeting in the Albert Hall organized by the London Inter-
Collegiate Christian Union and the World's Student Christian
Federation.

The same year the fifth Lambeth Conference met which
242 bishops attended. The results were not perhaps striking
to the popular imagination, but much useful work was done,
particularly in preparing the way for closer union with the
Eastern Churches, the Old Catholics, and the Scandinavian
Church. The Commission which was appointed at this
Conference began the labour and negotiations which have
recently issued in the entering into full communion with the
Old Catholics and the Church of Sweden. The Encyclical

Letter emphasized the aspect of the Church of God as
ordained for the service of men and recognized a stirring
of new feelings of responsibility for the evangelization of
the world and the Christianization of the social order. The
influence of the " Christian Social Union " and other similar
organizations is surely to be seen in the statement that the
Lambeth Conference " recognizes the ideals of brotherhood
which underlie the democratic movements of the century ".
The Conference had probably the Modernist movement
in view when it emphatically reaffirmed its adhesion to the
" historic creeds " and its firm conviction that the historical
facts of the Gospels are fundamental for the Christian faith.
" Without the historic creeds the ideas (of Christianity)
would evaporate into unsubstantial vagueness and
Christianity would be in danger of degenerating into a nerve-
less altruism." The Conference expressed, however, the
desire that a new translation should be made of the so-called
Athanasian Creed. The Conference condemned explicitly
and without reservation the practice of contraception, and
in this matter we may, remembering the last Lambeth
Conference, congratulate ourselves that it has never claimed
to be infallible. By a small majority the Conference expressed
the opinion that neither party in a divorce should be re-
married with the rites of the Church. A momentous
resolution concerned the revision of the Prayer Book. The
Conference laid down the following principles which should
be observed in any revision :—

(1) The rubrics should be adapted to present customs.

(2) Omissions should be made to obviate repetitions and
redundancy.

(3) There should be additions to the present services
by way of enrichment.

(4) There should be a fuller provision of alternatives.

(5) There should be greater elasticity.

(6) Words which are obscure or commonly misunderstood
should be changed.

(7) The Calendar and Tables should be revised.

It would be interesting to discuss how far these principles were observed in the actual revision which was produced in 1928.

This leads us to the actual beginning of the course of events which have had such important consequences in our own time. The so-called " disorders in the Church " and the agitation about ritualism and the impotence or reluctance of Bishops to deal with it had led to the appointment of a Royal Commission presided over by Sir Michael Hicks-Beach. In the autumn of 1906 the Commission reported, recommending that the rubrics concerning the ornaments of the ministers should be considered so that their meaning should be clear. " Letters of business " were issued to the Convocations ordering them to consider the desirability of a new rubric on this subject. The prospect of a revision of the Prayer Book drew nearer and was received by some with gratitude, but probably the opinion expressed by the editor of the official Church Year Book was more widely prevalent—viz., that it was " dangerous to throw the Prayer Book into the melting pot ". Both views possibly were right. We know now that it *was* dangerous ; but the end is not yet, and we may still come to regard the book which Parliament rejected as a milestone on the road to a Church and services fitted for the modern world.

The closing years of the reign present us with two events which signalize the passing of an old order and the beginning of a new. In 1909 a Bill for the Disestablishment of the Church in Wales was introduced and was opposed and denounced by most churchmen. Very few, I suppose, now would wish to go back to the old situation if it were possible. What seemed to many a disaster has been, in effect, a liberating of new spiritual power.

In 1910, two months after the death of King Edward, a great missionary conference assembled in Edinburgh. There was searching of heart among many Church people whether the Society for the Propagation of the Gospel could consistently take part in a congress which included all the Churches except the Roman Catholic. These scruples were happily overcome and the result was an increase of co-operation in the mission field which was of great value. Of still greater value was the mutual understanding and desire for comprehension which was fostered. The conference appointed continuation committees which worked in different parts of the world and prepared the way for the still more remarkable Jerusalem Conference which assembled after the War. It has often been said that the unity of the Churches will begin in the mission field. The South India scheme is a proof of this statement. The impetus to reunion in mission work comes largely from the Edinburgh Conference. We ought not to pass from this subject without mentioning the name of Dr. Mott, whose leadership and statesmanship was at Edinburgh, and has been since, a great asset to the Christian Church.

We have traced some of the external events of the ecclesiastical life of the period, but it may be asked how far was organized religion playing any considerable part in the life of the people ? We have seen the Church struggling and beginning to reform and adapt itself, but had it any meaning or interest for the masses ? We have a certain amount of reliable information on this subject. In 1902 the *Liverpool Post* conducted a census of the actual attendance at the places of worship in the city, and was able to compare the results with those of eleven years before. Somewhat surprisingly it was found that the proportion of churchgoers to the population in both years was almost identical. The following year the *Daily News* conducted a similar census in London, and here the results were far less encouraging. It was found that out of a possible church-going population of $4\frac{1}{2}$ millions just over one million attended some place of worship. It was also concluded that, whereas the Nonconformist churchgoers had declined only slightly in number, the Church of England attendances had dropped in an alarming manner. Where there had been four worshippers in 1886 there were only three in 1903.

But the most illuminating and authoritative source of information is Charles Booth's great work on *Life and Labour in London*. He summarized the effect of religious influence in London in a manner which must have penetrated the self-complacency of the most satisfied prelate. The purely working-class districts were, he reported, practically untouched by religious organizations. The middle-class districts had vigorous and spontaneous religious organizations which, however, were largely secularized and used for social purposes. Among the leisured and cultured classes there was much church-going, but very little church work. The able reviewer in the *Guardian* summed up the situation with equal frankness. " There are," he says, " really four classes : the poor, who are visited and bribed ; the working classes, who ignore organized religion and seek their ideals quite apart from it ; the middle classes, who use the church largely for social purposes ; the cultured classes, who go to church for worship but have no more to do with it." " It is," as he remarks, " a gloomy picture of failure ". We are perhaps surprised to learn that, in Sir Charles Booth's opinion, the Salvation Army in this period and area was not producing any marked effect. One comfort we may derive from this glimpse into the religious condition of London in Edwardian times. The revolt from organized religion is not a peculiarity of the post-war period. We have not declined perhaps from a better time as much as we had thought.

At the close of the reign a book entitled *Facing the Facts* was published which gives a candid examination of the religious situation. Dr. Kempthorne, the Bishop of Hull, wrote on the " present outlook ". He states the pessimistic case, pointing out the decline in public worship, the shirking of most responsibility, the declining birth-rate, the still disgraceful social conditions, the impotence of organized Christianity to cope with the situation on account of its inner conflicts. He finds consolation in the thought that, in the minds of many Englishmen, religion was a purely individual affair, "something entirely between themselves and their God," and hence that church attendance is no adequate criterion of the power of religion. He sees grounds of hope in the Edinburgh Conference and the growth of the Student Christian movement, also in the new spirit of self-criticism and the zeal for service which had been stimulated by Sir Charles Booth's book. Mr. H. G. Wood, writing from the standpoint of the Free Churches, has much the same tale to tell. He has a hint of the cause. "The pulpit is losing its influence as a moral and intellectual guide, partly because there is too much lip-service to old formulas, and pulpit utterances are too complacent in tone and insufficiently direct." "The work of readjusting the central message of the Gospel to modern conditions of thought has not proceeded with sufficient rapidity." He calls for a "master-theologian with the strength of a Calvin."

The future was to provide, not a master-theologian, but a world-war. There was one fact which these candid friends of religion did not face—they were not alone in their blindness—the fact that the whole international complex was in a state of unstable equilibrium. The tasks before the Church were even more difficult than they supposed. They wondered whether it had an effective message for a world confident of itself. They were confronted with the sterner test whether it had a message of power for a world in dissolution.

On the whole we have the impression of a time of religious decline. The "Victorian peace", such as it was, is ruined. For a time the impetus carries men forward in the old ways, but it is diminishing. The hopeful sign is that, in every communion there are men and women who are trying to face the facts and to prepare the way for an advance.

The intellectual movement of the Edwardian age in religion is of great interest. In it tendencies, prepared in the preceding decade, come to a head. The early years of the century saw the publication of a book by a group of Oxford tutors,

Contentio Veritatis, which, though not of such wide appeal as *Lux Mundi* or *Foundations*, showed the trend of thoughtful Christians. The present Dean of St. Pauls and the late Dr. Rashsdall were among the contributors. The writers are impelled by the need for reconstruction of the Christian faith. " There is," they say, " widespread unsettlement and uneasiness. There is a vague feeling that the old orthodoxy is impossible ; people suspect that much that was once commonly believed is no longer tenable, but they do not know how much, nor by what it is to be replaced " (p. v). The book did not create the sensation of *Lux Mundi* and produced only mild protests against what seemed to some critics a minimizing of the historical element in Christianity. Throughout the reign there were sporadic theological scandals concerning the Virgin Birth and the physical resurrection. In 1903 a long and confused controversy broke out over an address by Dr. Freemantle, Dean of Ripon, in which he was alleged to have denied the Virgin Birth. Much of the discussion seems to have turned on what Dr. Freemantle really said, a subject on which he himself appears to have been able to shed singularly little light. At the end it was agreed that Dr. Freemantle believed in the Virgin Birth but did not regard it as a miracle— surely one of the most remarkable instances of making the worst of both worlds. The same subject reappeared in a more acute form at the end of our period when Dr. Gore, then Bishop of Oxford, felt obliged to call upon Mr. Beeby to resign his benefice on the grounds that he denied this article of the creed. The irony of the situation in which the liberal of one generation became the hammer of the liberals of the next was not lost upon the general public.

The Edwardian age has to its credit much valuable work in theology. Probably its most important achievement was a provisional synthesis of the results of Biblical Scholarship. Hasting's *Dictionary of the Bible* and the *Encyclopædia*

Biblica were completed. The latter, though containing much valuable work, was vitiated by an excessively radical criticism and still more by the fact that Professor Cheyne, who was a large contributor, was unfortunately obsessed by the importance of the obscure tribe Jerachmell in Old Testament history. Hasting's *Dictionary* was an achievement of first-rate importance. It brought together the results of conservative criticism and placed before the mind of the ordinary clergyman and minister in a compendious way the modern view of the Bible.

The advance of scholarship was sustained in Biblical studies and the beginning of a wider view of the duty of the exegete may be discovered in the literature of the period. The evolution of religious ideas among the Hebrews was now seen to be a part of the general history of religion and the study of Comparative Religion made new conquests and its influence was felt among theologians. A notable contribution to the early history of religion was made by Dr. R. R. Marrett in his *Threshold of Religion*, in which he pointed out the importance of a type of feeling, called by him " Mana ", which appears to precede definite religious beliefs and rites. The field which Dr. Marriett opened up has been cultivated by many since, notably by Dr. R. Otto in his *Idea of the Holy*. Illuminating work was also done on the background of Christianity and more accurate knowledge was obtained of the religious and social conditions of the world into which Christianity came. Notable service was done in this field by Dr. Edwyn Bevan and Dr. T. R. Glover, whose *Conflict of Religions in the Early Roman Empire* had a great popular success. The research on the text of the New Testament also made advances and the problem of the Synoptic Gospels may be said to have been practically solved in these years. Dr. Sanday, of Oxford, and Dr. Stanton, of Cambridge, were the leaders of a group of distinguished scholars who devoted themselves to the Gospel text. Dr. Stanton's monumental *Gospels as Historical*

Documents deserves to be mentioned among the literary productions of the period.

Important work was also done on the lines of that recontruction which the contributors to *Contentio Veritatis* had demanded. Dr. Sanday did not confine himself to critical studies but in *Christologies, Ancient and Modern*, plunged into the deep waters of a restatement of the Doctrine of the Incarnation. Making use of the speculations of F. W. Myers concerning the " subliminal self " he suggested a new view of the relation between the Divine and Human natures of Jesus. The theory won few adherents, but the discussion which it aroused was of great value and brought to the notice of many who were plunged in " dogmatic slumbers " the problems with which modern theology had to grapple. Other contributors to constructive theology deserve mention. Dr. Tennant published a valuable collection of material illustrative of the history of the doctrine of Original Sin and in his book *The Concept of Sin* discussed with great acuteness the fundamental ideas of sin and guilt. Dr. J. R. Illingworth continued the series of volumes in which he based a Christian Theology on Idealism of the school of T. H. Green. A distinguished Nonconformist divine, Dr. Fairbairn, published during this decade his chief work, *The Philosophy of the Christian Religion*. In him we have an example of the contact with German theology which was certainly growing in this period. Perhaps the Free Church divines were more closely in touch with the dogmatic theology and religious philosophy of Germany than Anglicans, though the influence of Schliermacher and Ritschl began to be felt very widely. Dr. P. Forsyth should be named among Nonconformist writers who had a large circle of readers. His books were almost without exception directed towards a restatement of the Gospel of the Cross, and his weight counted for much as a counterpoise to the tendency in the New Theology and elsewhere to minimize the idea of salvation in Christian preaching. Dr. Forsyth commended his books by his epigrammatic style, but it is to be feared somewhat obscured his meaning. Much the same point of view, though less profoundly thought and imagined, was represented by the Scottish theologian, Dr. Denney, who defended and restated the old doctrines of Redemption in his *Death of Christ*.

These are some only of the important books on theology which were published during the Edwardian period and may be taken as evidence that there was great activity of religious thought. The ferment of ideas was of course also manifested in sermons and newspapers. We have already referred to the ministry of Mr. R. J. Campbell at the City Temple ; we must add the sermons of Canon Hensley Henson in St. Margarets, Westminster, which discussed the fundamental problems of religion and were not infrequently provocative. There can be no doubt that this ministry was an important factor in the movement of thought. Another symptom of the wider interest in religion as a subject of free inquiry was the beginning of the *Hibbert Journal* in 1902 under the editorship of Dr. L. P. Jacks and Dr. Dawes Hicks, who still in 1933 carry on their work with undiminished vigour. *The Church Quarterly Review*, under the editorship of Dr. A. C. Headlam, was changed in outlook and became a formidable champion of the liberal orthodoxy of the *Lux Mundi* type.

The Gifford Lectures had by the middle of Edward's reign begun to attract the notice of general readers as well as theological and philosophical experts. The prevailing philosophical theory represented by the lectures of this period was Absolute Idealism, and one of the most important of the series, *The World and the Individual*, by Josiah Royce, the American philosopher, presented the " new-Hegelian " interpretation of religion in its most cogent and attractive form ; but the most remarkable of the Gifford Lectures marked a complete break with the Idealist tradition and an attempt to build religious faith once more on experience and empirical evidence. William James, in the *Varieties of Religious Experience*, laid the foundation of a new psychological study of religion which was destined in later years to bear much, and various, fruit.

Two men who belonged to the Roman Church produced a profound effect on religious thought in this country— George Tyrrell, who was excommunicated, and Friedrich von Hügel, who was not. Both were affected by the remarkable Modernist movement which was exciting interest in France and Italy at the opening of the Edwardian decade, though Tyrrell was probably more thoroughly in sympathy with the principles of French Modernism than Hügel ever was. The leaders of this movement, in particular A. Loisy, attempted to combine a Catholicism, which was definitely opposed to liberal Protestantism, with the most thoroughgoing critical method in history and the interpretation of Scripture. Tyrrell was not so extreme a critic as Loisy and possessed a more mystical temperament which gave even his polemical writings a religious appeal which Loisy never approached. Tyrrell shared, however, the condemnation which the Vatican passed on the Modernists in 1907 in the Bull *Pascendo Gregis* and the new *Syllabus of Errors*. It is significant that while Tyrrell's funeral was performed by a Roman Catholic priest, a large proportion of those present was Anglican. The type of Modernism which he represented is, to all appearance, dead in the Church to which he clung even when it would have none of him— it is living in the Anglican Church to which he would not return. The last book which Tyrrell published, *Christianity at the Cross Roads*, though not perhaps a great work, is distinguished by a keen perception of the great problem which was to vex theologians in the coming years—the eschatological and apocalyptic elements in the thought and teaching of Jesus.

Baron von Hügel was perhaps never a Modernist in the sense of Loisy or Tyrrell. He was a scholar and philosopher with wide sympathies, and no less a saint. His immense learning and personal character gave him an influence far beyond the bounds of his own communion, and indeed, it would be true to say that his writings were far better appreciated by Anglicans and Nonconformists than by the authorities of his own church. His greatest book, *The Mystical Element in Religion*, appeared at the end of the Edwardian decade, though its influence is to be reckoned rather as a part of the history of the later years. He gave an impulse to the study of mysticism and the investigation of religious experience which is as yet far from being exhausted.

I cannot sum up the achievements of the Edwardian era in the field of religious thought. The scene is too confused : the voices are too various. Perhaps we are too near to them to grasp their full significance. I have the impression of a groping towards a new synthesis—towards a restatement of Christianity which shall retain all the ancient values and yet be in accord with the new world of science and democracy. This synthesis is being wrought out by many men along different lines, which may or may not converge. It is being attempted in the face of the bitter mockery of those who maintain that it cannot be done, that the religion of Christendom has finished its course and must make way for the non-religion of the future or the new religion of some distinguished novelist or playwright. It is being thought out while hungry sheep are looking up to be fed and perplexed shepherds are asking what food of the spirit still remains unsuspect. But it is being wrought out by men who have themselves no doubt about the permanence of religion or that it is the highest and " deepest exigency of man's nature " (Tyrrell). In short, the Edwardian religious thinkers were in a position very much like ourselves. We enter into their labours and their problems. We shall be fortunate if we acquit ourselves as well.

W. R. MATTHEWS.

IV

Domestic Politics

All who were living when Queen Victoria died in the first month of the present century must look back to that event as the beginning of a new era in our domestic politics. There was no outward sign of change, save the universal mourning. One constitutional sovereign succeeded another. The Unionist Ministry under Lord Salisbury remained in office. The South African War continued to exasperate the nation by its indecisive character and heavy cost. The party strife of " Imperialists " and " Little Englanders " or " Pro-Boers " was checked but for a moment. Yet everyone was conscious that something had happened to divert the normal course of home affairs, and that England would never be quite the same again.

Looking back, after thirty years, one can see that those who viewed the change of sovereign with apprehension were not justified. But at the time the new king, though very popular and greatly respected, was not understood. His mother was known to have exercised great, though unseen, influence over her ministers ; her correspondence, now published, confirms in the main the general belief of her contemporaries that she guided if she did not rule. The question was whether King Edward had the will or the power to maintain the Victorian tradition, whether he would not signalize his accession to the throne by insisting on some new development of policy, possibly even in a Liberal direction. It was thought by some that this shrewd and vigorous man of the world, who had for so many years been a privileged but inactive spectator of the political game, would wish to take a hand, now that the opportunity so long deferred had come. It was supposed in some quarters that the king, who

knew everybody and had been everywhere and whose social
pre-eminence was unquestioned, would be able, if he cared,
to exert a far greater influence over his ministers than his
aged mother had done. There were even those who imagined
that, although King Edward had no liking for his nephew,
the German Emperor, he might seek to give the monarchy
somewhat of the leadership that the Court of Berlin
unquestionably asserted in all departments of German life
and thought. Such anticipations, it can now be said, were
unfounded. King Edward doubtless impressed the virtues
of caution and moderation on all the statesmen with whom he
had to deal, but he never sought to enlarge the prerogative
or increase the power of the Crown. In contrast to his mother
who had long lived in retirement, he was much in the public
eye and revived the social functions of the monarchy.
But in politics, whether domestic or foreign, King Edward
never overstepped the bounds imposed on a strictly constitutional king. It was soon realized that he showed equal
favour to men of all parties. It was whispered abroad that
Mr. John Burns, then regarded as a Radical of the Radicals,
was one of the king's friends. The new era, then, had not
altered the position of the monarch, who was still to be the
impartial hereditary president of the state.

Nevertheless, the change of sovereign had a significance.
Many people felt that the confusion of parties which had
been increasing for years past must now be resolved. They
assumed, perhaps wrongly, that the party leaders had not
pressed their quarrels to the uttermost lest the venerable
queen's declining years should be embittered, and that in
a new reign such self-denial would not be shown. It is true
at any rate that political strife took on a sharper tone from
the accession of King Edward and raged unceasing till his
death.

The so-called "Khaki" Election of 1900, completed
a few weeks before the queen's death, had confirmed
Lord Salisbury's Government in power with the substantial

majority of 134 in the House of Commons—only 18 less than
the anti-Home Rule majority of the General Election of 1895.
It was doubtless desirable, on grounds of public policy, to take
the verdict of the electors on the South African War as soon
as the struggle seemed to be nearing its end.   A vote of
confidence in the Government was bound to disillusion the
Boers, some of whom counted on a Liberal victory and
expected that, as in 1880, it would mean a reversal of our
policy towards the Transvaal.   Until it was clear that the
British people meant to finish the war so unwisely precipitated
by President Kruger, the Boer leaders would not seek for
peace.   But for all that the appeal to the country was bitterly
resented by the Liberal Opposition.   They thought it most
unfair that the Government should snatch a party advantage
from a national crisis, and that Unionist candidates should
base their appeals on the argument, placarded everywhere,
that " A vote for the Liberals is a vote for the Boers ".   The
Opposition objected all the more vehemently because they
were sharply divided in their attitude towards the war.   Some
Liberals, led by Asquith and Haldane, regarded the war as
inevitable ;   others, led by Morley and Courtney, called it
a crime ;   while the remainder under Campbell-Bannerman
criticized the conduct of the war whenever an opportunity
offered for making party capital.   All, however, agreed that
Lord Salisbury should not have dissolved Parliament when
he did, and that patriotic sentiment had been improperly
aroused to prevent the usual " swing of the pendulum " at
the General Election.   The Opposition thus laboured under
a sense of grievance in King Edward's first Parliament, while
Unionists were apt to taunt Liberals with lack of patriotism.
Tempers on both sides were sorely tried, especially as the
war went on for another eighteen months.

Despite its electoral success, the Unionist Ministry was
by no means free from troubles.   The coalition between the
Conservatives and the Liberal Unionists, who left Gladstone
in 1886 because of their dislike of Irish Home Rule, had been

maintained with some difficulty in the country, but the entrance of Liberal Unionists into the Cabinet in 1895 had set up serious strains and stresses in that body. Mr. Joseph Chamberlain's forceful personality was by no means agreeable to some of the Conservative veterans. The memoirs of Sir Michael Hicks-Beach, afterwards Lord St. Aldwyn, who was Lord Salisbury's Chancellor of the Exchequer for seven years and a typical representative of the Conservative country gentlemen, show very plainly his distrust of Chamberlain's policy and methods. The Chancellor, true to his party tradition, stood for peace abroad and economy at home, and he viewed with ill-concealed alarm Chamberlain's readiness to run the risk of war in South Africa and his eagerness to initiate expensive social reforms such as he had advocated in his early Radical days at Birmingham. The outbreak of what proved to be a long and costly war confirmed Hicks-Beach's disapproval of his impetuous colleague, who had made it necessary for the Chancellor to increase the income-tax from ninepence to a shilling in the pound, and to introduce the first Budget that exceeded £100,000,000. In these spend-thrift days the taxpayer can but look back with admiration on that Golden Age, and wonder at Hicks-Beach's modest taxes. But economy was then taken seriously by statesmen of the old school. Gladstone had resigned in 1894 rather than agree to larger Navy Estimates. Hicks-Beach was as reluctant as Gladstone to increase public expenditure on any pretext. Chamberlain, reared in the hard school of business, had no such dislike of spending, if and when he thought it desirable or expedient. The difference between these two resolute men, each with his partisans, was fundamental. While Lord Salisbury presided over the Cabinet, such discords were repressed. When he resigned in July, 1902, a year before his death, his nephew and successor, Arthur Balfour, lacked the authority to control his colleagues. Hicks-Beach, indeed, had followed his old chief into retirement, pleading ill-health, but clearly foreseeing the quarrels that were about to break loose between the old-fashioned Unionists like himself and those who desired to move forward with Chamberlain on new paths.

The first important Government measure of the new reign, the Education Bill of 1902, brought out differences among the Government's supporters, comparable to, though not identical with, the differences in the Cabinet. The Bill was in the main a sound piece of reform, on which all English educationists look back with satisfaction, in that it co-ordinated all types of national education and set the county and large borough councils to supervise the whole. It also did tardy justice to the sectarian schools, Anglican, Roman, Wesleyan, and so forth, which had long been denied any aid from local rates and which had to eke out their modest Government grants with the help of private subscribers. But the rate aid now given to these sectarian or voluntary schools was anathema to the Nonconformists. They had beaten Gladstone himself on this issue in 1870, and they still maintained that it was unfair to call upon ratepayers of varying religions or none to subsidize schools in which there was a special form of religious teaching. The Nonconformists held that rate-aid implied control by the local rating authority. But the supporters of the voluntary schools objected to such control, which might and often would mean interference with the special religious instruction given by or under the direction of the parson or the priest. The Government, seeking to compromise, proposed that the managers of a voluntary school should be appointed, as to two-thirds by the school trustees, and as to one-third by the local authority. The majority would assure the appointment of teachers capable of giving the required religious instruction. The minority would see that the secular teaching was efficient. But the compromise did not pacify the opposition. The Established and the Roman Churches were, they said, being endowed afresh at the expense of the ratepayers. Some energetic Nonconformist leaders, like Dr. Robertson Nicoll and Dr. Clifford, began to agitate for passive resistance to the payment of the school rate. The welfare of the schools and the children was overlooked in the furious controversy that raged throughout the year.

The Education Bill, while encouraging a despondent Liberal Opposition, seriously weakened the Government Coalition. The Liberal Unionist party, which still maintained a separate organization, included many influential Nonconformists, especially in the Birmingham district. They brought much pressure to bear on Chamberlain, in the hope of getting the Bill modified or withdrawn. Chamberlain, who had strong Nonconformist sympathies, defended the Bill with reserve. " If the voluntary schools were crushed out, we should have schools without any religious teaching." He told the Duke of Devonshire in a private letter in the autumn that the Bill was disintegrating their party. The Duke, his fellow Liberal Unionist leader, preferred to accept and defend the measure. But both men foresaw that it would drive many of their Nonconformist followers away. On the other hand, the High Church party objected with almost equal vigour to an amending clause, inserted late in the long Committee stage at the instance of a Low Churchman, which provided that religious education in voluntary schools should be given in accordance with the trust deeds and under the control of the managers as a body, whether denominational or not. This, it was urged by its critics, would oust the parson from his rightful job and leave the religious teaching in the hands of laymen. Moreover, despite the large additional grants promised to the new education authorities, ratepayers, especially in the country districts, viewed with alarm the prospect of having to pay higher school rates. The Bill survived all these strangely violent quarrels because the Government majority, however restless, was supplemented on critical divisions by the full strength of the Irish Nationalists, acting in defence of the Roman Catholic schools. The venerable Archbishop Temple spoke for it in the House of Lords a few days before his death. But the end of the long session of 1902 found the Conservatives troubled by the dispute between High Church and Low Church, and the Nonconformist Liberal Unionists distinctly mutinous, while the Liberal Opposition, their unity to some extent restored by the ending of the South African war, had found a grievance and an election cry in the endowment of the voluntary schools without control. There can be no doubt that this sectarian controversy sent many Nonconformists back to the Liberal ranks and marked the beginning of the end for the Unionist Government. Moreover, it strengthened Chamberlain's determination to find a new fighting policy on which the Government could appeal with some confidence to the electors.

Chamberlain thought that he had found what he desired in the new fiscal policy upon which he now staked his political future. It had for him two aspects—the one Imperial, the other domestic. As Colonial Secretary from 1895 he had been profoundly impressed by his discovery of the British Empire. He shared in the enthusiasm aroused at Queen Victoria's Diamond Jubilee of 1897, which all the colonies and India took part in celebrating. His combative patriotism was aroused by the efforts of other Powers to enlarge and develop their colonial possessions, especially in Africa. He was deeply moved by the South African War, which convinced him that the Empire needed to be reorganized on a businesslike footing if it were not to fall to pieces. As an old business man he naturally saw in trade a means of strengthening the ties of Empire. The old colonial system, though damaged by the secession of the American colonies, had worked reasonably well for half a century longer, until the Free Traders swept it away. He would revive that system in a new and improved form, giving the colonies and receiving from them preferential tariffs which would, he hoped, greatly stimulate trade within the Empire and benefit the Mother-country most of all. His Imperialism, his interest in the growth of British civilization all the world over was, he knew, shared by many men on both sides of the House. Lord Milner, who had served as his chosen representative in South Africa, had as many close friends and admirers among the leading Liberals, like Asquith, Haldane, and Rosebery, as he had in the Conservative ranks. There was thus some reason to hope that parties might be realigned on this patriotic and Imperial issue, if it could be rightly presented, even if Imperial Preference meant a tax on foreign foodstuffs competing with those imported from the colonies.

Chamberlain attached no less importance to the domestic aspect of his programme. He had been a Radical leader in youth and middle age, and he was deeply concerned at the condition of the working class. He believed that we were losing our leadership in world commerce, that wages were unduly low, and that unemployment was tending to increase. He felt that social reforms, such as Bismarck had instituted in Germany, were overdue, and that new sources of revenue must be tapped to provide for such reforms. To revive industry and to provide fresh revenue he therefore envisaged a protective tariff. It would, he hoped, on both grounds attract the working class elector, while it would please the manufacturer, hard hit by foreign competition. Germany seemed to be prospering mightily under protection; why should not England adopt the same fiscal policy once again?

Chamberlain left England in the winter of 1902 for a political tour of South Africa, where he discussed the future of the conquered Boer States. He returned in the spring of 1903 full of new ideas for the benefit of South Africa and fully convinced that something must be done for the Empire as a whole. Two months later, at Birmingham on 15th May, 1903, he told his constituents that the time had come to strengthen the Empire by giving a preference to colonial produce and asking the colonies to give us a preference on our manufactures. The speech transformed the whole political situation. It divided the Unionist party while it reunited the Liberals. The Cabinet was rent in twain. Mr. Balfour, personally less influential than his uncle and predecessor, strove vainly to keep his team in hand. Ritchie, the Conservative Chancellor of the Exchequer, had virtually challenged Chamberlain at the outset by insisting that the trifling corn duty of a shilling a quarter imposed by his predecessor, Sir Michael Hicks-Beach (Lord St. Aldwyn), should be dropped, and Chamberlain had not felt it expedient to resist him in an uneasy Cabinet. As the summer passed the split in the Cabinet widened. King Edward advised Balfour to refer the fiscal issue to a Royal Commission but he declined. The Prime Minister was in general agreement with Chamberlain in so far that he had no objection in principle to a tariff which might be used to lower hostile tariffs, but he saw plainly that the country was not prepared to accept duties on foodstuffs, however small or whatever the alleged benefits to be received in return. By September it became clear to Chamberlain that he must be free from office to expound his new policy, and he resigned. He told the king that, before he made his crucial speech in May, he had discussed the fiscal question in Cabinet and thought that all his colleagues except Ritchie agreed with him— a strange belief that has not been explained. The king tried to have the announcement of the resignation delayed, but was too late. The four leading Free Traders in the Cabinet, not knowing of Chamberlain's departure, tendered their resignations. Ritchie, Lord Balfour of Burleigh, and Lord George Hamilton were allowed to go. The Duke of Devonshire was persuaded by Balfour to stay, but changed his mind and went three weeks later ; he explained pathetically to the others that his deafness had prevented him from following the Cabinet discussions and that he had not realized how far Balfour was prepared to go with Chamberlain in a Protectionist direction. These resignations excited much ill feeling and split the Unionist party into warring camps. Balfour displayed courage in filling the vacancies and much dialectic skill in developing a vague fiscal policy of his own, the main feature of which was retaliation on the Protectionist countries which imposed high duties on our exports to them. He thought, apparently, that if it were given time, the Unionist party, or the bulk of it, would accept at any rate the larger part of Chamberlain's programme. It was noticeable in 1904 that the party held together to pass the highly contentious Licensing Bill, which, by requiring the trade to provide a compensation fund for redundant public-houses, has gradually brought about a great reduction in the number of licensed premises. But with the rapid development of Chamberlain's Tariff Reform campaign and the counter-moves of the Unionist Free Traders, Mr. Balfour's followers became more and more confused and restive. A letter from Mr. Balfour's secretary, dated 20th January, 1905, which is printed in the recent *Life of Lord Carson*, shows that at that time the Prime Minister had abandoned all hope of retaining office after the next General Election. He could only seek to minimize the defeat that was clearly foreshadowed for a shattered and demoralized party.

As if to make matters worse, the Irish question obtruded itself anew. Balfour, in reconstructing his Cabinet, had brought into it his old friend, the gifted but highly temperamental George Wyndham, who had been Chief Secretary since 1900. Wyndham threw himself with his wonted enthusiasm into the task of settling the Irish land question once for all by a system of state-assisted purchase. If all the landlords were bought out and all the tenant farmers became owners of their holdings, rural Ireland, so Wyndham thought, would surely enjoy enduring peace and the Irish Nationalist party would lose its most popular grievance against the Union. The Irish Land Bill of 1903 gave effect to his ideas, and, as it was sweetened by a large Government subsidy, commended itself both to landlords and to tenants. Sir Edward (now Lord) Carson, who was then Solicitor-General, but who never forgot that he was an Irish Unionist, warned his Govern-

ment in a public speech that the Bill offered no permanent
solution. " I have been hearing of a last Irish Land Bill
and of a permanent solution all my life, and I have no doubt
that I shall hear of them again." But his warning, true enough
as we know now, was not taken seriously, and the Bill, as
a further instalment of the Unionist policy of " killing
Home Rule with kindness ", passed into law. Fresh trouble
developed almost at once. In the autumn of 1902 Wyndham
had persuaded Balfour, much against his will, to allow
Sir Anthony MacDonnell, a distinguished Indian civilian,
to be appointed permanent under-secretary for Ireland.
MacDonnell was an able and honourable man, but he had
strong leanings towards some sort of Home Rule for Ireland,
and therefore, as Balfour foresaw, was bound to arouse
suspicion among the Irish Unionists and thus to embarrass
the Government. A further disadvantage was that, owing to
Wyndham's rhetorical language, MacDonnell had been led
to believe that he would enjoy much more freedom to
initiate and develop a policy than was accorded to the ordinary
under-secretary. He was strengthened in the belief by the
king's anxiety lest he should, in the summer of 1903, accept
the Governorship of Bombay rather than stay in Dublin.
It was natural, then, that MacDonnell should feel justified
in co-operating with Lord Dunraven and other Irish landowners who sought to compromise with the Home Rulers
by what was called Devolution. In fact, MacDonnell helped
to draft, in Dublin Castle itself, the Irish reform scheme of
August and September, 1904. An Irish Council was to control
purely Irish expenditure, and exercise " such effective control
of purely Irish affairs as might be compatible with maintenance of the legislative Union between Great Britain and
Ireland, and with the supremacy of the Imperial Parliament."
MacDonnell believed that Wyndham knew what he was
doing, and he had told Wyndham by letter that he had
assisted in drafting the document. But Wyndham, who was
travelling abroad for his health, had not realized the situa-

tion until he saw the Irish reform manifesto in the newspapers and read the furious Unionist comments upon
" Devolution ". Wyndham at once repudiated all responsibility for the scheme. He could not, however, allay the
suspicions aroused, especially among the Ulster Protestants.
MacDonnell, feeling that he had been unfairly treated by
Wyndham, would not help him by resigning his post. Nor
did the Cabinet think it necessary or desirable to dismiss
MacDonnell, although they expressed their disapproval
of his action in assisting Lord Dunraven. But the Ulstermen
not unnaturally inferred that the Union was in danger
while MacDonnell remained in office under the nominal
control of so very romantic a politician as Wyndham. The
Opposition seized their opportunity to inflame the Ulster
suspicions when Parliament met in February, 1905, and
Wyndham, in trying to be loyal both to his party and to his
under-secretary, made matters worse. He was at the time
a very sick man, and he resigned a week later. But his
disappearance did not appease the Ulstermen, who continued
to hint that the Prime Minister himself was by no means
sound in the Unionist faith. There was, of course, no truth
in such suggestions. Yet they rankled in Balfour's mind
and caused a distinct coolness in his relations with those of
his colleagues who were more anxious than he to placate the
Irish Protestants. More than a year later, when Balfour
was out of office, the controversy was still proceeding.
When he was told by one of his colleagues that Unionists
in England as well as in Ireland felt " widespread misgiving
and uncertainty " about the MacDonnell affair, he replied
that the suspicions were " perfectly outrageous ". There
can be no doubt that Balfour's hold over his party, already
shaken by the tariff dispute, was fatally weakened by his
handling of this awkward Irish incident, in which he had
tried to shield an indiscreet friend. If his successor in the
leadership in 1911 made haste to emphasize his full support
of the Irish Unionist cause, it was at least partly due to

Bonar Law's remembrance of what Balfour had lost by seeming to think more of George Wyndham than of the Irish Protestants.

To complete the Government's misfortunes, it presented the now confident Opposition with a thoroughly popular election cry in Chinese labour. After the South African War, native labourers were slow to return to the Rand gold mines. The mining companies decided to import coolies from China, and obtained the approval of the High Commissioner, Sir Alfred Milner, and of the Colonial Secretary, Mr. Alfred Lyttelton. The coolies were kept in compounds, like the native labourers. Some of them were allowed to do semi-skilled work. The white miners complained of this, arguing that it would deprive some of them of employment. They initiated an agitation against the Chinese and gained the support of philanthropists who disliked the spectacle of coolies confined within enclosures. The suggestion that this was Chinese slavery found ready support among the less responsible Liberal politicians and the more credulous electors in England. A strenuous propaganda against the Government for permitting slavery in South Africa was carried on throughout the country in 1905 and unquestionably helped to make its defeat more decisive. A particularly venomous cartoon issued by the Opposition represented the ghosts of British soldiers killed in the South African War as pointing to the Chinese compounds and asking, " Did we die for this ? " It is now generally agreed that the importation of more Asiatic labour into South Africa, even for a temporary emergency, was a mistake. But from the domestic standpoint the episode is of interest as illustrating the bitterness of party feeling that was aroused by Balfour's continuance in office when public opinion had turned against him.

It was characteristic of the Unionist leader, who had clung to office for tactical reasons through two years of acrimonious disputing within his own party, that again for

tactical reasons he should determine to resign rather than
go to the country. When Balfour resigned early in December,
1905, he hoped—perhaps somewhat faintly—that the Liberal
Opposition would find it hard to form a Government.
During the South African War their domestic differences,
as has been said, were sharply marked, and even in 1905
many observers doubted whether Sir Henry Campbell-
Bannerman would be able to unite all the leading Liberals
under his leadership. The three chiefs of the Liberal League,
Asquith, Haldane, and Sir Edward Grey, were understood
to have no very high opinion of Sir Henry's statesmanship.
But when Campbell-Bannerman had undertaken to form
a Cabinet, the Liberal Leaguers soon found it expedient
to serve under him. According to Lady Oxford Asquith
made no difficulties but Sir Edward Grey tried to insist
that Campbell-Bannerman should go to the House of Lords
and let Asquith lead the House of Commons. The Prime
Minister's wife is said to have insisted that Sir Henry should
stand his ground. In any case the incipient revolt came to
nothing. The Prime Minister had the bulk of the party
on his side, whereas Sir Edward Grey was regarded with
suspicion by the more advanced Liberals. The experience
of 1880, when Lord Hartington, the Liberal leader, gave way
to Gladstone, the ex-leader of the party, was not to be repeated.
Campbell-Bannerman could not be ousted by any of his less
popular if more able colleagues. Within a few days the
Liberal Cabinet was formed. It was a strong combination,
in which room was found for all the leading Liberals—
always excepting Lord Rosebery, who preferred to remain
a detached observer. The Liberal Leaguers, Asquith at
the Exchequer, Grey at the Foreign Office, and Haldane at the
War Office, found themselves side by side with their old
adversaries, Morley at the India Office, Lloyd George at the
Board of Trade, and Sir Robert Reid as Lord Chancellor.
Past differences were forgotten—for the moment at least—
in the excitement of the return to office after more than ten

years and in the anticipation of a victory at the polls such as the Liberals had not had for twenty years.

The General Election of January, 1906, more than fulfilled their most sanguine expectations. At that time, of course, constituencies polled on different days within a period of two or three weeks. When Manchester, among the earliest boroughs to poll, rejected Mr. Balfour and its other Conservative members, there could be no doubt of the final result. Chamberlain's local popularity kept Birmingham solid for Tariff Reform. London and Liverpool, the Home Counties, and the South of England adhered in the main to their traditional Conservatism. But in the country as a whole the Conservatives, whether Free Traders or Tariff Reformers, were routed. Their domestic differences had fatally weakened them, whereas all the enemies that they had made in a prolonged term of office united against them. We have seen still more sensational General Elections since the War under adult suffrage, but in 1906 the Liberal victory was almost unprecedented in its magnitude. When the polling was ended, the Liberal Government could muster 377 supporters in a House of 670—an absolute majority—whereas the Conservative and Unionist Opposition had dwindled to 157, less than half its former strength. Fully two-thirds of the shrunken Opposition were avowed Tariff Reformers ; only eleven out of the whole number adhered firmly to Free Trade, and one of these was soon to cross the floor and vote with the Government.

The magnitude of this electoral triumph has to be emphasized because it affected the whole policy and temper of the new Government. First of all, it set the Liberal party free from the Irish incubus. Gladstone in 1886 and 1892 was dependent for a majority on the Irish Nationalist vote and therefore—apart from other reasons—had to introduce Home Rule Bills. Campbell-Bannerman in 1906 was completely independent of Redmond and his following and could afford to put the Irish question aside. Again, the size of its majority was interpreted by the Government to mean that the country disapproved of all that the previous Ministry had done, and wanted a complete change of policy. The verdict might have been taken as mainly negative— as an indication that the country preferred the solid benefits of Free Trade which it knew to the doubtful advantages of Tariff Reform. But an excited and triumphant Liberal party, once more in power after long years, could hardly be expected to take such a dispassionate view. They felt themselves empowered to undo all that the Conservatives had done and carry out the promises of the Liberal party programme. Such was the mood in which the Government presented itself to the new House of Commons in February, 1906.

There was but one small cloud on the Liberal horizon. At the General Election the Labour party, hitherto very small and but lightly regarded, had made its first serious effort to obtain representation, and it had succeeded in winning 29 seats. This compact little party had no mind to be treated merely as a section of the Liberal party, whose programme it thought antiquated and unreal. Moreover, it could not be ignored because it had 24 Liberal-Labour allies and was regarded with sympathy by the more Radical members of the orthodox Liberal majority. In the Cabinet Mr. John Burns, formerly a working engineer and now President of the Local Government Board, and Mr. Lloyd George, who had always paid close attention to the working-class movement, took a special interest in the new Labour group. The Prime Minister's first duty, after taking office, had been to receive delegates from a large crowd of unemployed who demonstrated in Whitehall, and he had promised them a fresh measure of relief. It was noticeable that the King's Speech included in the sessional programme several Bills designed to conciliate the Labour members, and that, when a Labour member introduced a Bill to provide meals for poor school children, it was readily supported by

G

Mr. Birrell, the Minister of Education. The principal Government measure in this category was the Trades Disputes Bill. A decision of the House of Lords in the Taff Vale case of 1901 had made it clear that a trade union might be made liable for damages for a wrongful act done on its behalf. The trade unions thenceforward demanded that the law should be amended, otherwise the right of their members to strike would be seriously impaired. The Liberal leaders had promised to remedy the grievance but were unwilling to concede the full Labour demand. This was made clear by the Attorney-General, Sir J. Lawson Walton, when he introduced the Bill on 28th March, 1906. The Bill, he explained, would limit the liability of trade unions to cases where the action complained of was that of the executive of a union or its authorized agent. There was to be no direct liability. But he could go no further, because Parliament " ought not hastily to transform the proletariat into a privileged class ". The Labour party was profoundly dissatisfied. Two days later, the chance of the ballot enabled a Labour member to introduce another Bill dealing with the same question. This provided that a trade union could not be sued for damages sustained through the conduct of its members. Admittedly, it put the trade unions above the law. But, to the general astonishment, the Prime Minister intervened in the debate and, throwing over his law officer, said that he would vote for the Labour Bill. At a later stage the Government Bill was amended in this sense, and those ministers like Mr. Asquith and the Attorney-General who obviously disliked the amendment had to choose their words with care. Sir Edward Carson summed up the Bill in a phrase : " The King can do no wrong : neither can the trade unions." That the Government had reason to fear the Labour vote was shown in the Committee stage, when a Labour amendment to remove all restrictions on picketing in a strike was narrowly defeated by only five votes. The great Liberal majority was divided on questions of this kind.

Looking back on that Parliament of 1906, one sees how the Liberal party, like its adversary, was the prey of conflicting tendencies. Most of its leaders still used the old Whig catchword " Retrenchment " and talked of reducing public expenditure, at a moment when Haldane's invaluable reorganization of the Army and the strengthening of the Navy made any such reduction of expenditure impossible. On the political side the Liberal Cabinet seemed chiefly anxious to undo what its predecessor had done, especially in regard to education and licensing. An English Ministry usually takes existing legislation for granted, though its administrative actions may be in sharp contrast to those of the Ministry which it has replaced. Thus Sir Henry Campbell-Bannerman lost no time in giving responsible Government to the Transvaal and in ordering that the Chinese coolies should leave the Rand as soon as possible.[1] But it is exceptional for a Government to devote its time to reversing the legislation of its opponents. However, in 1906 political tempers were inflamed, and the stupendous Liberal majority seemed able to do anything it pleased. Nearly one-fourth of the members were Nonconformists, more or less violently indignant at the Education Act of 1902 which had, as the saying went, put the Church and other sectarian schools on the rates. Liberals in general regarded brewers and publicans as so many Conservative agents and detested the Licensing Act of 1904 which had given owners and tenants a vested interest in their licensed houses, while saddling them, it is true, with contributions to a compensation fund. It is easy to see why the Cabinet was induced to yield to the clamour for revenge on Church and brewers. The alternative course was to embark on the positive social reforms which the Radical minority within and without the Cabinet, as well as the new Labour party, envisaged.

[1] Similarly, while Mr. Baldwin's Ministry had broken off relations with Russia, Mr. MacDonald, on taking office in May, 1929, immediately re-established the connection with Moscow.

But social reforms involved increased expenditure and higher taxes, and consorted ill with " Retrenchment ", so that for the time being they had to wait.

The first important Government measure was thus the Education Bill of 1906. It was certain to revive the religious controversy of four years before, since it provided that no school in which sectarian teaching was given should receive rate-aid. Much of the session was wasted in debate between the champions of what is called undenominational religious instruction and the supporters of the Anglican and Roman Catholic schools. No one was surprised when at the end of the year the Bill, after passing the Commons, was rejected by the House of Lords. No serious person, of whatever party, nowadays regrets the fate of that Bill.

At the time, however, the action of the Upper House was much resented, and all sections of the Liberal party made it the occasion for renewing the attack on the Lords which Gladstone had initiated before his resignation in 1894. That the hereditary Chamber should thwart a newly elected House with an exceptional majority was said to be intolerable. On the other hand, the Liberal Government had violated a well-established convention in trying to undo what its predecessor had done four years earlier. Moreover, constitutional disputes had seldom excited much interest in this country, except in the Reform Bill crisis of 1832. The Cabinet, swayed by its more cautious members, did not press the matter far. The session of 1907 opened with vague threats against the Upper House and the promise of a Licensing Bill to repeal, in effect, the Act of 1904. But the threats were not followed up and the Licensing Bill was postponed. The House of Lords amended some of the Government Bills freely, and much heat was generated in the controversy between the two Chambers, but in the end their differences were arranged. It was obvious that on the Bill to legalize marriage with a deceased wife's sister, for example, the House of Lords could scarcely be said to thwart the will of the people by insisting on amendments. Moderation characterized the Government's policy in finance. For the last time in living memory (if we leave out of account the abnormal post-war years) the Budget, introduced by Mr. Asquith as Chancellor of the Exchequer, showed a reduction of expenditure and a slight relief in taxation. Mr. Asquith, supported by the Prime Minister, still attached some importance to the idea of Retrenchment. To the demand for old age pensions, which many Liberals together with the Labour party put forward, Mr. Asquith's reply was that the country could not afford to spend twenty or thirty millions on a social reform of this kind. National defence against the ever-increasing menace of German armaments had of course to be provided for. But advanced politicians in those days preferred to turn a blind eye to the peril across the North Sea. It is difficult to understand, as one looks back to those years, how the storm-clouds lowering over Europe could have remained invisible to most Englishmen, so that the Liberal ministers who were reorganizing the Army and strengthening the Navy were exposed to the violent reproaches of their own followers for their extravagance. Such, however, were the facts. Comment is needless.

A marked change came over the scene in 1908, especially with the resignation and death of Sir Henry Campbell-Bannerman and the appointment of Mr. Asquith as Prime Minister, with Mr. Lloyd George as his Chancellor of the Exchequer. From this time onward the moderate section of the Cabinet and party lost ground, and the advanced men, the more Radical section, became more prominent. Personality doubtless counted for much. Mr. Asquith was an abler man than his predecessor, but he lacked Sir Henry's easy good humour which made him popular ; he also lacked Campbell-Bannerman's driving force and power of coming to a swift decision, whether right or wrong. Moreover, while " C.B." was perhaps lightly regarded by the intellectual minority of his party, Asquith was viewed with grave suspicion by a large section, who had never forgotten or forgiven his Liberal Imperialism in the South African crisis and who thought that he was unsympathetic to social reform.   By contrast, Mr. Lloyd George, with his magnetic personality, his readiness for adventure and his avowed desire for drastic political and social changes, was a more attractive figure in the eyes of the Radical section. The secrets of the Liberal Cabinet of 1908 and 1909 have yet to be unveiled.   But it may reasonably be inferred that Mr. Lloyd George was the driving force in the Cabinet's adoption of a more vigorous policy.   He saw, no doubt, that, while the Tariff Reformers were gradually gaining control of the Conservative party and while the new Labour party was demanding large measures of social reform, the Liberals could not remain content with a programme that was in part negative and in part antiquated.   Thus, while further attempts were vainly made to satisfy the Non-conformists on the schools question and the Temperance party on the licensing question, old age pensions were granted and the campaign against the House of Lords was resumed as a preliminary to the social reform Budget of 1909 in which Mr. Lloyd George revealed his policy.

Social reform was of course no monopoly of the Liberal party who had indeed regarded it with apprehension as costly and dangerous.   Their opponents, from the days of Disraeli and " Young England ", had tried to improve the condition of the poor.   Chamberlain's Tariff Reform policy was, largely though not wholly, designed to raise additional revenue with which to finance social reforms such as Bismarck had imposed upon Germany by similar means.   Sir Herbert Maxwell reports him as saying as early as 1895 that he would grant old age pensions and find the money by an import duty on wheat.   Thus the Tariff Reformers, who formed two-thirds of the Conservative Opposition in 1909, were not hostile to Mr. Lloyd George's social reform policy in principle.

They objected rather to the method by which he proposed to raise fresh revenue. The Budget increased taxes all round and imposed new burdens on landed property with the avowed intention of weakening if not destroying the landed interest and its political power. We can look back calmly on that Budget and wonder at the furious indignation aroused by imposts which, measured by the burdens of the taxpayer and property owner to-day, seem inconsiderable. We know, moreover, that Mr. Lloyd George's new land taxes, while they stopped housebuilding, proved so unremunerative that they were abandoned some years later with their author's consent. At the time, however, the Budget might well occasion alarm and resentment, for it increased direct taxation by a third and it inflicted the gravest injury on landowners great and small who were already suffering from Harcourt's estate duties and from agricultural depression. Mr. Lloyd George took full advantage of the political sensation which he had caused by delivering attacks on landowners as a class and on dukes in particular at Limehouse and elsewhere. He had, we must remember, first attracted attention in North Wales by championing the farmers against the squires ; class-warfare came natural to him, though it was uncongenial to English statesmen of either party. Meanwhile, to keep the Nonconformist vote, the Government had introduced a Bill to disestablish and disendow the Church in Wales.

Whether the Cabinet had, in fact, planned to provoke the House of Lords into rejecting the Budget is by no means certain, though it has often been stated as a fact. There had been much talk among Liberals of their " ploughing the sands "—that is, of passing Bills which the House of Lords could not accept—and of their " filling up the cup "— that is, of seeing how far the House of Lords would go in objecting to Liberal legislation. But it is certain that until late in the year 1909 no sober Conservative politician regarded it as possible or probable that the House of Lords would venture to reject the Budget, and it is highly doubtful whether Liberal ministers could have counted on what, from their point of view, was an astonishing stroke of luck. Much was said at the time about the theoretical right of the Upper House to reject if not to amend a finance bill. But it was well understood by everyone that the alleged right had been so long disused as to become virtually unusable. We have no written constitution, but we have very definite unwritten conventions which can only be defied at our peril. Thus, whatever the provocation offered by Mr. Lloyd George's Budget and still more by his speeches, the peers acted unconstitutionally in rejecting the financial measure which the Commons had passed after a long and stormy session. The shrewdest Conservatives warned the peers against such a course ; it is now known, for instance, that the late Lord Birkenhead, then a rising hope of the Tariff Reform Conservatives, advised his noble friends to leave the Budget alone. But the majority of the Upper House, swelled for the moment by a crowd of so-called " back-woodsmen " who rarely took their seats, disregarded the Conservative leaders and the well-known wishes of the king, and threw out the Budget by a decisive vote. Lord Milner, in colonial affairs so wise and far-seeing, had encouraged them by the violent speech in which he said, " Let us reject the Budget and damn the consequences." But it was, for them, a fatal blunder which surrendered all the advantages to the Liberal Government. Mr. Asquith at once made a solemn protest against the Lords' unconstitutional action and appealed to the country for authority, as it was expressed, to " end or mend " the Upper House.

The General Election of January, 1910, was fought with great bitterness, all the more because the Unionist party felt themselves to be taken at a disadvantage. They had hoped to make Tariff Reform the dominant issue and to profit by the widespread dissatisfaction of Churchmen and Roman Catholics, the licensed trade, and the average taxpayer with four years of Liberal administration. Instead, they found themselves faced with the cry of " The Lords or the People " and had to devote much of their energy to ingenious dialectic and fine-drawn constitutional arguments in defence of the Upper House. While the Opposition was half-hearted and angry, the Government was confident of success more overwhelming even than in 1906. The results, however, surprised both parties, for the Opposition made considerable gains where it advocated Protection, while the Government found the ordinary elector singularly unconcerned about the naughty peers and retained its hold mainly by Free Trade propaganda on the text " Your food will cost you more "—if, that is, the Unionists were returned to power. When the polling ended, the Government found itself still with a nominal majority.[1] But it had lost a hundred seats to the Opposition, whom it now outnumbered only by two votes, and was thus no longer independent of its Labour and Irish allies. Once again, as in 1892, the Liberals were to be maintained in office by the vote of the 82 Irish Nationalists under John Redmond. And it was made clear to them that they could remain in office only if, at Redmond's demand, they first abolished the effective veto of the House of Lords and then gave Ireland Home Rule.

The peers' blunder had thus led to worse evils than those which they mistakenly thought to avert. Asquith had no option but to introduce resolutions declaring that the right of the House of Lords to reject not merely financial measures but also other measures passed by the House of Commons must be severely limited. And he followed up these resolutions by introducing a Veto Bill. It was about to be debated when on 6th May, 1910, King Edward died, leaving his country in a state of political confusion such as had not been known for many years. The tragedy and suffering

[1] The new House contained 274 (373) Liberals, 272 (167) Unionists, 41 (46) Labour men, and 82 (83) Nationalists. The figures in brackets refer to the preceding Parliament.

of the War have since taught us all to be more tolerant, perhaps more indifferent, in matters of domestic politics, so that the younger generation can hardly realize the violence of party passion which raged in England at that time. The conflict between Free Trade and Protection, the development of class-warfare through the land and property taxes, the increase of labour unrest as manifested in miners' and railwaymen's strikes, the religious feud between Churchmen and Nonconformists over the schools, the political grievances of the unenfranchised men and of the women who were now agitating for the suffrage, were now complicated by a constitutional dispute and by the resurgence of the eternal Irish question which most people, and especially the Liberals, had hoped to forget. It was a sad end to a reign which, though begun in war, had been on the whole prosperous and had at least strengthened our international position for the trials that were soon to come.

E. G. Hawke.

V

Foreign Relations

It has already been said that the reign of Edward VII was a period of transition, whose nine hectic years offer a singular contrast to the spacious sixty-three years of the previous reign. It may be compared to a dissolving view, where the outgoing and incoming slides are simultaneously on the screen, and where to the imaginative onlooker other unsuspected details become apparent.

That the real break came in 1914, and that the four years between the king's death and the Great War may be regarded as a mere appendage to the previous nine, is even more obvious in foreign policy than in other fields. But with this difference that, before King Edward died, the series of transformations and readjustments with which we are to be concerned had been carried out, and a sort of lull followed, during which certain attempts—unhappily unsuccessful—were made to smooth off the edges of recent decisions, and to turn thesis and antithesis into synthesis, as between the two great political groups in Europe.

It will be my task to survey the successive phases of our re-entry into the whirlpool of Continental politics, and within this setting to discuss the much-disputed rôle of King Edward himself.

In the nineteenth century there were two main currents in our policy—interference and non-intervention. Neither was a monopoly of one party : for Palmerston and Disraeli were the chief exponents of interference—the first for liberal principles, the second for imperialistic prestige—while the Crimean War was fought by a coalition ; and again the Tories, first in the 'twenties and afterwards in the 'sixties, had stood for non-intervention until Disraeli converted them to a forward policy. Apart from this, there were certain guiding principles : the Balance of Power, to prevent the predominance of any one Power ; guarantees for the independence of the Low Countries ; and a pathetic belief in the reformability and eventual recovery of Turkey.

The first of these led us more than once to transfer our friendship, but was applied once more in 1914 and this time was blown sky-high. To the second we were true in 1831, in the 'sixties, in 1870, and above all in 1914. The third involved us in one unnecessary war, the Crimean, and very nearly in a second during the Russo-Turkish quarrel of 1877–8. On the latter occasion foreign policy became a party issue to an extent hitherto unknown since the days of Marlborough : and the rebound from this was, on the one hand, Britain's adoption of " splendid isolation " and, on the other, Continental suspicion of engagements with a country in which foreign affairs could become such a play-thing of passion, seemingly at the mercy of a passing parlia-mentary majority. A classic example of this may be seen in Bismarck's attitude to Gladstone.

Such suspicions, however, were fully reciprocated by Gladstone's rival, Salisbury, who was the greatest exponent of isolation and held resolutely aloof, save for the short-lived Mediterranean Agreements of the late 'eighties and for the abortive offer to Germany of a Turkish partition in 1895. Meanwhile after 1890 Russo-German relations were bungled by William II ; the Franco-Russian alliance came into being : and in proportion as British influence declined in Turkey—owing to our Egyptian and Cypriote policy, our protests against the Armenian massacres, and Salisbury's famous " wrong horse " pronouncement—Germany took over the old illusion of Palmerston and Disraeli as to Turkish recovery (this time, however, on a military basis), coquetted with the Moslem world, and thus added new complications to her relations with both Russia and Britain.

Outside Europe twenty years of colonial expansion meant

for Britain friction with other colonial Powers, especially France, and a vague fear of Russia in Asia. This culminated in Fashoda and the Boer War, and in the possibility of a Continental coalition. The death of Queen Victoria, then, occurred at a somewhat critical moment, when " splendid isolation " had reached its height, when its chief exponent's brilliant intellect was in noticeable decline, and he himself had become essentially negative, while his colleagues realized the dangers rather than the splendours of the policy and were anxiously scanning every horizon with a view to a possible change of course.

It is interesting to note at the outset that the first impetus to a new policy was given by the typical representative of middle-class industrial England (who twenty years before had been regarded as a revolutionary at any rate *in posse* and who was now going through the same evolution mutatis mutandis as Briand, Millerand, and Lueger) ; that the great change was effected by the head of one of the greatest Whig houses, now no longer Whig, the descendant of one prime minister and of one who could have been prime minister if he had chosen, but who himself had foreign blood in his veins and hence an unusually international outlook ; and that it was confirmed and elaborated by Liberal statesmen, chief among them being a representative of another great Whig house which had remained consistently Whig, but who by a curious contrast was " English of the English ", with fewer European connections than perhaps any previous Foreign Secretary. In other words the new policy, though challenged here and there in its details by the Left wing in Parliament, was in its essentials non-party and the work of all the main elements in the state. To take one example for many, the criticism directed against the Persian agreement with Russia did not mean opposition to a solution of unsolved issues between the two countries, but only a very proper desire for fair play for struggling Persia : and the criticism of Tsarism by the Left was only an indiscreet or exaggerated expression of the feelings voiced by Campbell-Bannerman in his famous cry " Vive la Douma ".

Already in 1900 Lord Salisbury had felt the strain of two offices and transferred the Foreign Office to Lord Lansdowne, fully conscious that the latter would initiate new lines of policy for which he himself was too old and too conservative. Britain felt her isolation as never before and was eagerly exploring new avenues. Fashoda, the friction in Central Asia, Russia's growing ambitions in the Far East, the vicissitudes of the Boer War and the possibility of a triple intervention in favour of peace—which has perhaps sometimes been exaggerated, but was by no means mere imagination— and finally the uncertainties in our relations with the United States, all this combined to produce nervousness and discomfort.

There is no little irony in the fact that the first Power towards whom our eyes were directed was Germany, with whom we had as yet never been in real conflict. Chamberlain's first informal overture to Hatzfeldt in February, 1898, had been rejected by Bülow and William II, who used it to poison the mind of the tsar still farther against Britain. His second overture in December, 1899, during the kaiser's visit to England, followed by a public speech, fell equally flat and was speedily countered by William II's appeal for a strong navy. The third came two months after the accession of King Edward, who said to the Anglophile diplomat Baron Eckardstein, " You know my view that England and Germany are the natural allies. But we cannot take part in the emperor's buckjumping." This was within a few weeks of William II winning British public opinion by smoothing the pillows of his dying grandmother, and of his unofficial speech at Marlborough House—" With an Anglo-German alliance, not a mouse could stir in Europe without our permission, and the nations would in time come to see the necessity of reducing their armaments."

In May, 1901, it got the length of a draft convention

of an Anglo-German alliance, prepared by Lansdowne, in spite of Salisbury's misgivings, and Mr. Chirol, as unofficial intermediary, talked with Holstein and Bülow. But no progress was made, and by the autumn prospects of success were ruined by the duel between Chamberlain at Edinburgh and Bülow in the Reichstag. " Let him alone," said Bülow, " he is biting on granite "—a famous quotation from Frederick the Great ; to which Chamberlain rejoined, " I withdraw nothing, I qualify nothing." As so often in private life, once there had been failure, the two sides moved rapidly apart, the propitious moment was lost, and the personal friction of the two sovereigns played an ever-increasing part.

Chamberlain had made it quite clear to the Germans that in the event of failure England would probably try to make terms with the other camp. But Germany misjudged the situation, taking it for granted that we could never win over either France or Russia. Under Bülow she retained Bismarck's old suspicion of an alliance dependent on a parliamentary majority, forgetting that that had not prevented Bismarck from certain definite overtures to England. Bülow was of course by no means the only factor on whom the decision rested : for there was the sinister Holstein spinning webs of suspicion in the inner recesses of the Wilhelmstrasse, there was Tirpitz planning the new fleet, and above all there was the erratic kaiser, arrogant, spiteful, rushing from one extreme to another and wooing every Power by turn. The best excuse that can be found for Bülow is that apart from his fears of German public opinion, then unquestionably anti-British, he supposed that Chamberlain's main aim was to secure Germany as ally in a war against Russia : and Chamberlain at this time was certainly Russophobe enough to justify some such reserve. Both he and the emperor, however, obstinately shut their eyes to the inevitable effect upon British opinion of their new naval policy. That they had a perfect right to build as many ships as they

pleased no sane person could deny. But that their building
them could only be directed against certain Powers, and
especially against Britain, and that equality would not,
and could not, be conceded and must therefore lead to acute
competition and rivalry, was far too obvious to escape their
notice : and that they knew quite well what they were
aiming at is abundantly clear from Tirpitz's writings, from
the emperor's marginal notes in *Die Grosse Politik*, and from
the " Willy-Nicky " correspondence.

Meanwhile there was in London a diplomatist of a nation
which has long made it its business to be uncannily well
informed in all political questions—who saw into the future
and now took occasion by the hand. Baron Hayashi saw
that Britain and Japan were each in dangerous isolation,
and that, so far as the Far East was concerned, their
co-operation would checkmate all the other Powers. His first
proposals were made in April, 1901, and sympathetically
received by Lord Lansdowne. Discussions were delayed
by the Marquis Ito, who favoured a Russo-Japanese alliance
on the basis—it is interesting to-day to remember—of
Corea as the Japanese " tit " for the Russian " tat " of
Manchuria. But Hayashi and Lansdowne between them
(and almost the entire credit belongs to them) at last over-
came all obstacles, and the Anglo-Japanese Alliance—the
first modern alliance of a European Great Power with an
oriental state—was concluded on 30th January, 1902, and
published on 11th February.

In its essence it was a guarantee to Japan against a fresh
coalition of Powers in a possible war with Russia, such as
had robbed her of the spoils after the war with China, and,
on the other side, a guarantee against any coalition of Powers
against Britain, such as might eliminate her from the Far
East and so injure her Chinese trade interests. Its motive
was the growing uncertainty of the Far Eastern situation,
in view of Chinese unrest after the Boxer troubles and of
Russia's steady advance eastwards. The British Cabinet

may therefore be said to have begun its new policy at that point of the world's surface where the possibilities of war were greatest. On the other hand, it must be said that the mutual disclaimers of aggressive aims were somewhat hypocritical, because Japan quite obviously aimed at the conquest of Corea, and the alliance gave her the cover without which she could not risk a conflict with Russia for that objective. It is well, however, to note, and to endorse, King Edward's remark to Prince Bülow at Kiel in June, 1904, when, in challenging the theory of the Yellow Peril, he declared, " The Japs are intelligent, brave, and knightly, as civilized as Europeans." It is unnecessary to remind you that William II on the contrary had painted a famous picture with the motto, " Peoples of Europe, preserve your holiest possessions," and was therefore furious at Britain allying herself with a " yellow " people.

The embarrassments that resulted from this alliance as soon as the inevitable clash came between Russia and Japan in 1905, can only be referred to in passing : they form a chapter or chapters by themselves. It may be argued that the new alliance cut both ways ; that but for it Japan would not have risked war. But could she have avoided it, the ambitions of the clique which at that time controlled the feeble Nicholas II being what they were ? It is surely far more probable that the alliance averted a general war. It is, moreover, certain that it stimulated the desire to clear up unsolved problems at issue with other Powers, and especially with France, just because the general situation was so precarious. France came first for a treble reason— because our relations with Paris grew increasingly difficult in proportion as the Russo-Japanese quarrel intensified, until we were each a benevolent neutral on opposite sides ; because an arrangement with France was more urgent and on the whole less difficult ; and because Germany had rejected our three informal overtures for an alternative alliance.

H

Before leaving the Japanese alliance it is important to note that, while William II, in his correspondence with Nicholas II, was constantly inciting him against Japan and imputing motives and suggesting bluff, Lord Lansdowne and King Edward in a quiet way behind the scenes were doing all they could to warn St. Petersburg and the tsar of the impending danger, and above all of the fact that Japan was in deadly earnest. They were not believed at the time, and their warnings were disregarded, but after the disaster they were remembered as a proof of good faith and sound judgment and contributed very materially, after the Björkö incident, to smooth the path towards Anglo-Russian understanding.

Even before 1905, however, events were drawing France and Britain together. Fashoda had been the culmination of a period of friction and served as a lightning flash to illuminate the abyss. It is far too often loosely affirmed that France and Britain were traditional enemies who came together again in 1904 solely out of jealousy towards the rising power of Germany. This is a superficial myth which ignores the fact that the two countries, though often disagreeing and sometimes acutely suspicious of each other (but generally, it will be found, owing to the tactlessness of an individual, as for instance Palmerston in 1840), had not fought each other since 1815, had fought on the same side in 1827, had formed an alliance in the 'thirties, two *ententes* in the 'forties, and conducted a joint war in the 'fifties. Egypt and lesser colonial issues had, it is true, divided them in the 'eighties and 'nineties, but it was now to become apparent that with a little good will these could quite well be adjusted.

It should be noted that on the British side perhaps the prime motive was the need for regulating the Egyptian situation, since neither financial reform nor operations up the Nile could make due progress until France had renounced her powers of blocking. The rôle of Lord Cromer behind the scenes of the coming *entente* is clearly outlined, but not yet fully emphasized, by Lord Newton in his *Life of Lord Lansdowne*.

Meanwhile, as the initiative for the Japanese alliance had come from Hayashi, so the initiative for the *entente* now came from Delcassé, who, it may at once be admitted, had very definite ulterior motives, but who saw far ahead and had long realized that the Anglophobe policy of his predecessor Hanotaux could only lead into a blind alley or something worse. To Delcassé's overtures the receptive Lansdowne at once responded : much of the spadework was done by Paul Cambon, while, incredible as it may seem, Delcassé did not consult his colleagues in the Cabinet till as late as January, 1904. A notable share in smoothing the path must be assigned to King Edward's visit to Paris in May, 1903, and President Loubet's return visit to London, which thawed the French atmosphere.

This lecture cannot concern itself with details : even the outline demands considerable space. The essence of the Anglo-French Convention of April, 1904, was the elimination of points of friction—the old-standing quarrel concerning the Newfoundland fisheries, a series of frontier revisions in West Africa, settlements in Madagascar, the New Hebrides, and Siam. But all else again centred round a tit for tat— this time Morocco for Egypt. Each Power disclaimed any intention of altering the political status of either country, but this must be described as somewhat disingenuous. Britain no doubt did not desire to do so at that moment, but she certainly wanted to be able to do so, in case of future need, without being tied and committed to France or other Powers ; while there can be no doubt whatever that France did want to change the status of Morocco in their own favour, sooner or later. That we fully realized this is shown by Lord Cromer's letter of 17th July, 1903, to Lord Lansdowne, in which he says, " Everything depends on our attitude as regards Morocco," and then asks, " Have we any objection

to Morocco becoming a French province ? " and answers
his own question in the negative, provided (1) that there is
a *quid pro quo* in Egypt, and (2) that France observes the
three secret conditions appended to the Convention.   Later
on, in November, Cromer writes, " *We must not fail*,"
because we need a free hand in Egyptian finance and in
the development of the Sudan.   In other words, we knew
what we were doing—namely, paving the way for French
absorption of Morocco.   This is the main ground upon which
the *entente* is open to criticism.

With regard to the secret conditions, however, it is difficult
to denounce them as very criminal in that age of secret
diplomacy, pursued by friend and foe alike.   They simply
contain (1) the neutralization of the Moroccan seaboard—
an obvious British interest, but quite unobjectionable except
to a Power which had hostile designs against Britain ; (2)
due insistence on regard to Spanish interests—an attitude
to which no one can take exception, and (3) a guarantee for
the future of British trade, which helped other countries also
indirectly by upholding the principle of the open door.
In actual fact, these clauses were made public in 1910 and
did not cause any serious heartburning.

The weakest spot in the Convention was the way in which
it tried to solve the Moroccan question by a bilateral arrangement—the assignment of certain " pickings " to Spain
might even be treated as a clever device for turning her into
an accomplice—and that it ignored Morocco's international
status   and   the   equal   rights   of   other   countries,
especially Germany, under the Madrid Treaty of 1880.
The French were of course entitled to argue that German
interests in Morocco were almost negligible and that they
themselves, with a contiguous frontier of 1,200 kilometres,
could not be indifferent to the growing anarchy at their very
doors.   But on a purely legal basis Germany's claim that
she had been wrongfully ignored, can hardly be denied :
and her people, being at this time in a peculiarly susceptible

mood about their " place in the sun ", were entitled to
protest.

On the other hand, it is essential to note that at first
Germany raised no objections. Bülow publicly treated it as
" an attempt to remove a number of difficulties by peaceful
methods : we have nothing, from the standpoint of German
interests, to object to in that." [1]   But within a year Germany
altogether changed her tactics, for various reasons good and
bad. The first was undoubtedly Delcassé's aggressive
attitude : his forward policy in Morocco, virtually ignoring
Germany, was felt by the emperor and his chancellor,
by Admiral Tirpitz and Herr von Holstein, as a blow to their
prestige. But while this was excusable enough, what really
decided them to move was the fact that in February, 1904,
Russia became involved in war with Japan and was slowly
beaten back by land and sea (Port Arthur fell on 1st January,
1905, the battle of Mukden was fought in February, and the
sea fight of Tsushima in May) ; while the strain at home
gave a fresh impetus to the parallel revolutionary and constitutional movements. As a result, Russia's interest was
diverted from Europe, and France stood alone.

Germany, then, used this new situation to check the
absorption of Morocco, to attempt to drive a wedge between
the new friends France and Britain, [2] and to win the sympathy
of the sultan and strengthen her hold at Constantinople
and the prospects of her Bagdad design, by the championship
of Islam in Africa. Her tactics were the February mission
to Fez, in March the landing of the Emperor William at
Tangier and his speech—as we now know—deliberately
prompted from the Wilhelmstrasse ; then in summer

---

[1] Bülow, *Denkwürdigkeiten*, ii, p. 107.

[2] In the words of Sir Francis Bertie to Lord Lansdowne on 25th April,
1905—" to show to the French people that an understanding with England
is of little value to them and that they had much better come to an agreement
with Germany. To this end the Emperor ' fait la guerre à l'Angleterre
sur le dos de la France '." *British Documents*, iii, no. 95.

growing pressure in Paris, culminating in the fall of Delcassé and France's acceptance of a conference on Morocco. It is interesting to note that the emperor enlisted President Roosevelt's mediation, and that the latter, to use his own words, " showed France the great danger of a war and the little use England could be, and that a conference would not sanction any unjust attack on French interests."

The agreed formulas given to the world based French consent on the conviction " that Germany will not pursue any aim which would compromise the legitimate interests of France or her rights resulting from her treaties " : and a phrase coined by the German Ambassador in Paris, Prince Radolin—*ni vainqueur ni vaincu*—obtained a wide publicity. In short, it was not clear what Bülow had gained, except to arouse intense distrust and resentment in France and almost automatically to force England closer to France, if only because she could not leave her new ally in the lurch, while pocketing her own advantages in Egypt, without ruining the whole basis of the *entente*.

Nothing illustrates better the bad psychology of the Germans and the miscalculations into which it betrayed them. They were too obtuse to realize that nothing was more certain to force the two countries together, especially with Russia in her then plight—to make a moral issue out of what, from one angle, (viewed without national prejudice and in the cold perspective of history)—might be regarded as a mere imperialistic combination without any moral basis. I can only re-echo the opinion of Dr. Gooch, who after condemning Delcassé's fatal blunder in omitting to " purchase Germany's assent in advance ", treats the Tangier demonstration as " a no less colossal blunder, for its inevitable result was to turn a limited obligation into a general defensive undertaking ".

The ineptitude of the kaiser and his advisers at the close of the Algeciras Conference is illustrated by an incident of quite a different character—the famous telegram of thanks addressed to the Austro-Hungarian Foreign Minister, Count Goluchowski, as Germany's "brilliant second on the duelling ground". As Goluchowski had shown surprising detachment and impartiality, many observers assumed the telegram to be sarcastic and prompted by ulterior motives. It seems more probable that it was the emperor's highest idea of a compliment. In any case, Goluchowski was politically dead from that moment, and Francis Joseph took the first chance in 1906 to replace him by the fatal Aehrenthal, who, however, began his career at the Ballplatz as a reputed Russophile.

Algeciras resulted in a certain temporary *détente* : but Germany's whole procedure during 1904–1905 had thoroughly alarmed all Europe and given an impetus to the tendency among the other powers to get together and remove points of difference, such as might otherwise be exploited by William II.

In this thumbnail sketch I am not attempting a narrative so much as a survey of general tendencies. A mass of cumulative evidence could be supplied for my assertion as to this distrust—some relating to the personal friction between uncle and nephew, where there were doubtless faults on both sides, but still more relating to the friction engendered by naval rivalry. We must not fail to note in passing Mr. Lee's famous speech at Eastleigh and "Jacky" Fisher's idea of "Copenhagening" the German fleet. It is, however, essential to remember—what Professor Kantorowicz has effectively pointed out in his courageous and critical book *The Spirit of British Policy*—that when the Emperor heard of this idea of Fisher, he told Beit that he admired Fisher and would have done the same in his place, whereas Fisher himself sadly records, "alas, even the very whisper of it excited exasperation . . . and the plan was condemned." [1]

[1] *The Spirit of British Policy*, p. 376 ; Fisher's *Memories*, and *Die Grosse Politik*, no. 6887.

To prove the assertion as to Germany's sinister policy in 1904–1905, it will suffice to quote in barest outline four incidents (their full treatment would require one or several lectures).

1. Prince Bülow in his memoirs recounts how the emperor on 21st January, 1904, received the tsar's telegram expressing the confident hope that war would be averted after all. At this William II was " very downcast " (niedergeschlagen) and feared Franco-British mediation, leading to a coalition. " I had hoped," he said, " that the warmth of my last letter would lead the tsar to throw his whole power against Japan." This speaks for itself : he was working for war.

2. In the " Willy-Nicky " correspondence we find the emperor in October, 1904, denouncing " Anglo-Japanese insolence " and " England's conduct ", proposing a German-Russian-French Treaty as a counterblast and, on the news of the Dogger Bank incident, assuming " foul play " and British suppression of the facts. Here again the facts speak for themselves : he was working to promote discord, not peace.

3. In Mr. Tyler Dennett's book *Roosevelt and the Russo-Japanese War* [1] we can study the emperor's attempts to prolong the war by his advice to the tsar, to achieve a Russo-German alliance, to prevent any British-American rapprochement, to sow distrust now of France now of Britain at Washington, and again his proposal for dividing northern China between Russia and Japan.

4. Most damning of all is the incident of Björkö on 24th July, 1905, when the emperor induced the tsar to sign a secret treaty between Germany and Russia, promising " help in Europe " if one or other were attacked by a European Power, no separate peace, and action on the tsar's side to initiate and win over France. We have here William II's detailed account of his conversation with

[1] Based on original material in the State Department : see also Thayer's *Life of John Hay* and Howe's *George L. Mayer*.

Nicholas II and his triumphant telegram to Bülow—" In fact Germany enters the Dual Alliance as third party." This was too much for the statesmen on both sides, behind whose back it had been signed : and, while Lamsdorff and Witte forced the tsar to repudiate it, asking each other, " Does His Majesty not know we have a Treaty with France ? " Bülow announced that he would resign unless the words " in Europe " were cut out. The main facts of Björkö were given by Lamsdorff to Dr. Dillon and thus transmitted to London, where they increased the tendency to follow up the agreement with France by clearing away current misunderstandings with Russia.

In view of the Björkö incident it has always seemed to me more than usually audacious of the German propagandist writers to write as they do of the later Reval incident, which as we shall see has been grossly exaggerated, but would be quite harmless by the side of Björkö, even if all they say of it were true.

It would not, however, be fair to pass on without some allusion to the alleged British offer of an offensive and defensive alliance to France, on the eve of Delcassé's resignation—including the blockade of the Elbe by Britain and the dispatch of 100,000 British troops to Slesvig. In disproof of this we have (1) the categorical denial of Lord Lansdowne to Count Metternich, who then wrote home of him as " incapable of deception " with such a clear denial (and it should be noted that we have both Metternich's own account of the conversation [1] and Lansdowne's account to Lascelles [2]); (2) the failure of Dr. Gooch and Professor Temperley to find any trace in the Record Office of such an offer ; (3) the marginal notes of King Edward—" How badly informed he is " and " Nearly as absurd as it is false " [3]—which an enemy might discount, if they had been written as an apology

---

[1] *Grosse Politik*, XX, ii, nos. 6858 (16th June) and 6864 (19th July).

[2] *British Documents*, iii, no. 99—16th June, to Lascelles.

[3] Ibid., iii, nos. 97 and 98.

to some one ignorant of the secret, but which are inconceivable as an ultra-confidential note to fellow-conspirators ; and (4) the explicit denials of Lord Sanderson and Lord Lansdowne to Professor Temperley in 1922.[1] As against this we must set the fact that Delcassé himself after the War, and some of his inspired apologists, definitely wrote of such a pledge, and again certain marginal notes of the emperor, which show that he believed the promise to have been made by King Edward himself, and not by his Government. The emperor's suspicions are the very reverse of proof, but according to Lord Newton the king actually wired to Delcassé in June, urging him not to resign [2]; and it is well known that in the previous April in Paris he had shown Delcassé marked and persistent attention and highly approved of his general attitude. It is therefore possible that the king used some incautious phrases, and that Delcassé's head was turned, or that he misunderstood the King (though it could not have been a linguistic *malentendu*). In any case anything like an official offer of this character from London to Paris, is a myth.

We now come to a decisive change in England itself— the Conservative defeat and the advent of a Liberal Government, with what till 1931 was regarded as an impossibly large majority. Sir Henry Campbell-Bannerman became prime minister, Sir Edward Grey foreign secretary. Lord Lansdowne's rôle is over, but as the creator of the Japanese alliance and of the third French *entente*, he has left his mark on British policy ; the Liberals are now to complete the transformation. And it is a very simple point, but one not usually stressed, that circumstances in Europe at their advent to power gave a powerful impetus to their future attitude. For, while laying down a general policy " opposed to aggression and adventure ", " C.B.," seeing the dangers and uncertainties of the Moroccan dispute, had perforce to lay special stress on the *Entente Cordiale*, in order to

---

[1] Ibid., no. 105.   [2] *Life of Lord Lansdowne*, p. 341.

reassure France as to continuity of policy. Hence—while affirming " nothing but good feeling " towards Russia and declining to see " in the case of Germany also " any " cause whatsoever of estrangement " (but what a lot can be read into that little word " also ")—he proclaimed, and undoubtedly felt, " real friendship " for France.

Another result of the situation of the moment was that Sir Edward Grey, no sooner was he at the Foreign Office, could not resist the urgent appeal of the French for military conversations between the General Staffs. Some people have read peculiar wickedness into this ; but I for my part entirely fail to see how he could possibly have refused, or how the Germans, in view of the history of their own General Staff and its relations with Austria-Hungary and Italy, can possibly take exception. In any case those who blame Grey for it should remember that it was expressly authorized by Campbell-Bannerman, Haldane, and Asquith, on the distinct understanding that it left the hands of the Government free for the event of war.

This is perhaps the right moment at which to consider the rôle of the king himself in foreign policy, for it coincides with the period when friction between him and his nephew was most acute. Here again I am not attempting a new treatment of this much vexed subject, but only a new perspective, when I deliberately take the two questions together—his influence over policy and his relations with his nephew. If the second has too often obscured the first, it is because the emperor, owing firstly to his own power, but still more to his peculiar character—restless, unstable, overweeningly self-confident, exacting, suspicious, self-centred, and convinced of his divine mission—was constitutionally incapable of understanding that his uncle, again both owing to his position and to his character, was not invariably the pivot round which everything turned, but that his ministers were the real power that shaped policy.

Certainly William II has a positive obsession that Edward VII controlled and even initiated policy, and doubtless the king's constant journeys and cruises, interlarded with discreet and tactful conversations with all manner of men from every country, acted on the nephew's nerves until the uncle seemed a sort of political jack-in-the-box emerging at the most unwelcome moments. The strange thing is that William II, whose own *marginalia* are the most fabulous self-exposure in all modern history, exceeding even the calculated memoirs of his chancellor Bülow, has none the less imposed this grotesque myth of the ubiquitous, all-pervading, all-powerful intriguant Edward VII upon the consciousness of the German people, who believe it even now that its authors are so entirely discredited.

The truth doubtless lies somewhere in the middle between the two extreme views. King Edward was not a man of profound intellect or original ideas, but rather one of tact, amazing social and political flair, and personal charm— at once jovial, familiar, and ruthless towards undue familiarity in another. He had a natural taste for politics and an interest in the men and affairs of the Continent, automatically maintained by close ties of blood with almost every court in Europe ; and, though very wrongly deprived for years by his jealous mother of due access to inside diplomatic information, he of course made good the deficiency by personal contacts of the most variegated kind in many social strata, and he also made good his dislike of reading by a remarkable gift for pumping experts on any given subject—a gift possessed by the very different Gladstone. In the eastern crisis of the 'seventies he confided to his friend Lord Carrington that when he came to the throne he intended to be his own foreign minister ; and a political lady, long since dead, once assured me that Campbell-Bannerman himself told her, on the very day when he was forming his new cabinet, that his choice of Sir Edward Grey for the Foreign Office was dictated by his own and King Edward's intention to keep the main threads of foreign policy in their own hands. When at long last he became king, he certainly insisted on knowing every detail, intervened actively in every question, and claimed a say in appointments and honours; while his knowledge of French and German and his connections with other reigning houses—Denmark, Greece, Portugal, Belgium, Spain, Germany, Russia—his friendship with Rudolf and Francis Joseph and with French politicians from Gambetta onwards, gave him weight and advantage in conversation with his own ministers.

That he was anything but a cipher in foreign policy could be illustrated by his attitude towards the Norwegian crown, the Serbian regicides, the Congo administration of his cousin Leopold, the promise of a Garter to the Shah of Persia. But that he ever held the threads of a consistent world-wide policy in his own hands, this is a German myth, even less convincing than the at least plausible theory of " Encircle-ment ".

Lord Newton in his *Life of Lord Lansdowne* prints a letter to the latter from Mr. Balfour, written in 1915 *à propos* of a war book of Professor Holland Rose, exalting the king's rôle. In this there occurs the passage, " So far as I remember, during the years in which you and I were his ministers, he never made an important suggestion of any sort on large questions of policy. I wish you would cudgel your own memory and tell me whether in this opinion I am right." No written answer is on record, but it is abundantly clear that the two Conservative leaders took for granted the king's subordination to the Cabinet in matters of foreign policy as a simple historical fact.

This anecdote may be clinched with a suitable extract from Lord Grey's *Twenty-five Years* : " A legend arose in his lifetime, that British foreign policy was due to his initiative, instigation, and control. This was not so in my experience. He not only accepted the constitutional practice that policy must be that of his ministers, but he preferred that it should be so." [1] This fits in with the evidence of the king's minutes on state documents, contrasting mightily with those of Emperor William. Very rarely do they go beyond the single word, " Appr^d—ERI " ; and, when they do, they are as a rule perfunctory and banal, though now and then strong feeling flashes out in a brief phrase. As Lord Grey puts it, " He did not care for long and sustained discussions about large aspects of policy, though he brought strong common sense and good judgment to bear on any concrete matter of the moment."

This, however, is only one side of the medal : the other was his immense prestige throughout the Continent, which has made of him a legendary figure and shows what miracles can be wrought by sheer personality. Thus though first Balfour and Lansdowne, then " C.B." or Asquith and Grey, never took their hands off the helm of state, the king contributed the all-important *imponderabilia* of many a situation, smoothed obstacles, added momentum, established contacts, created atmospheres—notably in his famous visits to Paris or Marienbad or Rome or Copenhagen or the Baltic —and often made possible what his ministers could never have done alone. It should be added that he was marvellously " covered " by a sagacious secretariat, which has handed on its traditions unimpaired to the present king.

The year 1905–1906 represents the height of the friction between king and emperor. At the beginning of the reign we have the authority of Lord Esher, and other no less qualified observers, that the king desired nothing so much as to be on good terms with Germany. But his alarm and annoyance grew, and here again it is necessary to emphasize the emperor's attempts to poison the tsar's mind, to deepen, not to bridge, the gulf between Russia and Japan, to set Britain and America or Britain and France by the ears, as the essential cause of the king's changed attitude, quite as much as any personal feeling, even on so poignant a subject as the treatment meted out to the Empress Frederick.

[1] *Twenty-five Years*, i, p. 204.

At the Kiel meeting in June, 1904, the king very earnestly denied all idea of isolating Germany by the French *entente*, and gave the frankest possible notice that he desired a similar understanding with Russia. He soon saw that William II was incapable of responding and full of secret ambitions and resentments. He described the Tangier incident in March, 1905, to Lansdowne as " most mischievous and uncalled-for "; the emperor was to him " no more nor less than a political *enfant terrible* ".[1] That August he objected to visiting at Homburg, told Lascelles " he doubts whether the emperor retains any affection for him ", resented " the tone of peevish complaint " with which William vetoed the crown prince's proposed visit to England—a true incident of which the emperor described to the tsar as " the finest lie I ever came across ".[2] By the end of the year Lansdowne told Lascelles that the king " talks and writes " about the emperor " in terms which make one's flesh creep " [3]; while the Emperor flared out to Lascelles and to Bülow, insisting to the latter that before all else " H.M. Ed. VII *has to make a personal approach to me* ".[4] When the Danish minister, Count Frijs, was sent to the king to discuss the dangers confronting Europe, the emperor wrote to the tsar about " the arch-mischief-maker of Europe "; while the king himself, though insisting on " a distinct will-to-peace tendency in Europe ", had to admit that " with a man of so impulsive temperament as the German emperor at the head of the greatest military Power in Europe, anything may happen ".[5]

In this phrase may be said to lie the key to our policy in these fateful years. William II was like an irresponsible child armed to the teeth, and it seemed advisable, as speedily as might be, to reduce the amount of explosives or powder

[1] Lee, *Life of King Edward*, ii, p. 340.
[2] Willy-Nicky Corresp., 22nd August, 1905.
[3] Newton, *Life of Lansdowne*, p. 335.
[4] *Grosse Politik*, nos. 6882, 6885, 3rd December, 1905.
[5] Lee, op. cit., ii, p. 358.

lying within his reach. But it cannot be too often repeated that while the erratic sallies of the Emperor William and the doubtful attitude of his ministers, especially in Morocco and the Far East, automatically speeded up the movement towards an Anglo-Russian understanding, London was from the first day, both under Lansdowne and Grey, ready and even anxious for a similar agreement with Germany ; and a whole series of tentative steps in that direction can be recorded. Yet the crux always remained the same—the absolute refusal to discuss seriously the limitation of naval armaments, and the logical outcome of this refusal, the inevitability of competition in building and the heightened value of alliances or agreements with other Powers. Despite the mass of material written on the subject—often tending, or indeed intended, to obscure the issue—that issue remained from the first very simple and logical. If Germany armed on a great scale, against whom could this be aimed ? Could the Power primarily affected neglect to follow suit ? And if so, could competition, if kept up long enough, end in anything save war ? There was the same underlying logic in the situation as there was at the Disarmament Conference of 1932.

These general remarks should serve to explain the urgency of an understanding with Russia, as it appeared to British statesmen in 1906. There were other supplementary reasons —the chequered career of the Russian Duma, which made the growth of a Russophile party in England possible and culminated in Campbell-Bannerman's famous cry " La Douma est morte, Vive la Douma " ; the advent of a Russian foreign minister, Alexander Izvolski, frankly in favour of Britain ; the abrupt end of the Austro-Russian *entente* and the beginning of a dangerous duel between Izvolski and Aehrenthal ; events in the Balkans and on the Golden Horn, to which only the briefest allusion will be possible in this already overcrowded lecture ; and all the time the Moroccan groundswell, in which, despite the cautious steering of

Clemenceau and Pichon, such incidents as that of Casablanca suddenly loomed up in the sea-fog.

The Anglo-Russian Convention came in August, 1907, and the initiative clearly belongs to Grey and Izvolski. But the way had already been prepared by the appointment of Sir Charles Hardinge as ambassador in 1904 (which the emperor tried to misrepresent to the tsar as hostile intervention), by the king's discreet talks with Izvolski at Copenhagen in the same year, by his cautious messages to the tsar in favour of " a more liberal form of government " in October, 1905, and by the many practical proofs accumulating at St. Petersburg that British advice on the eve of the fatal Japanese war had been as sound and well-intentioned as William II's had been perfidious. Tsar Nicholas was weak and not at all too intelligent, but he was not impervious to facts, and the urgent good offices of France, coinciding with a gigantic Russian loan in Paris, completed his conversion.

The Convention falls under three heads. (1) The territorial integrity and aloofness of Tibet is to be respected by both Powers. In effect, Russia is assured that the Younghusband expedition was an incident, not a prelude, and on her side renounces any advance from the north into Tibet or Chinese Turkestan—those regions on which her eyes seem again to be resting to-day. (2) Afghanistan is recognized as outside the Russian sphere of influence, while Britain is pledged not to touch Afghan independence or interfere inside her borders in return for a sort of control of Afghan foreign relations. (3) Persia's independence and territorial integrity are guaranteed by both Powers, but in effect Persia, which then seemed to be slowly degenerating into an Eastern. Morocco, was divided into three zones—a large Russian and a smaller British sphere of influence and a neutral zone in the middle of the country where the two reconciled rivals might compete. The Persian Gulf was left outside the Convention on the plea that this was limited to border regions between Russia and Britain ; but London's attitude on the

I

subject, as defined in the earlier statements of Lansdowne and Curzon, was clearly restated by Sir Edward Grey to Sir Arthur Nicolson for Russian consumption. The result was that what Lansdowne with unusual flippancy had described as " George Curzon's prancings in the Persian puddle " ceased, though he publicly criticized all sections of the treaty ; and the apprehensions of the Indian Government were certainly allayed, if not yet altogether dispelled. For the same reason there was no reference to the Treaty of Berlin or the question of the Straits. It was no doubt tacitly assumed that the elimination of causes of quarrel in the Far and Middle East would create a new atmosphere for the discussion of Near Eastern questions also ; and the knowledge that perhaps the supreme crisis in Turkish and Balkan affairs was imminent, certainly stimulated agreement between the two Governments.

The Convention contained nothing to which Germany could reasonably take exception, but it did very definitely affect the Balance of Power and revive those " coalition nightmares " which had haunted the dreams of Metternich and many another central European statesman and had prompted Bismarck's most daring feats of acrobatic diplomacy. It altered the whole focus of Europe, by ridding Britain of all reasonable anxiety on the Indian frontier and in effect creating a series of neutral zones all round India from Tibet to the Gulf ; and it reduced almost to zero the danger of any such combination as Shimonoseki or Björkö by the Continent against Britain. For Russia, on the other hand, it was the prelude to an active return to European politics, after the tremendous diversion of the Japanese War ; and this at once had its effects in the Balkan Peninsula, which was already seething with trouble. A further sign of her return westwards may be noted in the marked attention which Russia began to pay to Italy.

Its weakest point was, of course, the sinister treatment of Persia ; for, though it is important to note that no less a

person than Count Witte disliked the Treaty as making a
Russian annexation of Persia impossible, it is none the less
impossible to deny that Mr. Morgan Shuster's screamy
phrase " The Strangling of Persia " was largely justified,
and that there were direct designs on her independence, at
which we connived. In 1932 we, of course, know the historical
sequel and take note that Persia has not gone the way of
Morocco ; but the credit for this rests not on the Convention
of 1907, but on the diversion of the Great War, the temporary
eclipse of Russia, and the rise of a strong native ruler.

The part played by the Balkan and Turkish problems is
an essential factor in our survey, yet at this stage it is
impossible to do more than indicate its main lines.[1] There
were three definite stages of development during the period
in question.

(1) In 1903, after the Hamidian despotism had lasted a
quarter of a century, the Macedonian insurrection on the
one hand and the Serbian Revolution on the other ushered
in a new era of Macedonian reform and general unrest, in
which Austria and Russia went hand in hand and aimed at
a joint European mandate as a substitute for the cumbrous
methods of the European Concert. This did not suit Lord
Lansdowne, who put forward his own scheme in September,
1903, but it was forestalled—literally by a few hours—by
the so-called Mürzsteg Agreement, which for the next three
years was the real power behind the Concert.

(2) The substitution of Izvolski and Aehrenthal for
Goluchowski and Lamsdorff as foreign ministers of Russia and
Austria-Hungary speedily led to alienation and then growing
rivalry between the two ministers. With this we are not here
concerned, but it is instructive to note that while Grey used

---

[1] I may perhaps be excused for referring the reader to three articles of
my own, which deal fully with certain aspects of the Near Eastern problem :
" William II's Balkan Policy " (*Slavonic Review*, June, 1928), " British
Policy in the Near East " (*Contemporary Review*, June, 1929), and " Austrian
Policy under Count Aehrenthal " (to appear shortly in *Le Monde Slave*).

the success of the new Anglo-Russian Convention to restrain
Russia in all Turkish questions and so to promote the cause
of Turkish reform, Aehrenthal's main reaction was an
attempt to isolate Britain in the Macedonian question and
a disposition to let the Balkan peoples " cook in their own
juice " (his phrase to Baron Marschall) and to purchase his
betrayal of the Concert by special railway concessions from
the sultan.

(3) In 1908 the internal unrest came rapidly to a head in
the Young Turkish Revolution and the downfall of Abdul
Hamid, and this precipitated a long chain of events—the
Bosnian annexation, Bulgarian independence, the protests
and humiliation of Serbia, an accentuation of the national
movements inside Austria-Hungary, and the coalition of
the Balkan states against Turkey. In all this, and in face of
the personal duel between Aehrenthal and Izvolski which
added such dangerous complications to the general situation,
Sir Edward Grey's policy was simple and straightforward.
He, like King Edward, was naturally affronted and rendered
suspicious at the outset of the crisis by Aehrenthal's deliberate
falsehoods to our ambassador in Vienna, Sir Edward Goschen.
But his main criticism of Austrian action fell under two heads.
He opposed any unilateral change in an international treaty,
such as the annexation of provinces held by a European
mandate conferred at Berlin in 1878, and he might have
pointed out that on the last occasion when such a change was
attempted—namely, Russia's unilateral repudiation in 1870
of the Black Sea clauses of the Treaty of Paris—the strongest
protest came from a predecessor of Aehrenthal in office,
Count Andrássy. He also felt most strongly that such action
was likely to compromise and ruin the reforming party in
Turkey, whom he did not judge in any roseate light, but
rightly saw to be the only alternative to war and partition.
In a word, this whole Turkish policy was pacific and aimed
at averting partition and foreign complications ; and he
exercised a genuinely moderating influence upon Izvolski

in Turkish affairs. The best proof of his honest purpose was the frankness with which he made it clear from the beginning that Russia (and so indirectly Serbia) could count upon full diplomatic support, but not to the point of war (an attitude differing but little from that of France at this time), and Aehrenthal exploited this situation to the full, in order to inflict an open defeat upon Russia and Serbia.

This incident may be treated in passing as a classic instance of the disadvantage of defining one's political attitude before-hand. On this occasion it averted war, because Russia could not risk a war without allies and had to give way. One is tempted to wonder whether Sir Edward Grey was influenced by this experience when in 1914 he adopted the alternative attitude and left both sides in doubt as to Britain's inter-vention till the last moment. It is almost equally easy to criticize either alternative, but who shall deny that it is a dreadful dilemma.

In June, 1908, King Edward and the tsar, accompanied by Izvolski and Hardinge, had met at Reval, with the definite object of strengthening the Russo-British *entente*, and round this, the last notable appearance of the king in the sphere of foreign politics, there has gathered an amazing legend in Germany. His nephew, apparently reading into the king's mind the aims which he himself would have pursued if their positions had been reversed (as in the Fisher incident already quoted), and also, of course, ascribing to the king altogether exaggerated constitutional powers, afterwards treated the Reval meeting as having launched the whole Turkish revolution and perfected a definite design for the encirclement of Germany. Fortunately we now have the full confidential reports of what actually passed at Reval and can see that the main preoccupation was to avoid exasperating Germany and her incalculable ruler.

In our estimates both of men and of events we do not always sufficiently distinguish between their actual importance and the power of initiative which they may possess. The events which group themselves round the three great Conventions with Japan, France, and Russia are obviously of fundamental importance and could not but form the central theme of this lecture. But it should be remembered that the events which precipitated the final catastrophe were those of the Near East, and that initiatives which affected the whole world lay with men and events of secondary or even local importance, in the Balkan Peninsula. It is a failure to separate these two things—importance and initiative—which too often clouds the main issues and leads to false estimates, even now that we are all capable of drawing a distinction between the immediate and the ulterior causes of the Great War.

The events of 1908, then, may have been less important in themselves, but they were relatively even more decisive. The Annexation Crisis, and the way in which it developed into a personal duel of prestige between two men— Aehrenthal, falsest of the false, inelastic and reactionary, and Izvolski, vain, restless, bent on vengeance, until he could coin the incredible but well-vouched phrase, " C'est ma guerre "—and then at the end of the long crisis, the fatal twist which William II gave to German policy towards Russia, intensely disapproving Aehrenthal's action, yet afraid not to back him up and unable to resist the temptation of standing forth " in shining armour "—all this created a gulf between the two camps in Europe which it was increasingly difficult to bridge. After 1909 the rapids were very near ; the Balkan situation not only went from bad to worse, but envenomed Austro-Russian relations more and more, reacted upon the internal situation of the Dual Monarchy and fatally involved Germany on the side of Turkey. Yet even then a succession of brave efforts was made to bridge the gulf by a fourth and decisive understanding —cutting across all the main lines of division—between Britain and Germany. It must suffice merely to indicate four lines of approach. (1) The efforts to achieve naval limitation. Of these the Haldane mission to Berlin is the most important and much the best known, and, of course, had the full and active approval of prime minister, foreign secretary, and king ; but it would be unfair to omit reference to Mr. Churchill's offer or to Mr. Lloyd George's interview in the *Neue Freie Presse* in favour of a naval agreement, which is not so well known as his Agadir speech. (2) The efforts of Baron Marschall and Prince Lichnowsky, following on those of Count Metternich—all, it is true, handicapped by a series of naval and military attachés. (3) The efforts of many well-meaning and sometimes influential organizations in both countries to promote intercourse and better understanding. (4) Above all, the negotiations which took place between London and Berlin from 1912 onwards and which resulted in the two agreements—initialled though not yet ratified when war broke out—regarding the Portuguese colonies and the Bagdad railway, over which the two countries had haggled for twenty years. In all this Sir Edward Grey showed that he agreed with Mr. Balfour's assurance to Count Metternich in 1905 that " a war with Germany would be an act of perfect lunacy ".[1] He followed logically the general principle, adopted in 1902, of eliminating points of dispute and, while loyally supporting the friends towards whom we had engagements and even discussing military preparedness, tried also to extend the links between one group of Powers and the other. But now, as ever, the crux of the whole situation lay in the question of armaments and in Germany's steady refusal to accept a " naval holiday ".

It has not, however, been the purpose of this lecture to discuss the thorny problems of war responsibility or disarmament, but simply to sketch as briefly as possible the process by which Britain abandoned her policy of isolation for a system of alliances and friendships. I may perhaps be accused of not having given to King Edward his due share of credit or criticism or, on the other hand, of having

[1] *Grosse Politik*, xx (ii), no. 6855.

exaggerated the rôle of the Emperor William, thereby falling
into the very error for which I criticize some distinguished
German writers, as applied to our own king. It is, of course,
perfectly true that even William II had to give way to his
ministers on occasion and, indeed, often had much less
direct influence upon decisions than he himself supposed.
And yet I venture to affirm that his rôle as an unsettling,
disintegrating element in European affairs—often unconsciously or involuntarily, it may readily be granted—can
hardly be exaggerated. It is easy to discount the imaginative,
though exceedingly acute interpretation of Emil Ludwig
or even the more weighty and accumulative evidence of
Prince Bülow, that amazing message from a statesman's
grave, spiteful, suspect where not controlled from other
sources and certainly annihilating to Bülow's own reputation.
But these, when added to the self-revealing *marginalia* of
the emperor himself—spread over many years of *Die Grosse
Politik* and an infinite variety of subjects—and his own
more than mediocre memoirs, and " checked off " from many
contemporary first-hand memoirs and dispatches, combine
to produce what seems to me at least an overwhelming
case against him.

To-day any lecture on such a subject of controversy should
end on a different note. There can be no question of assigning
all the blame for subsequent disaster to one man or one
nation. All blundered, all were tarred with the brush of
aggression or territorial greed, and the real problem is one
of proportion or degree. Despite the appalling consequences
to which these rivalries led in the recent past—or, perhaps,
just because of them—it ought in my view to be possible
to-day for historians of the rival groups to discuss them
together, not, indeed, without keen feeling or without plain
speaking, but with mutual esteem, in the hope of reaching
conclusions as to the fundamental dangers inherent in the
international situation, with a view to avoiding them in the
future. For unless this be our aim, we are only uselessly

probing old wounds; whereas, with this aim always before us, the study of the history of our own times may become one of the greatest instruments of peace and international accord.

I would conclude by asking your indulgence for attempting the impossible. It was impossible to cover so vast a field in one lecture, and Dr. Gooch really had a better chance in ten than I in sixty-five minutes. I therefore almost of necessity, concentrated on the first half of the period, where great decisions were taken, rather than upon the second half, where the wheels were running along lines already laid down.

R. W. SETON-WATSON.

VI

The Empire

In the history of the British realms beyond the sea the reign of Edward VII is a more clearly marked epoch than in other political fields. Colonial matters were constantly in the public mind in the first half of the period, for they were one of the chief battle grounds in the struggle of British parties. The reign opened in the last phases of the greatest colonial war for a century wherein for the first time British and dominion troops were fighting side by side in the cause of imperial unity. Nine years later it closed amid discussions as to the organization of imperial defence that were to prove of vital importance in the World War. The change in the disposition and importance of the forces of the outer Empire in those two wars marked unmistakably the rapid growth of the self-governing dominions in the interval, and showed how, while remaining loyal and active members of the imperial circle, they had consolidated their individual nationalities with momentous bearing on the fortunes of the Commonwealth. In 1902 men still thought of the British Empire as consisting of the United Kingdom with various satellite communities of greater or less importance following humbly in its wake. In 1911 things seemed to have undergone an extraordinary change, though in reality it was not so sudden as it then appeared. The process of national differentiation had proceeded a long way before Englishmen began to realize it, and it did not reach its climax till 1919–1920. From being humble satellites of Great Britain in the higher spheres of world politics, the dominions between 1902 and 1910 grew to be co-ordinate partners in a league of free nations, and necessarily the intervening years were filled with events of prime significance.

Edward VII's reign was emphatically a time of transition in the history of the Empire. It saw the close of one great epoch and the opening of another—the change from the second British Empire that arose from the ruin of the old colonial empire by the American Revolution to the Empire Commonwealth of the Great War of 1914–18. Trains of events whose beginnings dated back to the early years of the nineteenth century were brought to an end—the Treaty of Vereeniging and the unification of South Africa which closed a chapter that started with the Great Trek; the colonial arrangements with France in 1904 which ended difficulties in Newfoundland that dated as far back as the Treaty of Utrecht in 1713, and bickerings over Egypt and Morocco that began with Mehemet Ali; the definite settlement of the last boundary disputes with the United States, and so on—and they affected not only the life of the Empire but were of first-rate significance in world politics.

But the reign was also a time of beginning. Movements started of which none reached their climax before 1919 and many have not yet come to an end. The Morley-Minto reforms which really began the momentous changes in Indian constitutional status; the organization and development of the Imperial Conference; the long discussions of imperial preference; the evolution of governmental and social policy for the improvement of civilization in tropical Africa—all these and many allied matters made imperial questions an important subject for public consideration such as they had never been before.

On the material side, too, the period was one of rapid change. The development of the goldfields of South Africa, the Klondyke and Western Australia had gone far before it began, but some of its results on the level of world prices had not fully disclosed themselves before the South African War. The development of the new electrical industry was to some extent hastened by the opening up of immense new deposits of tin in Malaya and Nigeria, while the nickel and copper mines of Canada and the zinc mines of Australia also supplied the demands of electrical invention. Malaya and Ceylon saw the rise of plantation rubber to be the raw material of the pneumatic tyre industry which began to revolutionize world transport. The West Indies were raised from the abyss of depression in which they had for long been suffering by the new agreements with Continental countries to remove their artificial bounties on beet-sugar, and by the introduction on a large scale of the cultivation of bananas. The Straits Settlements began to cultivate and export pineapples, and British Columbia canned salmon, while the improvements in the refrigerated meat trade which had begun a decade or two previously added greatly to the prosperity of New Zealand and Australia, which also began to export dairy products, especially cheese and butter. These developments made a marked change in the diet of the townsmen in Great Britain and thus aided in the improvement of public health which was a notable feature of the time.

But the most far-reaching change in the material sphere was the development of the prairie provinces of the Canadian West. It began during the later years of Queen Victoria's reign, but it proceeded at an accelerated pace under Edward VII and made the Dominion of Canada the greatest granary of the Empire. Where but a few years before there had been a wilderness roamed over by nomadic Indians and fur trappers, a constant stream of emigrants from the British Isles, the United States and the continent of Europe poured in a numerous population of farmers and agriculturists who brought new factors to aid in the building up of the Canadian nation. That flow of emigration both to Canada and to Australia and New Zealand was of immense importance in the life of the Empire, and it must not be overlooked in considering the changes in the outlook on imperial matters both at home and oversea which is perhaps the most striking and important development of Edward VII's reign.

The mere recapitulation of the more important movements and events of the time suffices to show how impossible
it is in the limited space at our disposal to attempt a comprehensive story of even the more significant happenings in
the outer Empire under Edward VII, not only because of
their multitude but also for another reason. To place many
of them in their true historical perspective it would be
necessary to go back and show whence they took their rise,
for only thus is it possible to understand why they came
about as they did. But space remorselessly forbids. We
must limit our aim, and since in history it is ideas that have
the most compelling force and ideas that set the stage for
events, we will confine our attention in the main to the growth
in the conception of the Empire, its management and
responsibilities that marked the period. Incidentally it
will appear that we are thus providing a setting for many of
the more striking events and casting some light on their
underlying causes. Here again, however, we cannot narrowly
limit our attention to the years between King Edward's
accession and his death, but our excursions shall be restricted
as far as possible.

The changes in ideas concerning the government of the
Indian Empire are inappropriate for our consideration, for
they have not at the time of writing reached their *dénoue-
ment*. We do not yet know whither are leading the movements that began to show their importance during the last
years of Lord Curzon's viceroyalty and came into prominence
with the Morley-Minto reforms. The piece is not played
out, and the time is not yet ripe for the historical critic to
attempt to summarize its plot. For another reason we shall
not concern ourselves with the influence of foreign affairs
on imperial development. That really belongs elsewhere,
for though the changes in British foreign policy which brought
about the *Entente Cordiale* with France had great influence
on the progress of Newfoundland, the East Asiatic, Pacific
and African dependencies, they cannot be studied indepen-

dently of the main currents of diplomatic history. The subject is dealt with elsewhere in the present work and here we must set it aside.

There remain the colonies of settlement or " dominions ", as we learned to call them under Edward VII. Besides them there are the colonies proper and the protectorates inhabited by people of non-European stock. Vital progress in the ideas connected with their administration took place during the period, but neither in Great Britain nor the dominions was it noted by the general public. Specialists were alive to the problems of the tropical dependencies, and extraordinarily valuable work was done, but not until after the close of the reign did such questions attract general attention and arouse active public debate on the policy to be pursued. However, the reign certainly saw the application on a wide scale of ideas whose origins could be traced back to the early years of Queen Victoria's reign, the great seed-time of the second British Empire. They had arisen in the fight for slave emancipation, the growth of the humanitarians in alliance with the systematic colonizers and the philosophic radicals. Now in the hands of the skilled experts of the Colonial Service the ideas were practically applied on a wide scale, but the results were hardly known.

By the British public until the period of the South African War the real character of imperial development had been largely overlooked or misunderstood. Sir John Seeley had called his most widely read book in the 'eighties *The Expansion of England*, and as such the process of imperial growth was almost universally regarded. Not until the painful shocks which the War administered to the self-confidence of the plain citizen did he come to realize something of what colonial history really taught and how colonial policy might vitally affect him. The reign of Edward VII saw the general awakening of an imperial consciousness in Great Britain, and the ripening to maturity of the fruits of ideas that had been planted long before. It was in relation to the colonies of settlement that the awakening came, and owing to the limitations upon our space, to that our attention must be confined.

Throughout practically the whole of the nineteenth century the general attitude of Englishmen towards the colonies of settlement was one of kindly condescension. They were regarded as detached appendages of the central realms and this view was recorded in the phrase " British dependencies " which was generally applied to them in official publications as late as the 'eighties. In the old empire before 1783 they had been thought of by most people as outlying estates to be managed by the central government—not only for the good of the nation at home, it is true, but also for the benefit of those who lived overseas. Englishmen were never so narrow in their outlook on the colonies as were the Dutch, the French, or the Spaniards with regard to their colonies whose main purpose was to subserve the interests of the home country. But undoubtedly the phrase " British possessions " did fairly represent the idea held in Great Britain concerning the king's realms oversea during the eighteenth century. The phrase continued to be used regularly throughout Queen Victoria's reign, but it gradually ceased to represent accurately the prevailing idea and came to be nothing more than a convenient label.

" Colonies " and " colonial " were terms involving some degree of kindly patronage. Patriotism was still a narrowly British patriotism and had very little of the wider imperial outlook with which we are happily familiar to-day. The men of English stock who lived oversea in Canada, Australia, New Zealand, or South Africa were naturally expected to look at the world through English eyes, and though they might have their own ideas about their own local affairs and be impatient of undue interference by the central government in that sphere, in great international matters they were instinctively expected to follow the English lead and to

acquiesce readily in the measures decided upon by British
statesmen and the Imperial Parliament. It was recognized
that there were other than English elements in the colonies,
and that the French Canadians or the South African Dutch
might be expected to look at things differently, but these
were unfortunate exceptions, and even down to the later
years of Queen Victoria's reign it was hoped that they would
sooner or later disappear and be absorbed into the predominant and more numerous British stock.

This attitude of condescension was exceedingly irritating
to men oversea who felt stirring within their communities
the growing pains of young nations. To Canadians and
Australians the words " colonies " and " colonial " had
become distasteful, for they seemed to be filled with unpleasant and derogatory implications. The first generation
or two of men of British stock in the lands oversea had still
had many ties with the old land. Most of the settlers or their
parents had only recently emigrated from the British Isles,
and they carried out with them an instinctive understanding
of British conditions and looked at the world in a British
way. But by the end of the nineteenth century those
generations had passed or were passing.

New generations had grown up and most citizens in the
prime of life knew little of Great Britain at first or second-
hand. The old country to the majority of Canadians or
Australians was ceasing to be looked on as " home ". That
idea was gradually but naturally fading, and a Canadian
or Australian national feeling and a dominion patriotism
came to replace the remnants of the old British patriotism,
though without irreparable loss, as we shall show later.

In Australia and New Zealand the stock remained over-
whelmingly British, but into the new Canadian provinces
that were settled during the later years of Queen Victoria
and under Edward VII there came an enormous influx of
settlers from the United States and Central Europe who had
no roots in the British Isles. Instead of the French Canadians

or the Afrikanders being absorbed, they were driven in upon themselves ; they consciously and deliberately set themselves to cultivate and preserve their isolated nationalism and, whenever the extreme nationalists would admit that that must be compatible with a wider patriotism, it was only a Canadian or a South African patriotism that they envisaged. But among their best and most far-seeing leaders a wider view prevailed, and they looked to the cultivation of an imperial idea in which all the young nations should contribute their influence, for none of them ever turned back to the old narrow British patriotism. They admitted that in the formation and maintenance of that imperial idea Great Britain must play a part of enormous importance, but it could only be as an elder sister among a group of young nations around her. When Edward VII came to the throne, the movement to-wards this new and comprehensive conception of the Empire had made very great progress over sea, but before the South African War it was not fully grasped in Great Britain, and its acceptance there was undoubtedly the most significant event of the critical years of the reign in the sphere of imperial politics.

The time was, as we have emphasized, a breathing space between two wars on the great scale, and we can best perceive the great change in public opinion that took place if we note the difference in the way in which the participation in the two wars of troops from the dominions was regarded. The dispatch of small dominion forces to take part in the South African war was taken both in the old country and oversea to be the assistance afforded by her daughter states in fighting out Britain's quarrel with the Boer republics. When the Great War began and infinitely larger forces were sent by the dominions to take part in it, most Englishmen at first spoke of their arrival in the same way and believed that the dominions were coming to aid the " Mother Country " in *her* danger, and because of their loyalty to the home land. But long before the War ended, it had come to be realized that

K

this was really a faulty interpretation. Canadians, Australians or New Zealanders who came to join in the vast struggle on the fields of Flanders or Palestine were not fighting England's battles. They were fighting their own. They were the forces of co-equal nations banded together to defend themselves and their own liberties. They were allies of Great Britain, not merely her followers. Local patriotism and the sense of nationality had been roused to a higher pitch than ever before, but they were integral with a wider imperial patriotism. Here allegiance to Great Britain could never have imparted such vigour to their efforts as the imperial idea. It had come at last into its own and the critical years of its preparation had been in the transition period, the reign of Edward VII.

The last twenty years of the nineteenth century saw a good deal of discussion in Great Britain of inter-imperial relations, but it was usually misdirected and mainly the affair of enthusiasts who were often out of touch with reality and had not grasped the significance of the growth of national ideas in the dominions. Their favourite remedy for colonial difficulties was the idea of imperial federation, to achieve which an infinite variety of paper schemes was suggested. They ranged from the schemes of the Imperial Federation League of the late 'eighties and early 'nineties to the elaborate plans of the promoters of the Round Table movement at the very end of King Edward's reign and in the early years of his successor. Some of the schemes attracted mild academic interest in Great Britain among those who specialized in such matters, but almost invariably they were regarded with suspicion and distaste in the self-governing communities across the sea, for they invariably involved a relinquishment of some of the autonomy of their rising nationality into the hands of a central Imperial Council. Men in the dominions thought of this as implying the restoration of the old hampering control of the Colonial Office from which they had escaped, and they would have none of it. The paper schemes of the amateur constitution-makers thus never found their way into practical politics either in England or the dominions.

Their advocates in Great Britain were drawn from the ranks of both the great parties, but they did not attract the support of more than a few statesmen of the front rank and imperial federation plans were left to be wrangled over by rival projectors. The feelings of the more responsible leaders of the nation were well summarized in the very lukewarm estimate of the movement which was made by the prime minister (Lord Salisbury) in 1887. " Imperial federation is a matter for the future rather than the present. These grand aspirations are doubtlessly hazy, but they are the nebulous matter that in the course of ages will cool down and condense into material from which many practical and business-like resolutions may very likely come." The movement petered out during the 'nineties and the Imperial Federation League was dissolved. The value of its work lay not in the abortive schemes it had promoted but in the dispersal of some of the abysmal ignorance of the average Englishman about the Empire and imperial problems in general.

The real division of political thought in Great Britain did not lie between the imperial federationists and their opponents, but between views that long had had a very tenacious hold and usually on opposite sides in the party battle. To characterize each of the rival parties by the taunting name bestowed by its enemies we may say that the essential division over imperial matters lay between the Radical " Little-Englanders " and the Tory " Imperialists ". Such a division stretched far back into the days of mid-Victorian Liberalism, but as a rule the parties had fought few of their battles over colonial questions. It was not until the latter days of the long duel between Disraeli and Gladstone that the struggle turned to some extent on their divergent views concerning the Empire, and not until the period immediately preceding the South African War did colonial policy become a major issue of British politics.

The Radicals derived their political ideas from the great leaders of mid-Victorian Liberalism. Cobden and Bright and the other great prophets of that time had prophesied the gradual effacement of national lines and the growth of an international policy infused with the ideas of individual liberty which they had formulated in their long and successful fight against privilege. They failed to realize the rapid and powerful growth of nationalist particularism either in European countries or the colonies, and their lesser followers drew farther and farther away from the world of hard realities into a cloudy and sentimental internationalism. By the turn of the century the essential and valuable portions of their teaching had won so full a victory that they had infused the thought of all statesmen and were no longer the sole possession of one party, though the new generation of Liberals still regarded themselves as the sole champions of British and colonial liberties and stigmatized their opponents as reactionary supporters of a bellicose imperialism. Many of them read the history of the Empire still with memories of the party battles of the American Revolution and saw the colonial problems of their own day as a repetition of the contest between liberty and despotism under George III. Perfervid Radicals proclaimed that the Empire had been built up by war and commercial greed and they pointed to the troubles in South Africa as evidence that such were still the dominant motives of Imperialism. Hence the bitter quarrels that marked the years of the South African War and the party rancour that fought the " Khaki " election of 1900 and carried the Conservative and Unionist party back to power with cries of " Pro-Boer " against their opponents and accusations of " Little Englandism " and lack of patriotic feeling.

When the war was brought to an end and the last Boer leaders sued for peace at Vereeniging in May, 1902, the liberality and magnanimity of the terms granted by the victors demonstrated the falsity of the wilder accusations of

their opponents, and commanded general approval throughout the Empire. The Boers laid down their arms and accepted
allegiance to the king, and the assurances that were granted
to them sounded the dominant note of the Empire's spirit
—freedom within the circle of the British realms. " Military
administration in the Transvaal and Orange River Colony
will, at the earliest date, be succeeded by civil government ;
and as soon as circumstances permit, *representative government, leading up to self-government*, will be introduced."
For a moment the quarrels of the rival British parties were
stilled and the approbation of a united nation was registered
to the settlement. But it was only for a moment, and the
dispute over colonial policy arose again almost before the
ink on the Treaty was dry.

The controversies over imperial affairs that had raged
with such bitterness since the Jameson Raid in 1895 had had
as unfortunate a result with the less judicious members of
the Conservative party as with the Radicals. Too many of
them claimed to have a monopoly of proper imperial sentiment and seemed to show a condescending tendency to
annex the Empire as a possession of the Conservative party.
To the dominions such claims were exceedingly distasteful,
for they knew instinctively their falsity and they hated to
see the Empire made the sport of British party politics.
They knew that responsible statesmen lent no countenance
to such an outrageous attitude as had sometimes in the heat
of the " Khaki " election been adopted by Unionist candidates
and the less responsible organs of the Press, but none the less
it made their statesmen particularly jealous to watch for the
revival of any schemes of imperial federation that might
be dangerous to their treasured autonomy.

During the later stages of the war the imperial federationists
again became active in pointing out the dangers of divergent
policies and the lack of co-ordination in schemes of defence.
On grounds such as these they found some support among
influential members of the Unionist cabinet. When that

ministry had been formed in 1895, Joseph Chamberlain,
the most powerful leader of the Liberal Unionists and a
statesman of international reputation, had chosen as his
post the secretaryship of state for the colonies, thus marking
the greatly increased importance of imperial affairs in the
formulation of world policy.   Until that date the colonial
secretaryship had been estimated as only an office of the
second rank, and it had never attracted an outstanding
personality.   Chamberlain had shown great initiative in
dealing with imperial matters and had consistently supported
Milner in his policy in South Africa. Both men had been
Liberals before the Home Rule split, and the defection of
the most active and able of the Radical leaders of the stormy
days of the 'seventies and 'eighties had never been forgiven
by his old associates.   Thus personal rancour augmented
the hostility of the Radicals to any policy advocated by the
renegade in the imperial as well as in any other field, and
this had a potent influence in the bitter controversies of
the time.

   Chamberlain had always been interested in imperial
federation schemes, though he had never committed himself
to details. In his work at the Colonial Office before the war
he had done more than all his predecessors to consolidate
the Empire as far as was possible in the absence of effective
machinery, and after the Treaty of Vereeniging he strove
to make a great step forward in the evolution of an organized
scheme of imperial defence which he regarded as the outstanding need in the face of a hostile world in arms.   The
war had witnessed such an ebullition of anti-British feeling
in every European country as to bring vividly home to our
statesmen the dangers of a situation in which practically
the whole burden of imperial defence rested upon the
shoulders of the United Kingdom. Chamberlain looked to
the Colonial Conference which was summoned to meet in
London in the summer of 1902 as an opportunity for
furthering constructive and unifying schemes, but it was a

bitter though revealing disappointment to him and the whole Cabinet.

In his opening speech as president of the Conference the colonial secretary had thrown out the suggestion of a Council of the Empire to which all questions of imperial interest might be referred. He admitted that for a time the functions of the Council might be merely advisory, but he held that the object at which he was aiming would not be completely secured until there had been conferred upon the Council executive functions and perhaps also legislative powers. The ideas of the advocates of closer imperial union had never before been voiced with such authority, but they were received with such unmistakable and determined opposition on all sides that it was clearly impossible to proceed further with the scheme. The attempt to persuade the colonies to take a share in the organization of an imperial navy and that of the War Office to set up an imperial reserve force specially entrusted with the task of imperial defence also met with almost unanimous disfavour. No further progress could be made on those lines, and though no full report of the proceedings of the Conference was ever published, its general failure was sufficiently obvious to give a most disconcerting shock to the enthusiasms that had been so fervently expressed during the war. It was the first step in the education of the British public to a comprehension of the realities of the imperial situation.

Within the next five years, before the Colonial Conference of 1907 assembled, that education proceeded apace, and especially so because Chamberlain turned all his energies to converting the British electorate to an imperial tariff system and to the abandonment of the Cobdenite system of free trade which had stood for nearly sixty years. The self-governing colonies were all strongly protectionist, but they had granted remissions of duty to British goods during the preceding decade, and Chamberlain believed that if a tariff system could be set up in the United Kingdom, it would be possible to reciprocate these imperial preferences and thus take a long step on the road towards a closer organization of the Empire. The first step in Bismarck's unification of Germany had been the formation of the *Zollverein*, and in the early years of the twentieth century Germany had made a spectacular rise to the front rank of commercial powers.

The progress and complete failure of Chamberlain's campaign for tariff reform played a commanding part in British domestic politics during the declining years of Balfour's ministry until the smashing defeat of the Unionist party at the general election of 1906, and they have been dealt with in another part of this work. Here, therefore, we need only touch upon the specially imperial aspects of the agitation and show how it aided the Radicals in their opposition to the Government's policy of reconstruction in South Africa, which stood in the forefront of their work.

After his rebuff at the Colonial Conference Chamberlain, still colonial secretary, determined to visit South Africa to see for himself something of the great work of reconstruction that was being done by Lord Milner and to assist in the reconciliation of our late enemies. This, the first visit to the colonies ever paid by a colonial secretary in office, was a significant new precedent. It did something to assure the Boer leaders of the sincerity of the promises of the British Government. " The terms at Vereeniging," he told them, " are the charter of the Boer people ; and you have every right to call upon us to fulfil them in the spirit and the letter ; and if, in any respect, you think we have failed, or that in the future we do fail, in carrying out those terms, bring your complaints to us and they shall be redressed. . . . I believe that with consideration on both sides, with a readiness to give as well as to take, before many years are over we shall all be one free people under one flag." In using such words he was speaking as the mouthpiece of the whole British nation with real effect for the assuagement of old enmities.

But there was another effect of his visit. Chamberlain had

had an opportunity of looking at the Empire from the colonial point of view, and in a way possible only in a colonial environment. He came back to England in 1903 convinced that it was necessary to embark upon a campaign for the enlightenment of the British electorate upon what he felt to be the only measure to prevent the disruption, or at any rate the rapid decline, of the Empire. He had, in fact, become a convinced imperial federationist, and with the practical mind of an experienced statesman he planned to reach his end by the most immediately practicable road which the preferential tariffs already granted by the colonies showed to be not distasteful to them. But when he returned, he found himself faced by immovable hostility to tariff reform among a large section of his own party and doubts and hesitations among most of the rest. Into the circumstances of his campaign and its effects in splitting the Unionist party we need not enter. That is a matter of British domestic politics, and we can do no more than emphasize the widespread educational effects upon the minds of British audiences of country wide debates upon imperial matters. The outer empire could no longer be regarded by the average Englishman as an appendage of the British Isles. He was forced, as never before, to realize how new nations had grown up round him with their own outlook upon the world and the same right to it as his own. It was the most lasting result of the campaign.

The agitation against free trade was, of course, a first-rate opportunity for the Radical party to recover its prestige and influence in defending the threatened system under which England had built up her world-wide commerce; but other measures of the Unionists in the outer Empire also gave them attractive rallying cries. The most insistent of these was in opposition to the Chinese Labour Ordinances in South Africa which were introduced by Lord Milner to supply the deficiency of native labour in the mines of the Witwatersrand. The importation of Chinese coolies under very strict restrictions was suggested to Chamberlain during his visit to South Africa as absolutely essential to get the gold-mining industry started again after its breakdown during the war. The colonial secretary was not at all favourable to the idea, but Lord Milner was convinced of its necessity and the Ordinances were promulgated, the first shiploads of coolies were introduced, and a policy that was repugnant to almost everyone in South Africa was thus begun.

The motives of its promoters were devoted to what they thought were the best interests of the new colonies in the restarting of the great industry which had added so much to the wealth of South Africa. But their policy lent itself readily to misrepresentation and the cry of " Chinese slavery " roused one of the deepest sentiments of Englishmen and stirred their humanitarian feelings as few other cries could have done. We have already spoken of the source of Liberal feeling in British public opinion which derived from the struggles against privilege and the fight for equality and individual liberty in the first half of the nineteenth century. Concurrent with those struggles there were two other great associated movements which left a deep impression upon Great Britain, the agitation against the slave trade and slavery, and the missionary movement which had such a potent effect in opening up tropical Africa to English influence. The religious impulse and the humanitarian had moulded the British Empire on quite different lines from the materialistic old commercial empire which looked upon Africa only as the source of a cheap labour supply for the exploitation of the sugar industry in the West Indies. To the humanitarian the traffic in flesh and blood was revolting, for all men, irrespective of race, creed or colour, were brothers, and to buy and sell negroes, to use them to death for the commercial profit of the white man was a sin against our common humanity and the essential tenets of the Christian faith. That faith taught that the Gospel must be preached to all mankind, and for nearly a century devoted missionaries had been carrying out that duty in South Africa and at the same time fighting into the very heart of the Dark Continent against slavery or any approach to it.

It is true that the Chinese were not slaves but labourers working under contracts by which they were paid wages and were assured of a free passage back to China on the termination of their contracts. But, while they were at the mines, they were confined to the labour compounds and ruled with narrow restrictions upon their liberty which could be speciously represented as slavery in a transparent disguise. We need not argue here as to whether the policy was well- or ill-designed or carried out. For our purpose it is sufficient to point to the undeniable fact that just at the time when Englishmen's minds were being turned to the problems of the self-governing empire by the agitation over tariff reform, their sentiments were roused against slavery and in support of the humanitarian treatment of native peoples as they had not been for fifty years.

The average citizen was moved at one and the same moment to think more of the self-governing empire than he had ever done and to realize that in the dependent empire with its primitive peoples he had a burden of duty laid upon him to see that they had a fair deal. It may seem at first sight that the question of Chinese labour was a specially South African one concerned solely with one part of Lord Milner's reconstruction policy, which is, of course, true. But there is little doubt that in regard to the formation of British public opinion on the Empire during the reign of Edward VII, which is the main subject of our study, the agitation against " Chinese slavery " roused much wider questions and turned men's thoughts to a new consideration of the whole question of relations with native races.

While the tide of unpopularity of the Unionist Ministry was mounting rapidly to the flood that washed it away in 1906, Alfred Lyttelton, Chamberlain's successor at the Colonial Office, was planning for a step forward on the road towards the fulfilment of the promise of self-government that had been given to the new colonies in the Treaty of Vereeniging. It was generally agreed that the crown colony government, which had been established when military rule was withdrawn, must be replaced as soon as possible. Lord Milner's administration of the new colonies, though it was admirably competent and produced great material progress in reconstruction, was repugnant to the feelings both of the Dutch- and the English-speakers who longed for self-government and felt degraded by autocratic rule, however efficient it might be. But there was an acute division of opinion as to what should replace it. In the view of Mr. Lyttelton, supported by a section of the English-speaking inhabitants of the mining area along the Witwatersrand, the immediate granting of full responsible government was filled with danger, and Lyttelton therefore determined that there must be an interval of representative government, that is, a form of government in which the legislative power should be placed in the hands of elected representatives, but the executive power should remain in the hands of the Governor and ministers chosen by him.

This decision aroused a storm of resentment in the Transvaal and in the Radical party in Great Britain. A strong Responsible Government Association was formed in Johannesburg by men of British stock, and, though the Boer leaders stood aside and took no active part, they let it be clearly understood that nothing but full responsible agreement could attract their support and ensure their taking an active share in striving to heal the deep racial antagonisms of the war. Mr. Lyttelton attempted to support his plan of representative government by somewhat ill-informed appeals to historical precedents, but his speeches and despatches produced a very unfortunate effect not only in South Africa but also upon public opinion in the self-governing dominions of the Empire. They seemed to show that the Colonial Office still looked back regretfully upon the grant of responsible government to the colonies of settlement and was desirous of restoring its hampering control whenever occasion should arise. The Unionist party, of course, had no such motive, but, coming as the proposals did at a time when Chamberlain had recently spoken of his ambitions for an Imperial Council with executive and legislative powers, and was pressing forward with his agitation for tariff reform as a first step towards that goal, it seemed that a great British party wished to turn the stream of imperial constitutional development back in its course, and was threatening the treasured autonomy of the dominions. The whole result was particularly unfortunate, and, though Lyttelton managed to secure the approval of a majority of the British House of Commons, his opponents had the best of the argument and his supporters were by no means enthusiastic.

Lord Milner left South Africa in 1905 and he was succeeded by the Earl of Selborne, who had none of his predecessor's unpopularity to hamper him in his efforts for conciliation. The letters patent for the introduction of the system of representative government were promulgated in the last days of the Unionist ministry, but they were never brought into effect, for before then the Radicals had come into power in Great Britain under the premiership of Sir Henry Campbell-Bannerman, who before the election of 1906 took place had publicly proclaimed his hostility to them and the intention of his party to proceed to responsible government for the new colonies in South Africa as soon as ever they got into power. One of the earliest acts of the new ministry was to take the first steps to carry out this intention, and Lord Elgin, the colonial secretary, announced that responsible government would be established with the least possible delay with the hope that it " would lead in due time to the union of the interests of the whole of His Majesty's dominions in South Africa ".

That such a hope was destined to so early a fulfilment was due to the welcome participation of General Botha and the best of the Boer leaders in the efforts of Lord Selborne to further the progress of a scheme for South African federation or unification. His celebrated Memorandum of 1907 is perhaps the greatest state paper of Edward VII's reign and its effect in furthering the movement for closer union aided by a well-organized campaign of propaganda throughout all the South African colonies resulted in the summoning of a National Convention later in the year. The Convention laboured against immense difficulties, but at last it reached agreement, and in 1909 a Bill for the unification of South Africa was presented to Parliament and passed through all its stages with little criticism and without amendment. The Imperial Parliament thus placed the whole responsibility for their own government in the hands of the people of South Africa and a new dominion came to take its place beside the great self-governing dominions of Canada and Australia. The development of the Empire as a commonwealth of free nations, leagued together under a single monarch, had taken another great stride forward, and in the discussions that had preceded it British public opinion had been brought to a far clearer realization of what was happening and what the Empire really was than had prevailed when Edward VII came to the throne eight years before.

It was not until after the close of the reign that that progress in imperial development was fully set forth in the speeches at successive Imperial Conferences both by dominion and British statesmen and their embodiment in formal documents and in the Statute of Westminster did not come until long after the upheaval and the many constitutional experiments of the World War. But even the Colonial Conference of 1907 differed fundamentally from earlier conferences. It was much more like a series of negotiations between the representatives of co-equal and separate, though closely associated, powers than they had been. The tone and temper of the colonial representatives at the Conference of 1907 were amiable and constructive in regard to matters of common interest rather than suspicious and distrustful of assaults upon their rising nationality by a well-meaning but over-officious mistress as they had been at the Conference of 1902.

After the election campaign of 1906, in which controversies over imperial policy were so hotly debated, such matters passed out of the realm of British party politics, to the great relief of all those who understood them best. The Unionist Opposition did not take up a partisan attitude in the debates over the South African measures of the new ministry, and the tempers of members on both sides cooled down. The affairs of the outer Empire came to be looked at from a national and not a party point of view, so that when the vital question of imperial defence came to the forefront in 1909 it was generally considered with a seriousness befitting its importance, as were the equally grave questions raised by the Morley-Minto reforms in India. The responsibility of office curbed the exuberance of all but the more extreme anti-imperialists among the Liberals. All but the more injudicious of the Conservatives ceased to claim to have a monopoly of imperial patriotism, and so, except among the apostles of internationalism among the new Labour party, the beneficient results of Britain's imperial work were recognized and emphasized as a glorious achievement which had been won neither by one party nor even by the people of one part of the Empire alone. When Edward VII's reign ended among the dark shadows of impending war, the essentials of the concept of the modern Empire-commonwealth of free co-ordinate nations had emerged from the controversies of that period of troubled transition.

ARTHUR PERCIVAL NEWTON.

VII

Education

The short space of years we are considering happens to coincide with a moment in the long and shrouded evolution of our national education when many detached but slowly blending forces achieved a stage of consistency such as enabled them to appear as visible form and structure. The beginning of the new reign and the beginning of the new educational phase coincide; but they are no more than coincident. Education is, of all our processes of national growth, the least advantageously affected by changes in government or in the personality of government. This is of its nature, and of the nature, happily, of our people. It was, therefore, even less liable than the course of our political or of our economic history to be influenced by activities principally concerned with the personal relationships of our own and other governments. The close of the reign and any further significant change in our educational evolution were not even coincident. Fully ten years after this close the ending of the Great War, with its abnormal and profound economic and social reactions, could only produce in our educational midst an agitated self-questioning. It could not initiate a new term, or even hasten development. With " unhurrying speed " and, we must trust, " majestic instancy " that development continued on its way, seemingly in its new phase of visibility exposed to, and deviating with, every breath of generational pressure but, as to its reality, still deeply hidden " in the labyrinthine ways " of the national mind.

Education as a national process—for we need not at the moment pursue it farther towards its origin in individual impulse—either as a system or without system, is one of several

parallel or complementary processes which together form
the life of a people. In its succeeding forms it is variously
conditioned by its relation to these concurrent developments ; to which we give the names of our social or political
or economic progress. With them, with their contemporary
phases, it forms an identity. So much so is this the case
that it is apt to be looked upon, contemporarily, as merely
a reflection of its collaterals when it emerges as a group
expression or a state system ; and its value is then measured
only by its success in reflecting their contemporary require-
ments. But it is more than this reflection. It has its own
essential growth and rate of growth, and its own independent
contribution to make to the collective progress. History,
with its wider angle of view, will measure the success of
a period by the extent to which these associated processes
maintained a simultaneous and mutually contributory
advance. It will measure the success of the education of
a period not only by the extent to which its self-formulation
was held to be contributory at the time, but by the extent to
which it was proved to have been anticipatory of the future.

To examine our education at a given point of time is, therefore, in effect, to cut through a stem, our life national, and to
expose a section discovering the severed ends, not of a single
continuity, but of a number of interrelated continuities :
our life political, our life professional, our life domestic.
We shall err—as we often do err—if we assume to be able
to isolate the one from the others ; and we shall not be
diminishing the error when we colour, for better distinctive-
ness, that part of the surface of activity which appeals to
our private judgment as primarily educational with the mild
wash of our own limited experience.

The educational process of a national life can be even
less easily distinguished, and more easily misread, after
it has attained maturity as a state system, than in the
uncorrelated movements of its infancy. No other process of
national life can be equally misleading. The reason is not

L

far to seek. Before the education of a people has achieved structural shape, among its sporadic local or voluntary activities, we can often be misled into identifying, as the main educational thread of a period, some one conspicuous movement; not improbably the efforts of some religious or philanthropic organization. Whereas the actuating educational influence of the period may have been exerted in some other form, less apparent: progressing through the guilds, exercised upon naval or military expansion, or concentrated in a local activity such as we might now call vocational. But, after it has assumed visible shape as a state system, the necessity under which an organized education lies of reflecting contemporary social or economic requirement can be even more bewildering in effect. And this is especially the case in the history of a race like ours, wherein political and social development have preceded our corresponding educational development through all the stages of national growth to full self-consciousness and self-responsibility. So that we might see in our history education, like a Cinderella sister, left to develop in a seclusion difficult to penetrate by the domestic hearth; or compelled to continue as the menial of the exacting service of elder processes, even after the attainment of years of discretion, and of a school organization. With the effect that, for whole periods, its own independent growth or, as we say, its cultural contribution to the national life has been proportionately lessened.

Because education has a twofold function to perform. It should reflect, but it must also prophesy, and, as a result, contribute. It should reflect contemporary demand, fashion its forms accordantly, and relate them placatingly to contemporary idealism. But it must also anticipate, and prepare for, a phase to come. And that phase will be the product of the interaction of *all* the processes of national growth. That is, education must contain within itself the power of predicting, and contributing towards, a whole of national evolution, of which itself forms only one part. This prophetic task, this sustained capacity of relating the part to the whole, the growth of method to the growth of idea, the present formulation to the ultimate need, the individual or generational interest to the progressive revelation of the purpose of the national life and, in the end, of human life as a whole is what we describe as its cultural function. Of this twofold and continuous process a view in flat section can only give an inadequate picture. A picture so seldom clear that we are often tempted to take refuge in our temperamental bias, to discover in the surface impression of some sympathetic movement or prophet the true educational expression of the time, and to proclaim that upon it, or him, the mantle of prophetic succession had fallen—in all but the semblance of wings. Against this temptation our only safeguard must be the retention of the distance necessary to the historical point of view. But, since it is not easy to keep the whole field of educational history in view simultaneously with our examination of a particular period—or, for that matter, simultaneously with our everyday educational practice— it is of almost equal help to keep a familiar image in mind. These lively processes, such as is education, which arise naturally out of human circumstance, follow the same order of development as the life of man. The parts in association develop function, and co-operation ; which in turn modify them. Nerve communications, or local exchanges, are established. In time the need of co-ordination evolves a central exchange, or mind, with a generalized awareness, or consciousness, but with only such limited control and initiative as may help and not hamper the local exchanges, specially developed to discharge their special functions. It would seem, indeed, that the life-force in a nation, like the spirit of life in an individual, can never trust more than a partial control to the terminable consciousness, in the one case of a single life, in the other, of a succession of brief lives. An individual is permitted only a restricted authority within himself, and a slightly larger area of awareness of himself. No stage in the development of a nation is entrusted with much more. If the prophetic mind has been conceded in addition, as necessary to the anticipatory function of the educational process, it was granted upon the terms that the weight of disbelief should always counterbalance its effect. Contemporary " common sense " weighs down the scale, lest an educational Cassandra might upset a natural order of development.

A national order of development must also be a natural order. It derives its energy of growth from the same continuous spirit of life that is enshrined in each individual and in humanity as a whole. But it is expressed in different terms of time. The historical standpoint will enable us to see that a longer view than was possible for any of the generations taking part in it has determined the history of national processes, including the process of education. At some future time we may be less concerned with national growth, and detect the longer view, and its determination, in the history of humanity. But, for the present, growth is still in national tutelage. And to our national evolution the image of the life of man as fitly applies.

As an organism, the education of the nation has passed through stages of growth very similar to those of human life in its approach to self-consciousness. But, as the dependent of related national processes, with ancillary functions to perform, its own independent growth has been periodically handicapped by their step-sisterly demands, by their imperious and often stormy stages of social and political adolescence. The prophetic function, the careful educational provision for the morrow, has been at times even extinguished by the social necessity of reflecting sympathetically the family mood.

The century preceding King Edward's reign embraced one of these vital, but tempestuous and therefore confusing, periods of change. The educational embarrassment which

resulted is often represented as due to a culpable delay on
the part of the state in centralizing control and establishing
an official school system. Synchronizing with the accession
of King Edward, the responsibility was acknowledged, and
education as a whole was recognized as, at least, under the
supervision of government. If the Victorian age is to be
blamed for arbitrarily delaying this culmination, through
dilatoriness or through some perverse dislike of correct
thinking or correct training for living, and the Edwardian
age is to be praised for reversing the decision, then in one
process of national development, our history contradicted
the order followed in all the others.

Our image of a life history can give us a different explanation : the picture of a gradual integration, handicapped by
circumstance ; of a progression towards the partial realization
that must precede full national awareness. In this picture
the Education Acts of 1870 and 1902 take their natural place,
as the undertaking in part and the undertaking in full, of
the responsibility attached to matured consciousness.

Originally, almost aboriginally, the early life of the child
was its education. When child life and after life were lived
in the same environment and atmosphere, all the formative
influences were contributory to the preparation for the
wholeness of life. With civilization, with the dislocation
of certain classes or groups from the soil and the ground-
work of living, natural preparation for life broke down ; and
the more completely because it had never been a conscious
system. Hence education for life very easily altered its
meaning to that of education for advantage in life, social
or economic ; a meaning it still retains. As educators,
the pedagogues, tutors, and vocational training replaced
natural circumstance. For a time, accident more than
intention kept them as part of the home-life ; environmental
training was unconsciously perpetuated. But the idea of
education as technical training, of knowledge as the basis
of advantage, and then of knowledge as an end in itself

inevitably gained ground. We can trace the conflict in progress at a later stage in the Athenian commonwealth, in the rivalry between the scientific and the philosophic schools. The former stood for the realistic pursuit of knowledge, and its advantage as vocational preparation. The latter unknowingly perpetuated an earlier tradition, of education as preparation for the wholeness of life. But if the philosphic schooling appeared to win in popular opinion, it was, with a few notable exceptions, at the sacrifice of the essence of that for which it seemed to fight. For it made of philosophy a branch of scientific pursuit, and attempted to formulate it as vocational preparation, before human life had acquired sufficient conscious experience.

All down the course of our history we can trace the efforts of education to reassert itself in its earlier meaning, and with its wider purpose in view. Naval and, on occasion, military training of their nature preserved a degree of environmental influence. The expansion of commerce revived it intuitively in the apprenticeship system. Even with the development of group and class schools, segregations which reflected social change, the use of the religious order and of the religious-minded as convenient educators for many centuries, bears indications of the same continuity of idea still present in the national mind. Beyond and below other more obvious qualification, they were accepted instinctively as the possessors of the prophetic mind. The nature of the religious life, in itself prophetic and preparatory, drew to itself in each generation a large proportion of those thus minded. They were professionally and morally concerned with the relationship of man to his future ; and they could be trusted, in the course of preparation for a future life, to secure by the way appropriate education for an earlier stage in that continuity.

This type of mind, continuous under different religious or lay denominations, remained often the only contributory educational force, as civilization progressed, and the phases of social dislocation succeeded one another. It maintained a thread of educational development, even through the period of detached group schooling; and at the beginning of the nineteenth century it alone, in individual prophecy or almost chance association, was able to make any headway against the confusion of social orders, the uprooting of group tradition, and the outcrop of new and deracinated populations, which followed upon the French Revolution and the Industrial Revolution.

Would an anticipation of the Act of 1902 have been a natural outcome, or even an appropriate national apparatus, at this stage? Collective authority under new pressures was in process of social transfer. Politically, we had barely yet attained self-respect. It was only a few years since a public man might still keep his public and his private sense of honour in different pockets. The great traditions of the Civil Service, and even of national loyalty or patriotism, were still in embryo. It would have been as surprising as perilous to our growth had our order of maturity in these processes been suddenly reversed, and an educational system been thrust upon our administrative immaturity and upon the new uncertainty of our individual need. As it was, educational progress was retarded; but it remained constant, and in the same quarter. The activities of the Society for the Promotion of Christian Knowledge and the Sunday School movement first made symptomatic appearance upon the surface. To be followed by those of the British and Foreign Society and the National Society, with the names of Lancaster and Bell in honourable opposition. In like honourable rivalry, the Church and Non-conformity made a new step forward, with the training of teachers. But, inevitably, with the changes proceeding in society, the demand for technical training, for knowledge as a weapon in the economic struggle, received fresh reinforcement, and challenged the divided educational counsels of the more prophetic-minded, themselves divided. It was

not " almost an accident " as we may read, but their response
to a clamorous need, which gave increase to Dr. Birkbeck's
Mechanic's Institutes.   The realism of the '51 Exhibition
set its seal upon this interpretation of education, and led to
the Science and Art Grants, to the work of the City and
Guilds of London Institutes and of the Science and Art
Department, and to an encouragement of a technical and
vocational bias which continued down to the close of the
century.

Under such conditions the prophets could do little but
cry in the wilderness. Education could be little more than
the reflector of immediate demand. And it was failing even
as a reflector, since the readjustments which it was called
upon to make could only reproduce old forms already in
dissolution, or new forms still uncertain of their purpose.
The primary schools were adrift, and rudderless. Higher
schools were fortunate if they could remain attached to some
group or convention which could offer them support. The
universities looked to be in mid-air, and under a clouding
sky. All the institutional forms of an earlier educational
tradition were deteriorating under that depression which
attacks the vitality of every corporate personality once it
becomes dissociated from a living demand.

The real growth was proceeding elsewhere. From the
new centres of local control, and from new voluntary associations in enlivening competition, the nerve-messages were
multiplying, and quickening a central awareness in the nation.
We can watch the inception and growth of the Adult School
movement; the foundation of the Y.M.C.A.; the purpose
of the Working Men's College under Frederick Maurice's
inspiration; the story of the Pupil Teacher system and
Kaye Shuttleworth's labours; the significance of the Co-
operative movement; University Extension, and its further
extension in the Tutorial Classes and under James Stuart;
Quintin Hogg's dream of the Polytechnic, and its rapid
conversion into official form by the Charity Commissioners

through the activity of Henry Cunynghame; Toynbee
Hall and Mr. Barnett's prophetic personality; the movement for Women's Education, Girton, the Women's Co-
operative Guild, the Club and Institutes Union, and the
practical idealism of Ruskin College. Nerve-messages in
a particular sense, for they were all communications from
a growing unity, or from impulses to further unity.

A new centre of national consciousness was responding
to them. In the successive Royal Commissions, always
indications of a pricking state consciousness, in Robert
Lowe's Revised Code, in the Science and Art Exhibitions,
in the Endowed Schools Acts, first acknowledgments of
the existence of a higher school problem, and, finally, under
the stimulus proceeding from the widest area of unco-ordin-
ated activity, in the Elementary Education Act. This marked
a national consciousness in being. The acceptance of full
state responsibility had still to follow.

We have still the picture of an organic life. The movements themselves, of diverse character, originated in very
lively, if dispersed, motor-centres. The forms they adopted
were those already existing in the native educational structure.
It was natural that these should be used. Modification
could only result from a further stage of unified development. If I might recall conversations with some of those
most instrumental in these movements of transition, with
Sir George White, Mr. George Cadbury, Mr. James Stuart,
Mr. Quintin Hogg, it would be with the youthful impression
still fresh, of how occupied they seemed with scholastic
and practical programmes on familiar lines, but how obviously
they were inspired by some far deeper educational intuition;
or it might be with the memory of the years darkened by
my father's disappointment—who, with a like intuition,
had been the most active promoter of a residential as well
as a teaching university for London—when the scheme
went awry by an accident of parliamentary succession,
an accident which can still suggest to us the incomplete

educational awareness present in the state, even at that late time.

But the century ended with the sense of central responsibility practically matured if still only on occasion indulged ; and with what we may consider an educational conscience stirring in the cells of new-formed local administration. In a relenting economic pause there was space, and hearing, again for the educational prophets. Mathew Arnold could be rediscovered as an educationalist. Victor Hugo and Alice Meynell—to mention only those most generally forgotten—could be found to have clarified our ideas of an oncoming generation. Childhood emerged again as in itself a respectable phase of a continuous life, and no longer, in accordance with a convenient group convention, as a blank copybook upon which the characters of the morrow's manhood must be written overnight. We were raking the earlier educational self-consciousness of our neighbours for experience on these new lines of interpretation, Pestalozzi, Herbart, Froebel. Our older universities even began to give modest cover to the training of teachers, and a shy undergraduate or two among us could be found to consent to receive it.

It was an educational ferment, at a point of momentous natural change : milder than the economic upheaval of a century before, but active in the inwardness of our educational process and no longer merely agitating the reflections cast upon its surface by other forces. As individuals, we were reproducing this dawning of a central consciousness, and we were responding similarly, to messages only vaguely understood, with means and methods indiscriminately adopted from the conventions of the past or the monitions of the prophets.

The Act of 1902 completed the phase. By establishing the Board of Education as the central authority, and at the same time by extending the educational function of the local authorities, the nation accepted responsibility, localized its

own share of authority in the Board—may we say the mind ?
—and acknowledged the conception of national education
as an organic whole, with responsibility and function in
like manner distributed.

The Board became responsible to see that the members
of this organization were treated as parts of a vital structure.
In the discretion of the Board it lay to adjust existing educational administration and provision to the new social
quantitative demands for equality and continuity of opportunity, to preserve diversity of preparation in so far as such
diversity might be adjudged contributory to the production,
or retention, of different qualitative values in citizenship,
and to effect cohesion and continuity as between old and
new schools and school types, while emphasizing their
independence of individual function. By its progressive
encouragement of variety in the higher grades of primary
school, involving the solution of the higher elementary
school problem which had been rendered acute by the
Cockerton judgment, and by the establishment of the free
place system, as a bridge between primary and secondary
school, the Board made an initial response to what we may
call the quantitative demand ; and by prescribing a minimum
four-years' course as the aim of the secondary school, it
gave guidance and support to the principle of diverse
qualitative preparation. If we now possess a school system
loose-jointed in character, perhaps chaotic to casual observation, but more elastic in its opportunities for individual
progress than do our neighbours, the credit—or discredit,
if we so think—lies with the policy of the Board at
this time. It succeeded at least in establishing in education
a reflection of the national mind. In so far, therefore, as
educational un-order continues to exist, it is due to our own
continued uncertainty as to what exactly we are preparing
for, or how that preparation can best be given. In so far,
also, as our school system remains loose-jointed or diversified,
it is the more adapted to accept alteration and enlightenment,

as our views with regard to purpose and method grow
clearer.

For the insight which at once produced and formulated
the Act, the nation owed much to Sir Robert Morant ; who
possessed the quality of the prophetic mind, and also of the
exceptionally energetic administrator. As president of the
reconstituted Board, he was also the first to discharge the
functions of the new brain, or central exchange. The story
of education in King Edward's reign consists largely of the
working out of the respective responsibilities of the Board
and the L.E.A.s, and it might equally be regarded as the
story of Sir Robert Morant's presidency. He brought to
the work an experience of the difference between the oriental
and the western mind, of value where so much depended
upon reconciling divergences of geographical, mental, and
traditional outlook, a great vitality and swiftness of decision,
and an excellent prevision of the relationships ultimately
desirable between the various members of the growing
educational body. He was helped by the accumulation of
information acquired by the ability of Sir Michael Sadleir ;
and he had for assistance men invaluable for their especial
gifts, the administrative quality of Sir Amherst Selby Bigge,
the tact and diplomatic accomplishment of the Hon. W. N.
Bruce, and the revolutionizing knowledge of the history
of our schools possessed by Mr. Arthur Leach. These three
had been assistants to the Endowed Schools Commissioner,
Sir George Young. They had shared with him in the
enlightened policy which the restricted powers under the
Acts permitted him to initiate, and they were transferred
by the Charity Commission to the Board, together with the
responsibility for the endowed schools, as, probably, not
the least important part of that transfer. Their names may
be taken as representative of a notable body of officials
equally conscious of the gravity and delicacy of the new task
of organization. Not very different, indeed, may have been
the anxious labour of the first human mind, when it was

evolved to act as moderating intelligence between members unruly because they themselves had called the rule into being.

Something of the nature of the work, in these first years, may possibly be suggested by a few words as to the experiences of one of the first body of secondary school inspectors brought into being by the new Act. Our new body included women, for the first time on an equal footing with men. And this important innovation in Civil Service tradition was made a success from the first owing to the happy choice of (Dame) the Hon. Maude Lawrence as chief of the Women's Staff. The divisions between the several branches of the inspectorate, and as between officials working at the Board and in the field, were also much modified, to the general advantage. The inspectorate, in this more sensitive and elastic form, was designed to act as an intelligence service, a network of nerve-communications to inform the brain no less than to inform the local educational centres and extremities. It might be claimed—in correction of criticism —that its action in those first years did even more to guide the policy of the Board than to establish any directory by the Board over the new local centres. It was composed of men and women of very varied experience ; and the nature of their service made them more subject to local influences than to bureaucratic tradition. If, for a space of subsequent years, the Board seemed to acquire increasing authority, and earned criticism thereby, the reason need not be looked for in the acquisitive autocracy of officialdom. It must be remembered that the Board, as the centre of channelled information of all kinds, assembled experience and formulated policy in accordance with it far more rapidly once unity of contact was established than could local bodies not primarily selected upon educational grounds, and with less information at their disposal. The Board, in this respect also, was much in the position of our brain when we reach manhood ; which knows, and can threaten

us with the consequences of much that our youthful senses
or muscles may wish still to undertake. We know the struggle
that may ensue ; and that we can even maintain a grudge, in
ourselves, against our own mind for the tyranny of its conscious direction. If, at a later date, there may seem to have
been a retraction of central authority, a greater freedom
left to local control and initiative, this was again the symptom
of ripening maturity, the consequence of increased co-
ordination. It is the business of the brain only to direct over
those areas where automatic or subconscious action is not
effective. And our conscious mind, as our co-ordination
matures, continues to surrender for local performance whole
combinations of movements as they become habitual.
Economy in a state system, or in a human system, insists
upon this. It would seem to us indicative of a prophetic
understanding of the lively nature of a state educational
organism, on the part of the new central administration,
if, at a distance of time, we can look back and trace this as
our curve of progress.

From the point of view of one of these state ravens,
released over the higher educational plane to inspect what
remained after the flood of social change, the picture presented
was distracting in its complexity, both of uneven decay and
of irregular fresh growth. Springing from the soil of national
life, and, where we should expect to find it first, in the new
elementary training of the new groupings of our people,
an energy of unsanctioned growth characterized the types
and methods of schools created, at our stage of partial consciousness, in compromise with group, or sectarian, or
generational convention. We were faced by the problems
of the provided and the non-provided schools, by the
controversies that raged around payment by results, by that
of the higher elementary school, and of the pupil teacher
centre. In our more immediate province we had, on the
one hand, the destructive competition between the older
urban grammar school and the new municipal secondary

school. On another, a premature local classification, such
as seemed to provide for everything except the fact that
growth is a continuous and not a stratified process.   On
another, the phenomenon of the old " group " school, so
long divorced from local life that it served nothing but the
sentiment of a dead tradition. On yet another, a weed-crop
of irresponsible examining bodies and tests.   On yet another,
the amorphous institutions produced by the technical bias
of the age of confusion just past, and by the lop-sided aid
given to science teaching, which had led many ancient
foundations to sink their endowments in laboratories as
unsightly as they were unsuited to local need.   On another,
the efforts, familiar but too often successful, of ambitious
head masters, by the ways of boarding-house elements,
school chapels, and imitation of the worser Public School
traditions, to inflate old local foundations above the means-
limit of the class and neighbourhood for which they were
intended.

The inspectorate mind was ill-informed in such matters
at first, but it groped sincerely for the truth.   The earlier,
amateur reports, before an official body was established,
suggested, indeed, the delighted surprise of discoverers.
" Cottingham is a large town in the Midlands," one might
read, " it is pleasantly situated on a river, contains 50,000
inhabitants, is served by two railways, and has the following
industries."   But the service once organized, it soon scrapped
every formula.   It set itself to develop a new art, the art of
keeping an open collective mind.   Upon this the personality
of a school or organization might impress itself as a whole.
Only when that impression became clear, might a judgment
be formed as to how far the personality was commendable,
or the purpose possible of its attainment.

As a compensation, from many localities and schools,
developed in independence, there was much to be learned.
And this knowledge was soon transmitted to other quarters
less well-directed or informed.   At one remote little east-

coast grammar school, more like a hedge-school with hornbooks in appearance, and reached after a long drive, a single-handed elderly master was giving to seven country boys the best English lessons, in the best English course, I have ever encountered. But at another, so novel and remote did Whitehall still seem, that a head master, upon the receipt of an unfavourable report, felt himself safe in denying to his governors that His Majesty's inspector had ever visited the school at all. Some governing bodies received the inspectors enthusiastically, as swallows preceding a summer of state subvention. Others, again, might take footing upon their medieval personality, and rise in a body to resign if ever we asked for an interview. But there were pleasanter moments. It was at Stratford-on-Avon that I had to listen to a nervous young man drilling " Treasure Island " into a class of sleepy country boys. It was a dull lesson, and I was inattentively speculating what Shakespeare, as a boy there, would have made of it, when I heard the question, " What *is* the wake of a ship, anybody ? " An awkward pause was broken by the shifting of a rough-headed boy on a back bench, and by the hoarse murmur, " Sir ! It's the part of the ship on which the sun shines first." Pure poetry !—and in that room we need not have listened, as a result, to five minutes' explanation of how silly the answer was.

On the teaching side, indeed, in method and practice, the change found us with little respectable tradition of our own. And our passage through the self-conscious age was marked by an aping of the fashions of our educationally maturer neighbours not seldom absent at such a time. Those of us who had, at about the turn of the century, obeyed the urge so far as to study methods of teaching abroad, may have come back a little disillusioned. There was surely something impalpable, say in Professor Rein's lecture-course upon " How to Teach Art ", if it could proceed for a whole Semester without requiring one concrete demonstration of a drawing or design ? But the catchwords of new method were not slow to spread far upon the wave of new interest. Intensive method, retention of interest (in the sense of excitement), activity of the learner, mental training by handwork (very vaguely defined), and, of course, the direct method in language teaching—we had plenty of laughable and plenty of melancholy examples of them all ; but two must suffice.

A few of us had invited the greatest of comparative educationalists of the era to tell us how to set our curriculum in order. After two hours of discourse, exquisitely phrased, we left, much impressed, and I asked a colleague tentatively what he thought it all came to. He replied after reflection, " The concrete part of it amounted to this : we've got to see that cloisonné enamel-work is introduced in IVth Form." At a later date, we were asked by the Admiralty to inspect the Naval Colleges, in whose creation by Sir John Fisher accident had allowed me a very small say. A very brilliant teacher was using the direct method with the senior year upon a French Classic dealing with the Three Unities of the drama. On the second day, I became uncertain as to the extent to which either the French or the subject matter was being communicated, and I was cordially invited to put questions. To my rather fundamental question, " What *is* the law of the three Unities ? " this answer was given by a scion of the Royal House then in the class, and it did great credit to the resourcefulness of the Senior Service, " La Loi des trois Unités, il est, qu'on n'ose pas mettre, sur le même étage, au même temps, Dieu, et le Fils, et le Conforteur."

In this field it is little wonder that the Board, with its advantage as the centre of information, could do much to encourage experiment and suggest method more native in character. The report upon the teaching of mathematics, associated with the name of Mr. Fletcher, still holds its place. To the acute brain and wide humanity of Mr. James Headlam, later Sir J. Headlam-Morley, belongs the credit of retaining for Latin a place in our secondary school

M

curriculum during years when local views upon education were still culturally uninspired.

It is illuminating also to remark the order in which legislation or regulation followed during these years. As a mind, we might say, in process of learning its business, the state began, appropriately, with the co-ordination of existing activities and with suggestion principally upon the intellectual plane. In 1903 the educational reorganization was extended to London. In 1904 the beginning of the registration of teachers gave access to a new area of schools, and greatly facilitated the transmission of information between the Board and the majority of schools, and between the schools themselves. Then the effects of the new universal contact with the actual life of the country began to grow more and more apparent; the national vision was broadening. In 1904 the capitation grants, reinforced in 1909 by the abandonment of centralized examining, set teacher and child alike more free to face their joint problems in their own atmosphere. In 1905 women had become equal members of the inspectorate. In 1906 followed the provision of meals for children. In 1907 their medical inspection and after-treatment. In 1907, also, the introduction of free places to secondary schools furthered a modification of a conventional school separation which no longer represented any real division in national life. In 1908 the Childrens Act, dealing with problems of neglect and unhealthy environment, took in new areas of responsibility; and the Mental Deficiency Act in 1913 filled in the outline of an increasingly humane interpretation of educational function.

It is equally illuminating to observe, over the same period, the direction taken by the voluntary activities of previously existing educational organizations, and the objects of new ones started. In the increase of strength discoverable in any such movement we have the best indication where national provision is still insufficient; in the diversion of its energy to a fresh purpose we have indication that its

original function is being discharged. Of the Victorian
voluntary organizations, many had their zone of activity
reduced ; some only continued to exist upon the surplus
of a greater numerical demand than the state could deal
with ; of yet others, the purpose was expressly deflected,
and the energy devoted to bridging some new gap.

Gaps, of course, persisted, and will long persist, more
especially in our provision for the later educational years.
For our higher schools and our universities were the
strongest surviving forms of our previous natural, but
unsystematized, educational growth. And if our own mind,
of its thought, might not add to our stature, no more could
a wise state ' brain ' seek to add hurriedly to their organic
structure. Even now, and even in the more plastic structure
of our lower school gradations, we are waiting upon the
event, to know whether the multiplication of types of school
produced by the Hadow Report, and which is designed to
satisfy all varieties of demand between the new primary
and the secondary school system, will prove to have been
a vital grafting, and survive in its present form ; or whether
a tendency, already noticeable in these new schools, to
reproduce older types, may not signify that there was something
natural to our illogical temperament in these older illogical
divisions. If that were so, the tendency to reversion might
be thought to be following naturally upon the conflict
between the newer conscious demand for equal social opportunity and an older ' racial ' desire to preserve qualitative
preparation. And it will not be satisfied until such ease and
appropriateness of transfer has been contrived between all
types of school as may appease both demands.

It was inevitable that the more conspicuous gaps should
remain at the top of the scale of educational provision. And
it was equally natural that the effort to fill them should
make the first call upon released voluntary energy. The
years when the individual is in immediate prospect of the
life before him are those which can best make their need

vocal. We are not supposed, as a people, to be interested in education. It is, therefore, interesting to note that at this stage, where it first comes into contact with the harsh reality of social and economic condition, our youth turns naturally to education for its weapons. It would seem as if we recognized, in spite of our neglect or criticism of its contemporary forms, that education with us is an integral process of national life, and that it is natural for us to have recourse to it when we become most aware of the need of reinforcing our own strength. This is not so, we may remark, with our more systematically educated neighbours; among certain of whom the adolescent years prefer to have recourse to any other process, political or economic, of national life, as their ally or remedy in setting the world aright for their generation.

No sooner did the school structure appear to be taking articulated form, under the combined guidance of local and central administration, than a rapid redirection of voluntary energy, with the powerful aid of Lord Haldane, produced in a short space of time a whole new growth of colleges, university colleges, and technical institutes. London university set its house in order; and practically no large town of importance failed to move either for its own university or for the promotion of its previous grade of institute.

The currents which had been furthering evening classes, working-men's education, and other branches of welfare work, upon philanthropic and social no less than educational lines, concentrated, in increasing combination, upon the area of adult education. The Workers' Educational Association was the product of their confluent streams, and the genius of Dr. Mansbridge gave to it direction and unity. The success of the Association, remarkable in itself, had a yet further meaning in the solution it presented of class antagonism and traditional group misunderstandings. It has been the experience of Europe since the war that it is in the early adult years, the post-graduate years of academic life, that our new generation most needs guidance and personal leadership, and more so, certainly, than our academic institutions of an older model are constituted to supply. And it is also in this period of awakening consciousness to the need of guidance that the harmonizing of group ideas is, under present conditions, most easily effected, and that an identity or sympathy of purpose between differently circumstanced individuals is discovered. Lord Baden-Powell's Boy Scout movement, was yet another product of the same wage of quickened, national self-provision. It owed its astonishing development to the educational gap which it was, almost undesignedly, able to fill : the lack, at an earlier stage in youth, for an active, disciplined release, over a wider field of personality than that contemplated by an older tradition of schooling.

During the same years, also, a change of accentuation rather than of express direction, is to be remarked in the work of the greater number of educational or semi-educational movements surviving the official re-organization. Instruction was supplemented by the developments of settlements, hostels, a corporate atmosphere, and by the encouragement of the influence of personal relationships. The change was significant of the same clearing of educational vision, of the better understanding of the lines upon which life can itself be borrowed, to be its own teacher.

If the meaning be extracted from these instinctive readjustments, proceeding internally in the organizations and complementarily as between official and voluntary effort, and effectively producing at one or two susceptible stages of growth community of idea if not equality of position, we may look forward more confidently to the possibility of obtaining from our schools themselves a broader and deeper work of training, and for all the impressionable years. If we can solve the technical problems of effective qualitative selection and of complete facility of transfer between all types of school, then each accepted type of school and college adjusted in teaching, pasturage, and environment to a single clear character of preparation, can do continuously and purposefully that which has been done remedially and with volunteer auxiliaries, at single points.

Before the close of the reign there were already signs that educational reform was having its effects in freeing the national spirit. It is unnecessary to dwell upon the improvement in educational machinery, system, and method; or upon the results, already becoming apparent, of the free passage of the most promising material up all the steps of the scale. Of more significance, perhaps, from the historical point of view, were the beginnings of a widespread recovery of interest in local drama, folk-dancing, and music. These had been natural interests of our people, as they are natural to any healthy form of living and training for life; and they had only lost their hold during the period of group schools and the artificial substitutes for that training. A further revival, in our youthful feeling for poetry, and even for art, may be expected to follow, when we have still further shed school conventions of emotional repression and intellectual misdirection, which we acquired in excess during our passage through the educational narrows.

The reign of King Edward covers the period of the dawning of an English educational consciousness, and of the beginnings of the expression of that consciousness in system and administration. It is tempting, to our primarily political mind, to consider it as the era of educational democratization, and to content ourselves with enumerating the many conduits of opportunity for our people cleared, created, or inter-connected during these years. In so doing we risk misleading; and we may confuse, in the history of educational machinery established, the less apparent thread of the manner of development of its motive power. From an educational point of view, it is the moment in time at which our national educational process reached its own stage of maturity, and began responsibly to set its house in order.

But not to build a new house. Idealists, our prophets, may regret this. It must be always a new regret, to those concerned in education, that so much of their work must still go in small contributions to things as they are, so little toward the foundations of things as they wish them to be. The only safeguard lies in seeing the educational process as it is, a natural order of development, inseparable from the political or economic progress of the nation; but with its own contribution to make to each succeeding stage of the national life, and with its own innate capacity for prophetic anticipation as well as for ancillary service. Educational idea cannot safely impose system in advance of the stage reached in a people's political maturity or social stability. We have examples about us. In such case it may even retard the rate of national development as a whole, which it was designed to accelerate.

For our own self-growing community there could have been no greater impediment than that the relative co-ordination in education, effected as a natural evolution during the Edwardian years, should have been formalized into a doctrine of full state responsibility. Education " of the nation by the nation "—if it means anything—means the binding of the ideas of a dominant contemporary group upon the nation as a whole, and upon its future. There is no contradiction between the conception of education as the release of individual personality, and that of education as the training for national citizenship. By releasing the individual personality we release also his portion in the national personality, that is, in the longer continuity of a people's life and purpose, of which he and his contemporaries are the only present expression and the only trustees for the future. In the agreement of succeeding generations of personalities so educated, both state structure and educational system can retain consistency, without sacrificing their capacity for necessary change. Education is for the wholeness of living, And to meet such a demand, as a system, and maintain its own prophetic vigour, it must continue to draw its vitality from the life of the nation, that is, from the multiplicity of demand, idea, criticism, and prophecy which is the utterance of the continued, and yet changing, life of a growing people. It is the function of our educational consciousness, central, local, and institutional, to reconcile ideals and conventions, and to harmonize forms and methods, for each generation. But that those ideals, forms, or methods should continue to be varied, mutable, even contradictory, need not distress us. Provided that we can continue to believe that contradiction and conservatism and change alike are inspired by real contact with the impatience of a natural development proceeding; and that we, individually, can feel that our own contribution draws inspiration from the same source, whether it is devoted to the application of an established form or method to-day, or to obeying the impulse which is preparing to change that form to-morrow.

GEOFFREY WINTHROP YOUNG.

VIII

Literature

What is Edwardian literature ? The question seems a plain one, to which a plain answer might be expected; it is the literature which made its appearance when Edward the Seventh was king. Yet, in the result, that would not be a very illuminating answer. Merely to draw up a list of books and authors, with due appreciation of individual qualities, would not in itself tell us what, if anything, *Edwardian* means in this connection, except as a matter of dates. The thing should be, if we can, to make out how that epithet *characterizes* literature : to show, in fact, how in Edwardian times the Spirit of the Age defined itself in terms of the art of literature. And that is not so simple as it sounds. Socially and politically the Edwardian decade seems to have a quite distinct character of its own. But it is not so easy to see the Edwardian spirit expressing itself in literature. For one thing we are still too near. In some ways there may be a certain advantage in this. The mere sense of contrast may be impressive. Very striking contrasts could easily be pointed out between literature in Edwardian times and the work of later days. But how can we be sure that this means anything more than differences between individual talents ? Theoretically, no doubt, you cannot point to individual talent without pointing to the Spirit of the Age ; since individual talent can only exist under conditions imposed by the Spirit of the Age. But it needs perspective to see what those conditions are and how they show themselves ; and it may be questioned whether we have the proper perspective yet for seeing that in the Edwardian age.

And then, for another thing, the period seems too short

for generalizations about it to be safe. As far as literature is concerned at least, an *age* is likely to be a somewhat arbitrary affair when it is limited to a single decade; there is hardly room enough in ten years for the Spirit of the Age to delineate itself in any clearly distinguishable fashion. And there can be no question that some of the most conspicuous talents in the Edwardian age only belong to it as a matter of brute chronological fact. Henry James, for instance, and Rudyard Kipling simply carry on in Edward's reign the highly characteristic careers they had begun in Victoria's; there is nothing specifically Edwardian about what they happened to write when Edward was king. The Spirit of the Age which has stamped itself on their work is the spirit of an age much more extensive than the one we have to consider; to describe it we should have to enlarge our survey very considerably. But would not that be true of *all* the writers who had in any way established themselves when Edward came to the throne? No doubt; and yet, in the Edwardian decade, something seems to happen in the career of a good many of them which may perhaps be regarded as characteristic of the age; especially as something similar occurs also in several of those authors whose careers begin or first become notable in this period. It is no very definite quality; nothing like what we at once understand by such terms as Elizabethan, or Restoration, or Eighteenth Century, or even that loose word Victorian, when we apply those epithets to literature. It is rather a tendency, which, as soon as we attempt to put it into general terms, seems so vague as to be hardly worth noticing. And yet I think it is worth noticing, and I believe it is truly Edwardian. I believe it belongs to the age, and may, without fantasy or ingenuity, be connected with other manifestations of the age—with its politics, for example. That prosperous age, so rich in its inheritance, so stable in its possessions, had nevertheless a strong inclination to go forward: it was not only progressive, it was even adventurous—but all the same it meant to keep what it had. And so in literature. From the many-sided vitality of Victorian literature, the writers of the time inherited, both in prose and verse, a rich and varied and solidly based tradition, and we find no sign of any desire to break with it. What we do find is that many of these writers not only make a decided advance in the development of their own individual careers; in so doing they also make a decided advance in the development of the art of literature. Something distinctly new in literary art emerges—new methods, new usages. Of course, it is a question of degree; something of the kind must always be happening in literature, even in its most conservative times. What distinguishes Edwardian literature is, first, that these innovations are noticeable, secondly, that even so they are not effected by breaking off the tradition and starting afresh; they are not revolutionary. Now this markedly progressive development of literary tradition seems to me the note of the Edwardian decade.

It sounds vague enough. Let us see how it works out. But it might perhaps be made a little more concrete first, in order to help us to see what we are looking for. And my instances will show that I am not thinking of developments of any particular kind or in any particular direction, but of little more than a certain general tendency to be progressive. There is perhaps no poet more avowedly traditional than Robert Bridges. That was the reason, I think, why his greatness went so long comparatively unrecognized, most readers failed to see how profoundly and subtly individual his serene command of the traditional poetic was. Nowhere can that be better seen than in his main achievement of Edwardian times—the masque *Demeter*, " written for the Ladies of Somerville College " in 1904. The Miltonic loveliness of its verse is a music as original to him as the significance of its Hellenic mythology. But it was in *Demeter* that some of his earliest uses of quantitative measures occurred; it was here indeed that he may be said to have first tried them on the public taste. The year before his friends had seen his first splendid outburst of English hexameters, and he was writing verse in quantity off and on throughout the whole of his Edwardian period. Now all this was not only a remarkable experiment in technique, and not only the occasion for some most notable poetry ; it was directly out of all this that the later Bridges proceeded, with his supreme achievement of *The Testament of Beauty*.

This, then, marks a very decided, indeed, a crucial advance in the development of his own personal career ; and in making this advance Bridges decidedly advanced the technique of English poetry. He brought into metrical form a whole new range of English rhythms : it was a real innovation in English poetics, as Tennyson's beautifully artificial adaptations of classical prosody had *not* been. But it was nothing revolutionary, of course. It simply carried on not only the classical tradition itself, but the attempts of the Elizabethans and of Tennyson and Meredith and others. But it carried them on to strikingly new results.

Now I shall not argue that there was some singular potency latent in the Edwardian age which promoted experiments in classical verse. The fact is that Bridges had long been meditating and discussing quantitative measures in English, settling in his mind the true method of them, facing their difficulties, exploring their possibilities. To trace out the history of this technical innovation of his would take us back far beyond Edwardian times. It is enough to note that the experiments did actually occur in Edwardian literature ; the mere fact of that occurrence is all we need in our search for the characteristically Edwardian thing in literature.

A single instance means nothing. Suppose we glance at fiction. The titles of four novels occur to me at once—and I think they would probably occur to anyone—as outstanding achievements in the art of fiction during the Edwardian period : *The Way of All Flesh*, *Kipps*, *Lord Jim*, and *The Old Wives' Tale*. *Kipps* and *The Old Wives' Tale* mark an

extraordinary and decisive development in the art of
Mr. Wells and of Arnold Bennett; *Lord Jim*, however, is
rather the first full and expansive triumph of the remarkable
technique Conrad had been evolving since the 'nineties, and
The Way of All Flesh, of course, is Butler's only novel.
But I think it would be generally agreed that these four
novels are not merely of capital significance in their authors'
careers; each one of them is also an important development
in the art of English fiction. Their authors, however, are
not in the least rebellious against tradition. On the contrary,
they heartily—indeed, Conrad and Bennett delightedly—
accept tradition, both English and foreign, and plainly
carry it on. But they carry it on a remarkable step forward.

Once more, though, we must note that this need not be
ascribed to any force residing actually *in* the Edwardian
age as such. It is enough for us that its mere occurrence is
an Edwardian event. We are a little too apt, perhaps, to
think of the Spirit of the Age as a sort of genius or demon,
potently presiding over his appointed province; we take
the metaphor rather too literally. For some reason or other
we pick out a certain term of years and call it a *period*.
Naturally, into this period there run all sorts of tendencies,
forces, movements from the preceding years, some of which—
currents perhaps which have long been flowing and growing
underground—now first come to the surface. These
emergings we call, quite rightly, characteristic of the period—
these, rather than the well-known streams that run into it
plainly and openly in the light of day; for it is these new-
appearing springs that differentiate the period. We generalize
the nature of the forces that thus now reveal themselves, and
rhetoric calls our generalization the Spirit of the Age.
Charmed by this figure of speech, we then proceed to hypo-
statize our generalization, and to invoke the Spirit of the
Age as the power which *causes* this or that particular event,
whereas it is nothing but a summary formula of the tendencies
these particular events exemplify. I do not say—it would

be grossly absurd to say—that literature, or any other
activity, may not be profoundly influenced by the things
going on round about it. Thus, it is possible that the new
development which Wells and Bennett gave to the art of
fiction in *Kipps* and *The Old Wives' Tale* may have been a
direct response to the age itself, though that which was so
effective *in* the age probably flowed into it from beyond it.
But certainly what was new in *Lord Jim* and *The Way of
All Flesh* was not produced by the age. Butler died just
after the Edwardian period began, and *The Way of All Flesh*,
which was published after his death, had long been on the
stocks. And *Lord Jim* was but the logical, though a magnifi-
cently generous, development of the peculiar art Conrad
had been practising and improving several years before the
momentous accession of King Edward.

At any rate, in all four novels, if their innovating quality
is to be regarded as truly characteristic of Edwardian
literature, that is not because the Edwardian age was the
cause of it, but simply because it was in the Edwardian age
that it made its appearance. That is what we shall find all
through. What is characteristically Edwardian in literature
is that which conspicuously *appears* in Edwardian times,
no matter what its origin. If we look for a Spirit of the Age
as a power out of which characteristic things emanate, we
shall be hunting for a phantom. But if we are content to
look for a Spirit of the Age which is simply a generalization
of certain things specially occurring in the period, then
I think we shall find it. That is to say, there are sufficient things
happening in our period of a rather peculiar kind to make
the generalization of them characteristic of it. We need not
trouble ourselves whether they belong to it in any other
sense ; that is the only sense that matters.

There can be little doubt where a survey of Edwardian
literature ought to begin. The commencement of the period
was greeted by the art of literature with a formal and highly
elaborate salute. This was William Watson's *Ode on the*

Coronation of King Edward VII, and it is very much to our
purpose now. Nothing could better illustrate the rich and
varied and solid possession of *good* which the age inherited,
and which makes those ten years, as we look back on them
now, seem one of the supremely fortunate periods in
history.

> Sire, we have looked on many and mighty things
> In these eight hundred summers of renown
> Since the Gold Dragon of the Wessex Kings
> On Hastings' field went down ;
> And slowly in the ambience of this crown
> Have many crowns been gathered, till, to-day,
> How many people crown thee, who shall say ?
> Time, and the Ocean, and some fostering star,
> In high cabal have made us what we are,
> Who stretch one hand to Huron's bearded pines,
> And one on Kashmir's snowy shoulder lay,
> And round the streaming of whose raiment shines
> The iris of the Australasian spray.
> For waters have connived at our designs,
> And winds have plotted with us—and behold,
> Kingdom in kingdom, sway in oversway,
> Dominion fold in fold . . .
> *So great we are, and old.*

It is easy to see, too, in these deliberately lofty lines, and
their masterly technique, a symbol of the great and complex
tradition which the art of Edward's time received from
preceding ages ; we may take as it were a datum-line for
our survey such well-tried cunning of diction as that which
celebrates

> seats of puissance where,
> With long grope of his desultory hand,
> The ocean, prying deep into the land,
> By Morvern and the legends of wild Lorn,
> Repents him, lost about Locheil ;

or the easy polysyllabic grandeur of versification which
could hail England as she

> Of high and singular election set
> Benignant on the mitigated sea.

It was natural, with such a poet as William Watson, that the
Ode should give a very clear and very fine warning of the
danger of being content with wealth. As it turned out,
the warning too was to prove itself characteristic of the time
politically : the age was not content merely to be wealthy ;
and just so, artistically, it was not content merely to receive
tradition, however splendid. It is not in William Watson's
sounding periods that we shall discover that, but the audience
that heard the Ladies of Somerville College recite the masque
of *Demeter* ought to have been aware of it, as soon as the
Chorus of Oceanides began to chant

> Gay and lovely is earth, man's decorate dwelling ;
> With fresh beauty ever varying hour to hour.
> As now bath'd in azure joy she awakeneth
> With bright morn to the sun's life-giving effluence.

Probably they did not quite realize what it was they were
listening to—English choriambics ; and if they did, probably
a good many of them would have refused to admit either
that these measures were choriambic at all, or that they were
anything but theoretically choriambic—of no resemblance
to Greek and of no value to English poetry. These things,
in effect, were said : it was but reviving against Bridges
the old verdict which prejudice and ignorance have recorded
in our history books against Sir Philip Sidney's choriambics.
Equally disturbing, too, to received opinion about both the
nature of classical measures and the metrical limits of
English rythm, were Bridges' hexameters, the first batch
of which had been privately printed the year before *Demeter*,
but which, with other classical meters, he continued to write
all through our period :

> What was Alexander's subduing of Asia, or that
> Sheep-worry of Europe, when pigmy Napoleon enter'd
> Her sovereign chambers, and her kings with terror eclips'd ?
> His footsore soldiers inciting across the ravag'd plains,
> Thro' bloody fields of death tramping to an ugly disaster ?

Was this what hexameters ought to sound like ? Were these

rhythms tolerable in English verse ? But we must not let ourselves be caught by these controversies just now. What is certain is that the metrical tradition of English poetry received in Edwardian times a remarkable jolt : or so it seemed. Really, it was no more than a remarkably bold development, which was to lead on eventually to the still bolder but quite different and more acceptable development of English metre in *The Testament of Beauty*. History will surely note this last as an innovation in English poetics of extraordinary importance ; but the thing for us to note is that the process out of which it came began in Edwardian days—and, as I suggest, it is characteristic of the Edwardian period that it should have done so. For Bridges' experiments with metre were not the only ones of that time. They are but the capital example of much new interest in English prosody and much new handling of English verse. Walter de la Mare had begun those delicate liberties which were soon to lead him on to the subtle incantation of

> Is there anybody there said the Traveller,
> Knocking on the moonlit door ?
> And his horse in the silence champed the grasses
> Of the forest's ferny floor.

And what were John Masefield's experiments then are no longer experiments to-day, when everybody's ears have accepted the enchantment of them :

> Quinquireme of Nineveh from distant Ophir,
> Rowing home to haven from sunny Palestine,
>   With a cargo of ivory
>   And apes and peacocks,
> Sandalwood, cedarwood, and sweet white wine.

What is perhaps even more remarkable is that blank verse itself—which might be called the most traditional of all forms of English metre—blank verse itself was being thoroughly remodelled by the sensitive craftsmanship of W. B. Yeats, to fit it once more to the living voice in a new

N

effort in poetic drama : firm-set as blank verse might seem, with all its possibilities explored, it proved once again plastic in the right hands, and new possibilities were found in it.

But it was not only in technique that Edwardian poetry showed itself progressive. The crucial moment in Mr. Masefield's career falls just outside our period. I mean his discovery of that vigorous narrative power of his in *The Everlasting Mercy*, and the opportunity this gave him, in that poem and its successors, of setting poetry to work on the harshest and grimmest realities of things. Doutless, however, this ambition really belongs to his Edwardian days, though its success came a little later ; and in this very matter Wilfrid Gibson had by a few years anticipated him, with less passion than Masefield, but with far sounder and subtler knowledge of human nature, finer insight, and much more scrupulous art. It is, indeed, a phenomenon which we should now be prepared to recognize as characteristically Edwardian, to find Mr. Gibson suddenly at this time giving over writing poems about Arthurian queens in romantic castles, to create the poetry of everyday life. I say *create*, for that is what it comes to : the poetry of present, actual everyday life, which is just that and nothing but that, is really Mr. Gibson's creation ; no one before him who had attempted anything like it had relied so completely and absolutely on the subject itself, and so rigorously avoided getting poetic effect by any sort of decoration. This was a very notable advance : the discovery that poetry, and poetry of no doubtful or diffident kind, but wholly admirable and vivid, could by the sheer power of structural form, truthful insight, and plain words always lively with the force of *speech*, be made out of the lives of colliers, shepherds, clerks, shopkeepers, mechanics, and convicts,—this was a real conquest of new territory. Mr. Gibson has maintained it, by dialogue, narrative, idyl, and lyric, ever since his Edwardian days ; from the *Stonefolds* and the *Daily Bread* of that time he has gone on, through such masterpieces as *Bloodybush Edge*, to the

culmination of the matter and manner which are so peculiarly
his own in *Krindlesyke*, one of the few great poems of our day.

A very different poet, whose reputation to-day seems
somewhat clouded (most unjustly), also set out in Edwardian
times to conquer new territory for poetry—very different
territory from Gibson's. This was John Davidson, whose
conversion from a vigorous kind of æstheticism (in which
premonitory symptoms might be discerned) to the pro-
clamation of a new religion was first decisively announced
with the series of monologues which he called Testaments,
dating from 1901 to 1908—*The Testament of a Vivisector,
of a Man Forbid, of an Empire Builder, of a Prime Minister,*
and finally *The Testament of John Davidson*, who by this
has become indistinguishable from the god of this new
religion. For the god is Matter, Matter is the Universe;
and John Davidson is " the Universe itself become aware ".
Poetically, this is magnificent. Matter for Davidson is not
what you or I might mean by matter; it is a glorious conception for which he makes science responsible. He deifies it
superbly; and it then provides him with ethic as well as
metaphysic, both of which he proclaims with the loftiest
sort of passion—intellectual passion. All this might be no
more than individuality of exceptional kind and degree.
But the very nature of his ambition compelled Davidson
to make a large poetic invasion into the domain of science.
Towards the end of his tragic career, he sometimes suffered
the worst accident that can befall an artist; his inspiration
ran away with him. But if ever we have a modern Lucretius,
John Davidson will be among his ancestors; he at least
showed how intellectual passion can transmute science—
its facts, its theories, even its nomenclature—into the stuff
of poetry.

But the Edwardian age can show us something perhaps
even more remarkable than a poet invading science: it
can show us a great scientist who was also an excellent poet,
whose art moreover could accompany the most momentous

of his researches with a most moving and profound comment on the mind and the intention and the end of science in this divine world. I mean Ronald Ross—too good a scientist to deify an equivocation like matter, as Davidson had done, but a poet whose god is the god of a scientist's worship and belief :

> He is the Lord of Light;
> He is the Thing that Is;
> He sends the seeing sight;
> And the right mind is His.

Ronald Ross's philosophical poem on his own investigation of the fearful problem of malaria is, with its severe technique, a striking example of tradition put to new use—and new not merely in the sense of being individual. As the poem is Edwardian in time, so it is Edwardian in character.

But remember how short that Edwardian time was ; and remember too that I am not pretending to show how the Spirit of the Age governed its writers. I am simply pointing to a very general kind of thing which (whatever its cause), merely by happening then in a noticeable way and a noticeable number of times, thereby makes itself characteristic of the age. Inevitably, therefore, I must pass over several admirable talents that were at work in the period. They were certainly not inferior in quality to those poets I have mentioned ; but in such a wide variety of quality as they show, nothing specially Edwardian seems to appear—unless it be that variety itself. The poet who exclaimed—

> A rainbow and a cuckoo—Lord,
> How rich and great the times are now !

might have exclaimed that at any time. W. H. Davies's open air lyricism with its exquisite alliance of spontaneity and artifice is in our period, but not of it. I have mentioned Walter de la Mare's development of metrical tradition : but in his matter, that magical mood of reverie, there seems nothing Edwardian ; any more than in the deliberate beauty of Flecker's Parnassian imagery, or the intellectual, emotional, and technical curiosity with which the early Rupert Brooke was all on fire. Some day, history will see all these varied qualities as peculiarly expressive of the age in which they occur : but it will be of an age a good deal larger than our limited period. Besides, it was not so much to individual quality I was pointing, when I singled out the poets I take to be characteristically Edwardian, as to the fact that, to express their quality, they showed a tendency to some remarkable kind or degree of innovation. There must be a certain innovation in all poetry that has any individuality in it—and what poetry has not ? The poets whom I have cited as specially Edwardian add some distinct development to the tradition of their art. But there are other poets of the time—and as poets they may be just as good—who do not need to express their quality by that means.

But in this matter of poetry, I have left my heaviest broadside to the last. It might indeed seem sufficiently to characterize the Edwardian decade to describe it as the age in which *The Dynasts* and *The Dawn in Britain* appeared. Now that is something well worth pondering very gravely. It was just about then that critics were beginning to say, as they have gone on saying ever since, that poetry in the modern world can only be lyrical. " For Nature brings not back the Mastodon " : so Tennyson himself had said, in one of his admirable moments of semi-humorous magniloquence. Tennyson's Mastodon, however, was not so much epic poetry itself, as the epic of Homer and Virgil ; and in his anxiety not too seriously to contravene the laws of geology, he adopted the Alexandrian method of idyls, in his ambition to write a long poem of epic intention. The result was some exquisitely beautiful poetry : but nothing like an epic. The fatal thing was, that the matter he chose could not have the true epic effect for his time or the time that came after him. Nor were any of the Victorians in this respect more successful than he was. They wrote remarkable long poems that were nowhere near epics, as Browning did : they wrote remarkable essays in the received manner of epic, as William Morris and Matthew Arnold did. All this was admirable ; but the authentic Mastodon remained apparently extinct. It was left for Thomas Hardy and Charles Doughty to show, in Edwardian times, that the laws of poetry are quite unlike the laws of geology : that the poetic Mastodon is capable of reincarnation ; that, though epic poetry can never again be Homeric or Virgilian, it is still possible to compose an epic which will do for its time what the epics of Homer and Virgil did for theirs. With that, indeed, the comparison ends. For in the first place, as regards the immeasurably important quality of *diction*, nothing but sheer insensibility could put Hardy's or Doughty's work beside the epics of antiquity. And in the second place, if it is a most remarkable phenomenon—and I think it is *the* most remarkable phenomenon in Edwardian literature—to find two poets simultaneously continuing—or rather renewing—the ancient tradition of a kind of poetry the appearances of which have always been " like angels' visits few and far between " ; what is equally remarkable is the way each of these poets proved himself—each in a totally different way—an innovator on tradition : each of them re-created the epic tradition to serve his own extremely individual ends. The two poets represent the two opposite poles of the sphere of the poetic conception of things : the analytic and the synthetic. Hardy makes the utmost possible use of the invaluable method of the *dramatic poem* in order to give a highly analytic version of the tragic idea of a universe of absolute monism or determinism, in an immensely organized series of separate scenes : in which the Napoleonic wars affect a huge variety of persons, and many aspects of the significance of this are declared, philosophized, and deplored by a family of phantom intelligences. Doughty's even vaster panorama is of pre-history (suggested, I suppose, by archæology) rather than of history : and the spirit of his poem proceeds not from science, but from faith. Here, accordingly, we have the early world presented in a colossal narrative synthesis by one who detested modern life, modern thought, modern language —all, for him, vitiated by the vice of analysis. In his passion to vindicate the synthetic habit of mind, Doughty in his great poem even undertook to re-create the English language, hoping to force its essentially analytic forms into a more primitive synthetic syntax : and in the result it may be said of him, as was said of his beloved Spenser by Ben Jonson, that he " writ no language ". Yet his power triumphs over this idiosyncrasy : how grandly, those who wish to begin on him may best realize perhaps in his other Edwardian poem—that noble thing, his dramatic poem of the " loss of Eden ", *Adam Cast Forth*. Well, if anyone wants a type of what is meant by *Edwardian* in literature, here, I suggest, he has it : in either of these two epic innovations. Not so much in the particular nature of them, as in the tendency each of them so remarkably exemplifies to develop tradition. And yet neither of them can be said to have been caused by the spirit of the Edwardian age : they rather go to constitute that spirit. *The Dynasts* seems to have been written in Edwardian times ; but it was already an old project in his mind when Hardy set out to compose it. And Doughty seems to have started work on *The Dawn in Britain* soon after *Travels in Arabia Deserta* had proved so disappointing to the Cambridge University Press in 1888. But a book enters into literature when it is published : the three parts of *The Dynasts* in 1903, 1906, 1908, *The Dawn in Britain* in 1906 (all six volumes of it). At any rate, these two poems form a *massif* of Edwardian poetry with which nothing can be properly compared unless we go back to *The Prelude* : and since *The Prelude* is such a highly specialized kind of epic, perhaps we might say that nothing can be profitably compared with either of them unless we go back to *Paradise Lost*.

It is not in the nature of poetry to make so public a stir as drama ; and there was much stirring activity in the drama during our period. In theatrical history, probably the most important fact is that England as a whole was now ceasing to be dependent on London for its drama. Just when the old provincial stock companies had all but disappeared, " repertory " theatres began to emerge in Manchester, Birmingham, and Liverpool, and round them a good deal of original dramatic activity collected : most of which, however—e.g., *Hindle Wakes*—falls just outside our limits. But the two chief sources of energy in Edwardian drama—which have notably enriched our dramatic *literature* —were the two " managements " associated with the names of Granville-Barker and W. B. Yeats—the first in London at the Court Theatre (but also at the Savoy and the Duke of York's), the second in Dublin at the Abbey Theatre. The tradition of the Victorian drama of manners, which had come down, with occasional contact with real things, and great respect for technique, from Robertson through Henry Arthur Jones and A. W. Pinero, to Oscar Wilde's exquisite *reductio ad absurdum*, had been torpedoed in 1892 by George Bernard Shaw with *Widowers' Houses* : instigated partly, perhaps, by Ibsen. Shaw's irruption brought into the drama, first (and by far the most important), a genuine concern with the practical actuality of things : though with him this was inextricably involved with his own peculiar humour, fantasy, and eccentricity. But his plays were also examples of very unconventional but masterly stagecraft, and of vivid dramatic language, full of the force of living speech, finely controlled. From him the new tradition of English drama proceeded ; and the Edwardian age saw its full development in Granville-Barker's theatres in London. In such plays as *The Voysey Inheritance* by Granville-Barker himself, or Galsworthy's *Strife* and *The Silver Box*, there was not merely a concern with actuality : it seemed as if actuality itself had come upon the stage, with all its technical

as well as its human details. Yet in their structure these
plays were just as exactly designed as the most well-made of
Victorian plays, and much more interesting ; and they were
also (except for Oscar Wilde) infinitely better written. But
this admirable Edwardian drama was not much infected
either by Shaw's humour or by his fantasy : " Life is real,
Life is earnest " was the motto for most of it. Yet it was
capable of that deliciously preposterous little masterpiece,
Prunella, which certainly ought to be revived ; a fable that
enchantingly needs no moral, a whimsy absurdly significant.
And in St. John Hankin it found a writer of first-rate
comedies who could make the cruellest realism not only
laughable but genial. Nor should it be forgotten that the
Edwardian age first saw that famous improvement on the
theatre's traditional Christmas entertainment, that remarkable concentration of all the romancings of childhood,
Barrie's *Peter Pan*.

But it was the Abbey Theatre in Dublin, under the potent
inspiration of Mr. W. B. Yeats, one of the major creative
powers of our time, that brought the most original and
unexpected contribution of the drama to Edwardian literature.
Unexpected : for who, after the Eighteenth Century, the
Romantics, and the Victorians, could ever have expected
poetic drama to be again a living force in our theatre ? Yet
that is what Mr. Yeats made it. He came to this achievement
gradually. *The Countess Cathleen*, his most splendid and
perhaps most original imagination in dramatic form, belongs
to an earlier part of his career, and was written without any
theatrical experience behind it : yet it has proved itself
nobly on the stage, though never quite native there. It was
in Edwardian times that he first perfectly combined the
loveliness of poetic import with theatrical efficiency : and
what he did in *The King's Threshold*, *On Baile's Strand*, *The
Shadowy Waters*, *The Green Helmet*, and *Deirdre* was something absolutely new in poetic drama. Moreover, it was he
who opened the way for the greatest modern master of tragi-

comic satire, who was also the greatest modern exponent
of dramatic nationalism, John Millington Synge, with his
superb enlargement of the scope of prose dialogue both in
beauty of rhythm and phrase and in emotional expressiveness,
grave or ludicrous, and his profound instinct for design in
dramatic action.   All Synge's plays belong to the Edwardian
period : it could have no higher distinction—and it is a
characteristic distinction.

I can but touch on the fiction of the time. The stream
of tradition is, of course, much more voluminous here, and
the occurrence of modification in it must be therefore less
remarkable.   Besides, in fiction, the art itself is much less
definite than elsewhere in literature ; and changes in it
therefore define themselves less clearly. Yet here too we
find, as I have already indicated, unmistakable cases in which
striking development of individual talent was also a development of the art it practised.   In some of these, the *direction*
of this development resembles what we have noticed in the
drama—a development in the power of rendering the actuality
of things.   Sometimes this may seem mainly a question of
degree, as in Arnold Bennett's masterpiece *The Old Wives'
Tale*, the completion of which came just after the most
entertaining of his extravagant comedies, *Buried Alive*.
But the real thing in *The Old Wives' Tale* is the magnificent
structure it builds out of common material.   With a much
more sudden turn the exact imagination of H. G. Wells,
which had already showed how wonderfully it could make
scientific fantasy and social prophecy both plausible and
thrilling, plunged into the most exquisitely minute realism
of everyday things in *Kipps* : but it was not only the loving
minuteness that was new, and will surely be immortal,
but the lavishing on every moment of this of elaborately
energetic phrasing, and the consequent magnifying of every
least thing into humorous importance.   Samuel Butler's
imaginary biography of the author of *The Fair Haven*,
the finest thing he ever did in pure irony, must have told

him what he could do in fiction if he chose : and the result
perhaps was *The Way of All Flesh*. Here the art of the novel
faced actuality with a vengeance ; and it would not be
surprising if future historians should ascribe to this profoundly witty book a good deal of at least the desire of the
modern world to adjust its *morals* to things as they are.
But romance too had its great opportunity in Edwardian
times, when Joseph Conrad in *Lord Jim* developed to the
full his knowledge of danger and strange adventure up and
down the world, his singular power of improving the significance of his story by ingeniously dislocating its chronology,
and above all by transmitting his narrative through the
subtle and many-coloured mind of Marlowe, his ideal
commentator on the picturesque futility of man's affairs.
Something, too, in this connection, should be said on W. H.
Hudson's unusual employment of the art of the novel in
Green Mansions, with its circumstantial portrayal of extraordinary life, and in the midst of this its lovely new version of
the child of nature in Rima ; but, long before, Hudson
had shown similar powers in *The Purple Land*, as he was
to show them again most admirably in an English setting
in *A Shepherd's Life*. Something, indeed, should be said
about many authors of Edwardian times of whom I have
said nothing. But I hope I have said enough, at least, to
show what the epithet *Edwardian* may be taken to mean,
when it is used of *Literature*—a tendency to innovate decidedly
in literary tradition without a revolutionary breach with it.

LASCELLES ABERCROMBIE.

N.B.—For a summary account of the chief writers of
the period, the last chapters of L. Cazamian's *Histoire de
la Littérature Anglaise* (Hachette : English translation
published by Dent) may be consulted.

IX

Science

However important the first ten years of the present century may have been in the history of the then reigning monarch, it is scarcely at first sight to be expected that a period of time, chosen at random as far as science is concerned, should possess any outstanding significance. This is, however, to adopt a needlessly superficial view. For science resembles a chain forged by society, a connected movement within the social structure, exhibiting at all stages features of a theoretical, an experimental, and an essentially practical nature. On any link in this chain, therefore, we must expect to find three distinct characteristics—(1) the consummation of past theory and experiment in the form of social application, (2) the inception of new experimental activity emerging from problems that arise in that application, and (3) the initial stages of new theories and new principles offered to explain and expand the outcome of this experimental work. These then are the features we shall have to seek in our present survey.

To many this may seem to be rather an extended, even an unjustifiable, interpretation of the scope of science. To them it offers simply a logically coherent description of the processes of nature. Social effects that may follow on the application of these laws in practical form to serve social needs are not science but sociology; it is an intellectual pursuit divorced from social change. From this angle the history of science would be the history of scientific thought, the history of a succession of ideas, and the creations of a series of great thinkers. In these days, when the writers and expositors of science are largely drawn from the physical and mathematical fields, and the theoretical advances, startling as they are, are interpreted in precisely this form, the layman is rather inclined to accept the tacit assumption that science implies only physical science, and even there only mathematical physics. However one may value the achievements implicit in the theory of relativity and wave mechanics we have to recognize, historically at least, that the dominance of the mathematician is of comparatively recent growth. It is, indeed, an aftermath of the Edwardian period. For while the nineteenth century had its share of great mathematicians, its Clerk Maxwells, and its Kelvins, many of its mathematicians were also its engineers. Kelvin himself is known perhaps more for the imprint he left on engineering than on mathematics. It had its great experimenters like Faraday—who was anything but a mathematician—Rayleigh both experimenter and mathematician, and its great systematic biologists like Darwin and Wallace, with their suggested mechanism for the origin of species. The social atmosphere of the late Victorian era was that of an intense engineering activity, correlated as it was with the whole Industrial Revolution internally, and with the supply of new imperial markets externally. Within the scientific movement it saw not merely the detailed examination of the numerous mechanical principles associated with the names of Newton, Hooke, Helmholtz, Clausius, Faraday, Clerk Maxwell, Kelvin, to mention only a few at random ; principles associated with the laws of transformation of energy from one form to another, but a gathering concentration on direct applications to production and to the machinery of production. Science, in fact, during the period just prior to the Edwardian era was to all appearances much more intimately associated with industrial practice than one might at first sight suppose. The hammer of mechanical principles on the anvil of industry, beating out new social applications, did, in fact, continue to resound throughout the first decade of this century, as we shall see in a moment, but, side by side with it, there burst forth an intense activity in experimental science, on a scale and with a vigour not previously experienced by the scientific movement. If, therefore, we are inclined nowadays to believe that science is largely absorbed in highly theoretical problems concerning the ultimate structure of the universe, the nature of space, and the inner constitution of the stars, we have to remember that this local colour has followed on a phase of intense experimental research during the Edwardian period, while that itself was preceded by, and contemporaneous with, an extended period of mechanical invention and discovery.

It is important, therefore, in estimating the nature of the material that may justifiably be grouped under the heading *science*, and in assessing the relative importance of its parts, that we should not take too parochial a view. We have to see science as a feature of society and continuous with the social movement. We have to recognize its various facets—its internal properties in the form of the theories expounded, and its external properties in the form of its social repercussions. For the period under review saw vast changes in the amenities of social life. These arose principally from the applications of the new science and the new technology to social convenience. One illustration alone must suffice. Many of us remember the ill-lit streets of the late nineteenth century and the early twentieth, dim gas jets, fish-tail burners, and later the tremendous improvement that was achieved by the installation of gas mantles, and acetylene lamps. Even so, there was little attraction to wander about in the grudging half-light of an evening. The setting of the sun to all intents and purposes was the signal for the population to retire indoors. To realize the change that has been effected since that day we have simply to think of the blaze of multi-coloured light in Piccadilly Circus and the surging crowds that seek their amusement nowadays in theatre and picture house. The introduction of street lighting alone has effected a revolution in the customs of the population, with it a revaluation of

the whole ethics of amusement, and a drastic change in the
nature of the nation's leisure.   It was the Edwardian period
that effectively saw this transition.   The larger houses and
the dwellings of the better-class artisan, moreover, that
were built at this period were wired for electric lighting
and the click of the switch indoors replaced the hissing of
the gas jet.   Innovations of this nature take a generation
to penetrate into the structure of society for the full introduction of this form of lighting has even yet not been achieved,
but the extension of the National Electrification Scheme
within recent years assures us that in a comparatively short
time electric lighting and electric power will be available
in the remotest corner of this country.

The new era in illumination was not without its more
remote effects.   The better lighting of theatres, for example,
and the advances in the technique of stage illumination
made possible artistic developments that had hitherto
been impossible.   Coupled with a perfected photographic
technique and the invention of the moving picture it has now
brought into being a vast new industry whose products are
consumed literally from China to Peru.   If we can appreciate
the extent to which the new technique of illumination has
gradually insinuated itself into every nook and cranny of
social life and industrial practice, from pocket flash lamps
to motor head-lighting, from street signs to flood lighting,
from medical instruments for exploring the interior of the
human body to searchlights, from the tiny switch in the
domestic coal cellar to the scientific illumination of factory
and workshop—we shall the better be in a position to
appreciate what a revolution has been effected by the new
form of electrical power.   For electric lighting, one of its
most trivial consequences, developed during the first decade
of this century side by side with the centralization of electric
power production.

The extent to which science has begun to permeate
social life and to constitute itself an essential condition

for the continuance of society could hardly better be appreciated than by a brief survey of the quite extraordinary nature of the engineering applications of old and new principles that were brought into being during this comparatively short period. So numerous were they, in fact, that it would be quite impossible to make any attempt at comprehensiveness in the time at my disposal. We choose merely a series at random, without even suggesting that these are the more important. We have simply to realize that already in the period prior to this the theory and experimental practice of electrical power in all its manifestations had been securely established, the thermodynamics of heat engines had received thorough investigation, fundamental chemical discoveries and new processes for the production of chemicals at the laboratory stage had followed one another in rapid succession. On the biological and bacteriological side the discoveries of Pasteur and his co-workers, originating from attempts to improve the quality of French beer, had opened up a vast new field of investigation in connection with ferments. The theoretical essentials were there and had been for some time. What was required was the transformation of these principles into eminen.y practical form to adapt them to social use. Thus 1901 opened with the production of the Diesel oil engine, and by 1908 oil engines of this type of 1,000 h.p. were being produced, although it was not until 1912 that the first Diesel-engined vessel, the *Sealandia*, was launched. In 1892 Moissan working at the Sorbonne with electric arcs had conceived the idea that here, between the poles of the arc, was a possible source of great heat, and from that idea there sprang one of the most important industrial developments, the electric furnace of 1901. Eight years later enormous quantities of steel were being produced by this means. The same year, 1901, saw also the consummation of many years of metallurgical experiment, the large scale extension of aluminium production, and because of its resistance to acids, its use in the manufacture and storage of foodstuffs, while on account of its lightness its employment in motor-cars, airships, and scientific instruments. Cold storage and artificial production of refrigeration were, of course, already well established.

Turning to a different field that same year saw the first wireless signals transmitted by Marconi across the Atlantic, from Poldhu in Cornwall to St. Johns in Newfoundland, confounding the mathematicians and theoretical physicists by surmounting the great hump of the ocean which rose between his two stations to a height of 125 miles. Marconi was indeed bring' ıg his arduous labours to fruition. He displaced the old-fashioned coherer by a magnetic detector in order that the feeble currents from his aerial might be induced to work a telephone, and at the same time prevailed on shipping owners to instal wireless. It was the beginning of a new era indeed. Meanwhile a revolutionary movement of a differer' nature was in process in America, where in this same y ar Wilbur and Orville Wright succeeded in hopping a di tance of 600 feet with their aeroplane, literally a first flutter into life.

In the next year Marconi was again to the fore. With improved apparatus he was now able to receive readable messages on board a vessel 1,500 miles from his transmitting station at Poldhu, and Morse messages at 2,000 miles. Wireless had already proved its worth for ships in distress. That same year, 1902, saw arrangements completed for the erection of transatlantic stations, and in the following year, 1903, the First International Wireless Convention was held. Meanwhile the brothers Wright were still busy and had so far improved their plane as to remain in the air for a full minute.

On the industrial side innumerable new processes were rapidly being inaugurated. From the development of the electric furnace already referred to there emerged a number of by-products and one more chapter on the utilization of waste began to be written. It was recognized, for example, that the white powdery substance calcium carbide formed from the lime between which the poles of the furnace lay, and from the carbon of the electric poles, was itself a useful commercial product, and when combined with nitrogen at 1,000° C. formed calcium cyanimide, a valuable manure. The nitrogen was, of course, obtained from the air. Thus was inaugurated a new industry for the capture of nitrogen by means of the electric furnace. Meanwhile the new manures were themselves stimulating further research. The Agricultural Experimental Stations immediately undertook a series of intensive experiments on the effects of nitrogen compounds on the yield of crops. These valuable experiments lasted for many years and threw a flood of light on the effect of bacteria on crop growth. Thus we see science passing from social practice through experiment to theory, then through experiment back to practice, and the unity of theory with social needs stands out clearly.

Meanwhile in this same year, 1903, numerous minor engineering feats were under way. Tunnels for underground railways were excavated in London and elsewhere by means of the new Compressed Air Greathead Shield, whose success was finally vindicated by the driving out of the Charing Cross–Hampstead Railway. When the two shields, starting from opposite ends, met midway there was found to be an error of only $\frac{1}{8}$ in. in level and $\frac{1}{4}$ in. in direction, so accurately did these excavators work true to requirement. 1903 saw a vast extension in electric generation by the establishment of electric power stations, while Norway and Sweden harnessed their waterfalls to provide themselves with cheap power. Meanwhile the brothers Wright were still persevering. By 1905 they had succeeded in flying for 38 minutes, thanks to new developments in engine power, and three years later Wilbur Wright at last clinched the future of the aeroplane by flying in France for 2 hours. At this the newspapers awoke to the publicity value of the new transport, and the attention of society was focussed upon it. Next year, 1909, Curtis won the Aeroplane Speed Race at 47 miles per hour at Rheims, using a motor-car engine of 50 h.p., while Farman remained in the air for more than 4 hours. Meanwhile, as already indicated, the illumination engineers and their scientific colleagues were busy. In 1905 the first successful metallic filament lamp— the tantalum lamp — was produced, succeeded in the following year by tungsten filaments. I have already suggested something of what this has meant for the amenities of social life.

In 1905 Marconi invented his directional aerial, and the following year the seal was set on the use of this new method of communication by the simple adoption of the international S.O.S., and by 1907 the wireless stations to the west of Ireland and in Nova Scotia were opened for public service. During all these years electrification of industry and the erection of power stations was proceeding apace. By 1908 in this country over 200 miles of single track railway were worked wholly by electricity, and an equal number worked partly by steam and partly by electricity. In London alone there were 138 miles of electrified line, but other forms of transport were steadily evolving along new lines. By the end of the period under review there were already nearly 200,000 motor vehicles on the roads of England alone, and the era of keen competition between electric trams and motor buses had commenced. Bleriot had flown the Channel and thereby demonstrated the latent possibilities of the aeroplane as a weapon of offence. Shortly after that, in fact, France was already committed to spending £1,000,000 on aircraft and Britain £850,000.

Britain was of course not alone in the conversion of already established principles to social and industrial ends. Germany and the U.S.A. had already more than made up the leeway of the nineteenth century, arriving later in the field but with less obsolete plant.

To illustrate the enormous output of various commodities we may note that at the close of this period the annual quantity of iron produced in the world would have formed a band two square feet in section right round the world.

It is now time to withdraw ourselves from this feverish rush to apply well-established principles to social practice, in order to examine, in slightly more detached manner, the experimental and theoretical investigations that were maturing during this period. For from these in due course would the next stream of discovery and invention be expected to pour forth. We turn in fact to an examination of the internal properties of the scientific movement and away from its external social properties.

There are two such internal properties that must repay examination. One concerns itself with the personnel of the scientific movement and its internal administration. That is to say it deals with the steps that were taken to provide the human material, the scientific machinery for the pursuit of research, and the nature of the channels along which this knowledge should flow if it is to act consciously as a reinvigorating influence in industrial practice. The other is concerned primarily with the scientific ideas themselves, and the trials and travails of scientists in their efforts to produce a logically coherent statement of natural processes as they are exposed in experiment, in such a form as to provide predictions and pointers for further practice. We turn first to the latter aspect of this question, and for purposes of illustration, and because it is the region with which I am best acquainted, we shall deal mainly with physics.

In this field we have to appreciate the outlook of the world of classical physics, and its preoccupation with the ether. The ether from being a verbal convenience throughout the eighteenth and nineteenth centuries had gradually become an accepted physical fact. Permeating all space, it had also permeated the minds of scientists. It was the medium for transmitting vibrations of light and all forms of electro-

magnetic action, a sort of universal jelly, sufficiently tenous
for us and the earth to slip through almost with perfect ease,
or it through us. Yet so strong was it, that it could withstand
without rupture the tension set up by the collosal forces
of gravitation that were exerted between the huge masses
of solar space. It was a happy hunting ground for the
explanation of every new physical phenomenon. When
occasion demanded one required merely to accord it an extra
ad hoc property. Even matter itself as Kelvin tried to show
could be regarded as vortex rings in the ether, and since
vortex motion in a perfect fluid was shown mathematically
to be indestructible there, to hand, was the indestructibility
of matter. It was the medium for the flux of Clerk Maxwell's
energy, and the seat of Faraday's tubes of force. It was
the absolute, the stuff of the universe, relative to which,
the ether being at rest and filling all infinite space, all
phenomena occurred. True there were difficulties. Gravitation, for instance, did not appear to be transmitted with
the velocity of light as did all other etherial effects. It scarcely
seemed to have a velocity at all. It was in a sense
instantaneous. Moreover, there were ambiguities as between
uniform motion and accelerated motion in this medium.
Newton's laws of motion for material bodies applied as
between two bodies when they were in uniform speed relative
to each other. In such circumstances it was immaterial
which was taken at rest in the ether and which in motion.
With accelerated motion it was different, for such an acceleration according to Newton implied the existence of an active
propelling force localized on the accelerating body, but
whether a relatively accelerating body was accelerating with
respect to the ether was not known. Thus, during the
centuries since Newton, there had accumulated quite a
literature concerning this question of absolute and relative
motion, and the validity of the mechanical laws in relation
to it. Intimately bound up with this whole discussion was
the assumption explicitly stated by Newton " Time flows

uniformly ", a statement inherently incapable of experimental verification. Time and space were apparently two separate and completely isolated features of the universe. The fact that they were never separately experienced, neither capable of measurement except in association with each other or in association with matter did not apparently affect the issue. They were independent absolutes, all three, time, space, and matter. Thus began the quest for determining an absolute motion. The electromagnetic theory of light, evolved in the middle of the nineteenth century, at last seemed to provide the experimental means for detecting absolute motion in space, if it existed at all, inasmuch as light was presumed to be carried through the fixed ether. For a study of the propagation of light between the planets from a moving earth would decide whether the velocity of the earth round the sun really corresponded to an absolute motion in space.

A series of such tests was undertaken, the most outstanding and the most accurate being those by Michelson and Morley in 1881, and in 1887, and again by Morley and Miller in 1905. Assuming that light travelled in a fixed ether and that the earth's orbital speed of 1,000 miles per minute relative to the sun represented a motion through this ether, by delicate experimentation it should certainly have been possible to detect certain differences dependent on whether the earth was approaching the source of light or whether it was receding from it. No such effects were discernible. Whatever the reason, it was impossible to avoid the conclusion that the velocity of light as measured by an observer situated on the earth was independent of the earth's motion. This startling result, contrary to the accepted principle of the addition of velocities and, therefore, contrary to all scientific expectation, immediately gave rise, as usual, to a crop of ad hoc explanations. These we need not here pursue. It suffices merely to state that once the consequences of this conclusion were faced it seemed impossible to avoid the inference that an absolute space, separate and distinct from an absolute time—the same for all observers—could not consistently be embodied in the logical and experimental framework of science. There did not exist a unique time-table of events in the universe which all could consult. It was in 1905 that Einstein resolved these paradoxes by propounding his special theory of relativity. Assuming the principle that *any* object may be regarded as at rest and others in motion, assuming the findings of the Michelson-Morley experiment as universally valid, that all observers irrespective of their own motion always measure the speed of approaching light as the same magnitude, he developed a scheme for a chronology of world-events from which each observer could deduce his own particular version of the cosmic process and set out his own particular time-table. All of these versions would have an equal validity. Nothing in the universe of science was known to give one pre-eminence over the other, while the particular one corresponding to an *ether at rest* had no special status at all. The absolute space of Newton and his uniform flow of time had lost its apparent necessity. The Michelson-Morley experiment and the deductions therefrom by Einstein had destroyed it. The theory of relativity even in its restricted form applicable to systems in uniform motion relative to each other was immediately of profound importance in the epistomology and in the methodology of science although it was passed almost unnoticed at the time except by Planck. At one sweep it unified whole branches of apparently diverse fields. In electrical theory, for example, there existed electrostatics, the field of force due to electricity at rest ; electrodynamics and electromagnetic induction, the theory of electricity in motion, as expounded and developed by Faraday and his contemporaries ; and finally the theory of electromagnetic waves as developed by Maxwell, where the energy is alternately electrostatic and electrodynamic ; all three branches became unified, each derivable from the other. In the sphere of mechanics it involved a restatement of the principles of the conservation of momentum and mass, and predictions based on this restatement applicable to rapidly moving electrons have been verified. A complete parallelism in fact was exposed between what is called material mass and the *so-called free energy* of light and electromagnetism.

The completion of this story in the general theory of relativity cannot be entered into here. That was not launched on the scientific world until 1913 and is, therefore, outside the scope of our survey. It must suffice to say that the contradictions regarding accelerated motion tacit in the Newtonian laws, the anomalous position held by gravity, the meaning of inertia, and a host of other difficulties were smoothed away or rather consistently interwoven to form one logically coherent descriptive scheme, by throwing the burden of these needs on a detailed and equivalent mapping out of a space-time geometry for world events. Of the significance of such mathematical explanations I shall have something to say later. For the moment we recognize the essential fact that the explanation of mechanical and electrical phenomena was thus being expressed in an intricate mathematical form ; and the criterion of validity of this resolution was not so much the experimentally verified truth of each element of the theory as the fact that, accepting the mathematical formulation, it resolved existing contradictions, made certain predictions, and found them verified.

If the Edwardian era saw the first step in a totally new orientation to the scientific laws of the macrocosm, it saw also the inception of the first revolutionary move in the reorganization of our knowledge of the microcosm. There is, of course, no special beginning to any such step, but let us work back a little if only to acquire the atmosphere of the period. It was about 1895 that it began to be realized seriously that in some way not yet understood electricity was closely identified with the intimate structure of matter.

Röntgen had discovered that X-rays, a new penetrating radiation, was emitted when an electric current was passed through a vacuum tube and made to impinge on an obstacle inside the tube. In 1906 Becquerel, on examining whether phosphorescent salts also threw out such rays found that a new form of radiation was emitted from uranium salts. By 1898 Madame Curie and her husband had isolated radium, with more than a million times the radiation intensity of uranium. The succeeding years, throughout the whole period under review up to the present day, bristle with discovery after discovery of the nature of the radiation and the charged particles that could be dislodged from the interior of the atoms of which matter was composed. Experimental work, however, cannot usefully proceed without some theory of the action that is to be expected, just as no fruitful theory can be constructed except on the basis of established facts, and thus as more and more information poured forth concerning the behaviour of the charged particles that were dislodged at terrific speeds approaching that of light, a clearer and clearer picture—a model of the inner structure of the atom—gradually took shape. This has not been attained without the exposure of many inconsistencies in our preconceived notions of these matters. The initial stages were comparatively easy. It was recognized that, if a substance be heated to luminosity, then, according to the electromagnetic theory of light this luminous radiation would be emitted by the agitation of electric particles or electrons. Thus at first the atomic structure that was pictured appeared to fit this scheme. The difficulty, however, was this, that when the light emitted was examined through the spectroscope, certain regularities—spectral lines they are called—were mapped out, yet no mechanism of the type initially suggested could conceivably have produced these. Here was the atom, pictured as a miniature solar system, composed of a central charge of positive electricity with a collection of negative charges rotating round it. If such a system radiated energy, how could it remain stable in such circumstances ? The simple picture demanded stability, the energy radiation the opposite. Why did not the negative charges fall into the central nucleus, just as the earth would drop into the sun if it lost its energy ? Moreover, the radiation emitted even from such a system would not be selective, it would produce a continuous coloured medley quite contrary to observed fact.

This was the state of affairs well into the period under review, but so breathless was the chase for experimental knowledge in the new field, so thick and fast did new information emerge, that the revolutionary suggestion made by Planck in 1900 at the very beginning of this period passed with little comment at the time. If anything it aroused a slight derision, so extravagant did it appear. We have to realize, of course, that the idea of continuity in physical phenomena, in the flux of energy in the ether, for instance, had so long been assumed true by physicists that it had become almost second nature to them. Discontinuities were regarded rather as the invention of the mathematicians. Planck proposed a revolutionary doctrine. It was revolutionary in the sense that it broke with the tradition of the time. Far from energy passing as a continuous flux like a stream of water where any amount, no matter how small, may be tapped off, he suggested that discharges of energy took place in jumps, in definite quanta, like a trigger action. It was definitely an atomic theory of energy in action, implying that no radiation of energy could take place except in a series of gulps. By 1905 Einstein had adopted the quantum theory seriously and by its means sought to explain the anomaly of what is known as the photoelectric effect, the effect of light on chemical substances. In this it is not so much the intensity of the light that determines the action, as the frequency or the colour. There is a threshold of frequency, for example, below which a chemical substance will not be affected in this way by the light in question.

A photographic plate for example will not be affected by intense red light, but blue light, no matter how faint will, on falling on the chemical surface, eject electrons from it and start the chemical action. The significant point is that the speed of ejection is unaffected by the intensity of the light. That depends simply on the fact that at least one quantum of the radiation has been absorbed. More intense light simply ejects more electrons at that speed. It does not increase their speed. The success of the quantum theory in a number of crucial experimental cases of this nature succeeded in producing such a confusion in the scientific explanation of the microcosm as can be paralleled only by the corresponding state at the same time in the macroscopic sphere. Side by side there existed as it were two totally different and apparently mutually contradictory views of the nature of light. On the one hand light was a continuous wave motion of an electromagnetic nature on the basis of which whole regions of scientific facts had been co-ordinated and explained. On the other hand light had a definite atomic structure ; it was composed of numbers of small but discrete packets of energy. If both views were to be reconciled it was essential that any unified theory should embody at one and the same time a set of mechanical laws and a set of wave laws for such a system. The attempts that have been made to effect this reconciliation under the title of the wave-mechanics scarcely concern us directly since their full development did not commence until after the Great War. Here we may simply note that once again as with the theory of relativity we are dealing with a range of phenomena that are in many respects outside the region of detailed examination. The theory as it is propounded in explanation and for the purposes of prediction takes a highly mathematical form, and in the nature of the case, no attempt can be made successfully to interpret the full significance of every term in such an explanation. The quantum theory like the wave theory of light necessary as they each were to explain aspects of the behaviour of radiation have jointly led to a form of reconciliation that in outward form at any rate is more mathematical than physical.

A few words about a relevant aspect of biology. As far as biology was concerned the period opened with a comparatively startling and fertile development. Already in 1858 Darwin had published his *Origin of Species* involving, as the motivating principle of change, the process of natural selection. The extraordinary success of this theory in reconciling numerous outstanding contradictions and the extent to which it appeared to undermine established belief deflected the thought of the time from the testing of the theory itself and its consequences by direct experimentation to acute controversy and finally to biological stagnation. What should have become the beginning of a period of fertile experimental work became the closing stage of an epoch in morphology. Mendel alone, an obscure monk, set about a study of the principles of heredity and in 1865 his paper containing the fundamental law of the science of genetics was published in a small journal in Brünn. It was, however, not the obscurity of the journal that was responsible for the neglect of Mendel's work. It had been submitted to Nägeli of Berlin, one of the foremost biologists of his day, but he saw nothing significant in it. The reason lay, as I have said, in the settled outlook produced by the dominance of Darwin's theory of natural selection, as the mechanism of evolution. From 1866 to 1900 there was one reference only to Mendel's paper in a book on plants by Focke in 1881. It was this reference that finally led to the rediscovery of the paper in 1900, at the time when three separate scientists of note, De Vries, Correns, and Tschermak, independently rediscovered the law before reading the paper. These experiments setting out a law of inheritance in simple numerical terms marked the inception of a hectic period of experimentation, that is still increasing in intensity, leading as it has done to a systematization of knowledge in plant and animal breeding and to the formulation of an extensive mathematical theory dealing with the crossings of genes in the chromosomes. The Edwardian period on the genetical side of biology represented in fact the conversion of a qualitative theory of evolution as propounded by Darwin, intrinsically incapable of verification by measurement, to a quantitative and measurable stage. It had at last entered into the field of the numerical sciences and marked the beginning of a new and important epoch.

If we look at these theoretical and experimental developments in retrospect, and contrast them with the feverish activity evinced in the engineering and more definitely applied sciences during this period it is amazing how remote they seem from the practice of everyday life. The theory of relativity need never have been propounded for all the practical effect it is likely to have on the life of the layman. Its importance lies less in the realm of social practice than in that of ideas. It is a contribution to cosmology and in that sense is to be classed with much of the later development concerning the expanding universe and even the greater part of much that treats of the internal constitution of stars and nebulæ.

In spite of certain similarities the quantum theory is on a different footing. It is too closely linked with the field of experimental physics of electrons and radiation to be without its effect on all those aspects of electrical application that is associated in the popular mind with valves and wireless.

Those who have attempted to follow the trend in scientific thought during this last decade must have been struck by the emergence of a curious feature in scientific explanation. Particularly has it shown itself in connection with the theory of relativity and with wave mechanics. Since both of these developments found their inception during the Edwardian Period it may not be out of place to say a word or two on these puzzling features.

In modern scientific writing it has become a common-place to state that the day of mechanical models is at last gone. Whereas it was possible during the great days of Kelvin to describe the processes of nature in simple mechanical form, either by visual machine-like models or by diagram, that day has now passed, and only by means of the most abstruse mathematical formulæ, whose detailed interpretation by pictorial images defy the imagination of Man to conceive, is it possible to *explain*—note the continued use of the term—and to predict many of the most fundamental processes of nature. The space-time curvature of the relativity theory, and the wave-particle activity of the electron—a wavicle it has been called—are cases in point. Now it must be admitted at once that to persist in the use of the term " explanation " for the complicated mass of mathematical symbols, with their not infrequent use of imaginary quantities, and used successfully for making predictions in this field is to stretch unduly, if not to destroy, the meaning of that term, for the cure as it were appears more serious than the disease, the explanation more complicated than the original problem.

It is important that this trend should be properly appreciated, for it is a very significant feature of modern scientific thought and likely to remain so, but it is a feature that has, in fact, never been absent. Only since the beginning of this century has its presence manifested itself at all prominently.

Let us go back in the first place to the Kelvin days, the hey-day of the engineer. For the purposes of scientific inquiry, for the purposes of prediction, it sufficed for the investigator after his detailed examination of any apparently complicated process, to abstract or to isolate from it what were to him and to other scientific men of his day the guiding principles at work ; to strip as it were, all that mass of extraneous features that were irrelevant as formative factors and to retain a skeleton whose mode of operation could be clearly set out. Kelvin, a great representative of this school, in fact maintained that a process was not understood until a working model of this nature could be constructed. We have to realize, however, that models have always been of two very different kinds—even to Kelvin who was both mathematician and engineer. To understand the mechanism of an eclipse, for example, and to predict when such an event would take place and over which part of the earth totality would be observed, it sufficed in the first place to set up a model of the sun, the earth, and the moon to scale, and to set them in motion with their appropriately observed rotations about each other, and so, by running the system ahead of the present time to make the necessary predictions. This would constitute the mechanical model. Quite a different procedure has, however, been adopted and one which is not usually recognized as one relating to models at all. A series of algebraic symbols are taken to represent the separate heavenly bodies, the measure of their masses and their distances apart. The effect of masses on each other's motion are represented by writing these symbols in connected form on a sheet of paper, and the set of symbols are allowed to be moved about in relation to each other according to rules which ensure that the changes made in their arrangements follow, when interpreted, the physical principle at work, the same principle in fact that has been seen in operation in the actual physical model. This grouping of symbols and the transformation in arrangement of these groupings that are permissible provides what is usually called the equations of motion, but what I prefer to regard as really a symbolical model. As the changes are rung on the symbol groupings the model is in fact being made to run through its possible motions. The process of solving the mathematical equations is a process of model movement, but the model is now entirely an isolated one of symbols, none the less real since it is a series of black marks on a sheet of paper, like a drawing of the original machine.

Ever since the days of Newton and Galileo and even prior to that, this form of mathematical model has existed side by side with what we have come to regard as the physical model. In an extended sense of the term this mathematical model is a symbolical physical model. In putting it through its paces it provides the answer to the question " What next ? " if it is an accurate model. For a model need not be a geometrical pattern of the original. A model to determine the stresses in the blade of a propeller when it is distorted, for example, has been usefully applied in the form of a soap bubble stretched across a hole whose shape is that of the propeller section, and puffed out under air pressure on one side of the film. The deviations of the soap bubble measure the torsion in the propeller blade. This then is a physical model of a totally different outward type from the original. In precisely the same way the collection of black marks that represent the mathematical model can function to make predictions and this is what is called applied mathematics.

Now the special feature of the mathematical expressions in the quantum theory is that the operation of the mechanism in the interior of the atom is incapable of detailed examination. They are in the main outside the scope of accurate measurements and yet mathematical models have been produced—mainly it must be admitted by guess work—which, on being put through their paces, provide the correct answer. If, therefore, we regard the mathematical tendencies of this period from this standpoint we recognize at once that there has been no break but an actual continuity in the interpretation of explanation.

We appear to have travelled a long way from the heavy atmosphere of the engineer during the period under review when we have entered the rarified ether of mathematical physics. How has it arisen, we may legitimately ask, that these highly abstract questions have now pushed their way to the fore in succession to the eminently practical problems of their predecessors ? Whence is to come the necessary impetus to development at the next stage ? While it is not true to say that the great body of scientific workers are concentrating their attention on questions of theory so remote from application that in some respects it is scarcely to be distinguished from pure speculation, it is correct, I think, to say that there are nowadays a much greater proportion of workers on what has come to be called fundamental research than in the past. This, I think, partly arises from the fact that the scientific profession itself and the administration of science in the community has been allowed to develop in a form dangerously unregulated when we consider how great a power for good or for evil science may be.

In 1914 at the outbreak of the Great War, when it became clear that the assistance of technicians was essential to the successful prosecution of the fighting, when in fact it became evident that the potent and indeed the determining factors were likely to be associated with the extent to which the belligerent armies were armed and supplemented by inventions of scientifically destructive weapons, scientists were enrolled in army categories as mechanics and labourers. In estimating the public prestige and state of development of the scientific profession during the Edwardian period it is perhaps not legitimate to take as an index of that valuation the state of mind of the traditionally conservative army chiefs thirteen years after the commencement of that era, but the surprise with which we now regard the status thus allotted to what is now recognized as a very fertile source of industrial practice and of philosophical speculation is itself an index of the change that has taken place in the interim. It is impossible to give an exact indication of the number of scientific workers who were engaged in research in the early days of this century. Certain it is, however, that full-time research workers, apart from engineers, were few and far between. With the exception of Brunner Mond and one or two minor concerns of a similar nature with close connections with German firms who were much more advanced in this respect than British industrialists there were practically no industrial research laboratories in existence. Whatever scientific research was being done was mainly in association with the universities. There was the elementary form of our modern National Physical Laboratory, then situated at Kew with a mere handful on the scientific staff. If we wish to visualize the tremendous change that has been effected since that day we have only to pay a visit to the huge mass of buildings at Teddington constituting the present National Physical Laboratory, the Admiralty Research Station, and the Chemical Research Laboratory, with their special blocks for aeronautics, ship research, engineering, acoustics, modern physics, metallurgy, electrotechnics, etc., and the numerous institutions like the Shirley Institute for Cotton Research, The Boot and Shoe Research Association, The Fuel Research Association, The Food Research Board, the many Agricultural Research Stations, the Electrical Research Association, etc. Many of these are now either directly or indirectly under the ægis of the Department of Scientific and Industrial Research. While the number of full-time scientific investigators in 1910 ran perhaps to several hundreds in this country, there must be at the present time something in the neighbourhood of 40,000.

The scant attention that was given to establishing Institutions for Industrial Research during the period under review exposed a distinct lack of alertness on the part of industrial magnates, and a failure to appreciate the changing face of industrial practice throughout the whole world at that time. Until 1900 Britain had been on the rising wave of imperial expansion. Its markets, found with comparative ease among the regions of the globe that had been parcelled out as Britain's sphere, were scarcely showing great signs of contraction. If they were not still markets for manufactured commodities they were, at any rate, suitable markets for heavy machinery to manufacture these commodities on the spot. An intelligent industrialism would have seen the necessity for the systematic development of new needs in these regions in order that their markets could be maintained alive. The vast populations of the East must of necessity be led to follow the standards of the West just as the standards of the West would themselves require to be steadily raised if they were yet to offer new fields for exploitation. The easy lead acquired by British industrialists in the early days of the nineteenth century over their Continental rivals was not to be held in the face of a spreading industrialism in the East or of an increasing efficiency of technique of the West. The selfishly enlightened attitude would surely have been to use the initial advantage accorded to Britain by her geographical isolation, to acquire a new advantage in technical and scientific manufacture by the intensive development of industrial research. The tradition that new markets were always to be discovered merely by looking for new geographical areas was, however, too powerful to allow such a far-sighted industrial policy to be seriously considered. The consequence was inevitable. It was Britain's rivals who first felt the need for such a venture and it was Britain's rivals who set the lead in the expansion of Research Institutions. Later, too late in fact to maintain their old advantage, the British industrialist turned after the War to this possible new weapon. I am not suggesting that the present international impasse in industry would not have emerged even then, I am certain it would, but rather that industrial policy was at that stage not alive to its next obvious step.

To summarize then. The well-established principles of mechanism and energetics that had been evolved since the time of Newton and particularly during the preceding century had been applied in very practical experimental forms to the development of power units. Sources of steam power energy were already well established, but now there rapidly emerged machinery of various types driven by gas

and oil.   The principle of combustion within the cylinder
itself, to provide the mechanical drive, passed out from the
experimental stage to full fruition to set free a whole new
expansion in locomotion and transport.   The full fruits of
that development on land, sea, and in the air, we at this
stage are now experiencing.   The theoretical discoveries in
electro-magnetic theory by Faraday, Clerk Maxwell, and
others, became transformed into a totally new and, in a sense,
revolutionary form of energy unit.   The fact that although
the production of electrical energy requires to be centralized
it is nevertheless capable of easy transmission to a series of
sub-stations, and directly to individual factories and to
households, brought a reaction to a process that had been
proceeding steadily during the previous century of steam
power.   During the Industrial Revolution it was essential
that factories and workshops should be situated as closely as
possible to the source of power—the coal centres.   Since
it was equally essential that the dwellings of the workmen
should be in close proximity to their work, the rapidly
growing towns of Britain were located in the coal mining
districts.   With the advent of electrical power, however,
a centripetal force set in.   New sites for factories were
cheapest in the less congested areas, electrical energy could
be distributed from the power stations to distant points at
comparatively little cost and a slow movement away from the
black spots became apparent.   While the effects of this
technological factor on population and urban distribution has
not yet reached its maximum strength, an enormous speeding
up in our own time will in all probability become discernible
under the national electrification schemes that are afoot.
The Edwardian period saw the beginnings of a technological
advance whose fruits we in our generation may possibly
pluck.

Side by side with the new forms of energy distribution
and of power sources there has emerged almost a complete
transformation in social life and social habits.   With the

advent of the motor car, made possible by the internal-combustion engine, with the success of the aeroplane, transformed from a mere glider to a medium for transport and a violently destructive weapon in warfare, with the revolution in illumination, both internal and external, in the home, in the workshop, in the public streets, and in places of amusement, there has been effected a far-reaching change both of the whole system of goods distribution and in some respects of workshop practice, and a transformation in the atmosphere in which the younger generation has grown up. Almost every day saw new luxuries and new needs created. To those in their thirties, born and brought up in the first decade of this century, there has been such an acceleration in speed, light, and amusement, as was undreamt of by their parents. With an enormous choice in the employment of leisure, for those who have the spare time to employ, problems of education and of social culture have become complicated rather than simplified. The mechanization of social life has dragged in its train a vast complex of new problems that cry aloud for solution. Towns spread to suburbs, suburbs became new towns, stretching out their tentacles just as far as the convenience of the daily load of workmen could tolerate the train and motor-bus journey to their places of employment. Even the deathly stillness of the quiet Scottish Sunday became desecrated by the clang of the electric tram and the raucous hoot of the motor car. In a new mechanical environment a new balance of social ethics began to show itself, and has continued to this day. Electro-magnetic waves, the toy of simple scientific men, became in the hands of Marconi a speaking tube that carried its message across the Atlantic. The period that saw the insulation of Britain from the Continent destroyed by Bleriot's flight across the Channel saw the isolation of America break down by the wireless signals of Marconi from Poldhu to Newfoundland. Political frontiers might persist for a few more generations but the first decade of this century

saw the loosening of forces that in their time must expose
the economic interdependence of the nations of the earth.
Science had set going a deeper and more far-reaching
revolution than any of its discoverers could have dreamt
was possible.

H. LEVY.

X

Social and Political Ideas

Although the dialectic of ideas bears little relation to the occupancy of the throne, it yet happens that the Edwardian era corresponds to a fairly definite chapter in the history of English political theory. The reign is approximately coincident with the interval between the first and second editions of Bosanquet's *Philosophical Theory of the State*, and during that interval several distinctive movements of thought resulted in an appreciable alteration of the intellectual climate of the 'nineties. The " new Liberalism ", for example, was seeking a coherent social theory (the lack of which had been glaringly revealed by the failure of the Newcastle Programme) to replace the now discredited doctrines of mid-Victorian individualism. Simultaneously, H. G. Wells, Ramsay MacDonald, and the Fabians were developing the implications of the idea of a " planned society ", and their popularizations were reaching sections of the community that would have been untouched by the more academic speculations. Above all, a remarkable revival of interest in the psychological approach to politics— perhaps the most important of all the intellectual movements of the period—bore fruit in works which still greatly influence our social and political reflections ; works, indeed, which in themselves make a significant cleavage between our own habits of thought and those of the 'nineties.

I

A marked spirit of pessimism suffuses much of the political writing of the Edwardian era : a sense of disappointment and disenchantment. Nor is that spirit confined to the

writings of those with Liberal affiliations. Conservative
and Unionist journalism, as well as the few books of Conservative political polemic, betrays a similar sentiment;
and even Mr. Kipling (after his return from the hospitals
and battlefields of South Africa) is now heard singing in
the minor key, so that in reading *The Five Nations* (1903)
one is made aware of the very real change that had come over
Imperialism since the more blatant days when *The Seven
Seas* (1897) appeared. Even *The Times* noted the change,
and commented (with unconscious irony) on the " deeper
earnestness and humility " of the later volume. Kipling,
with that strange capacity he once had for catching one phase
of the national mood, has embodied this spirit of disenchantment in his poem *The Return*, and in so doing has expressed
the temper not merely of post-Boer War Conservatives or
Imperialists but of the majority of politically conscious
writers and thinkers throughout these ten years.

> I did no more than others did,
>   I don't know where the change began ;
> I started as an average kid
>   I finished as a thinking man.
>
> If England was what England seems,
>   An' not the England of our dreams,
> But only putty, brass, and paint,
>   'Ow quick we'd drop 'er !
>   But she aint.

There is scarcely a reputable book of political speculation
produced during the reign which does not embody in its
own way that same disillusionment begotten of the antithesis between a new sense of social reality and " the England
of our dreams ". L. T. Hobhouse, J. A. Hobson, Graham
Wallas, C. F. G. Masterman, and the dozen or so others
who determined the trend of the Edwardian mind all show
a similar mood, and each tries in his own way to analyse
and explain the fact itself.

Every age loses its faith, in the sense that it puts off its traditional beliefs and comes into its own with throes and struggles, and backward looks of longing to a past from which it must part, and with apprehension of what lies before it ; but something more than the normal apprehension of the future must be invoked to explain the prevalent pessimism. Anyone who is at all familiar with the correspondence and writings of Francis Place and his circle during the eighteen-twenties and thirties must have been struck by the underlying sense of certainty and of confidence in all their thoughts and efforts. However much individual temperaments in that circle may have differed, there is yet a dominating optimism of outlook among them. They had a clear-cut philosophy of social life, they knew what they wanted to achieve, and they had a tolerably clear sense of how to achieve it ; they were sustained, moreover, by the exhilarating sense of co-operation with a movement of progress which they believed predestined to triumph. This spirit of certainty which originally characterized the philosophical radicals had gradually spread to the Liberal party as a whole and eventually became the dominant spirit of mid-Victorianism in the so-called era of complacency. It was left to Tennyson to apply this optimism to the universe and to discern in the cosmic process the " one increasing purpose ". Lord Bryce, in his *Hindrances to Good Citizenship* (1909)—that dignified lament for vanished convictions which is itself but one of the expressions of the prevailing mood—thus recalled the fact : " From 1830 to 1870 the general attitude of most of the powerful intellects, and nearly all the finest characters, among the thinkers and writers of Europe was a hopeful one, expecting immense gains to human progress and human happiness from the establishment of free institutions." Now, however, he went on to say, the clear convictions of a generation ago have been clouded over, and the pristine enthusiasm has been disappointed by events. The " new Liberalism " had scarcely any of

the confidence of the old, for the new Liberals were not sure
where they were going though they hoped they were on the
way. " What is peculiar to the modern reformer," wrote an
anonymous reviewer in commenting on the fact that C. F. G.
Masterman's *The Condition of England* (1909) was a melancholy and anxious book, " is that the dawn which he greets
in his sanguine hour is so very gray and ambiguous a twilight.
This is the chief difference between him and his antecedents—
the change from confidence to misgiving, from hope to a
brooding doubt. All the certainties of politics seem to
have melted in the interval." Whether or not such a comment is applicable to the politicians, it is certainly a pertinent
reflection upon the political writers with, perhaps, the single
exception of Mr. G. K. Chesterton whose " blasphemous
optimism " Masterman criticized in *In Peril of Change* (1908).

The cause of this intellectual pessimism is not far to seek ;
it is writ large in most of the works dealt with in this essay.
It may be summarized in a formula by saying that the
Edwardian intellectuals were disappointed with the results
of the extension of the franchise during the previous seventy
years ; that events had revealed certain false assumptions
in the thinking of the fathers of Liberalism which now
appeared to be bearing unexpected fruit ; that the silent and
chilling force of a new realism was bringing home to thinking
men a fresh and intenser sense of social problems to be solved
and of their vast complexity ; and above all, that there was
no adequate or coherent body of social philosophy at hand,
such as the philosophical radicals had possessed, to guide
reformers through the rapidly accumulating mass of social
data. The day of the simple verities in politics was over.
" Modern observers," wrote the editor of the *Speaker*,
" to whom every political question presents a thousand sad
and baffling riddles, are amazed at the secure and easy
psychology which dictated, for example, such a document
as the Report of the Poor Law Commission of 1834, or the
political anticipations of William Godwin."

The disappointment with the results of democracy was patent. It was the central theme of three such diverse works as H. G. Wells's *Anticipations* (1901), L. T. Hobhouse's *Democracy and Reaction* (1904), and Bryce's *Hindrances to Good Citizenship* (1909), and lesser works echoed the same sentiment. The gains from democracy have been considerable, wrote Bryce, but not nearly so extensive as expected; although some general improvement in the material comfort of the masses has been secured, " yet the friends of democracy are disappointed," for larger, quicker, and deeper gains were hoped for. The Liberals were disappointed at the long-continued preference which the electorate showed for the Conservative party; but most surprising of all, and least explicable in terms of individualistic utilitarianism, was the phenomenon of Imperialism. Dicey, in *Law and Opinion in England* (1905) commented upon it as the most remarkable of the unforeseen consequences of democracy, and Hobhouse agreed, in *Democracy and Reaction*, that the vogue of Imperialism meant that certain illusions would have to go; the belief for instance, that a people enjoying self-government could never be imperialistic. " That was indeed a hasty belief, for it implied an expectation that self-government would change human nature." We shall be under no illusions about democracy, he wrote, " the golden radiance of its morning hopes has long since faded into the light of common day." To men such as L. T. Hobhouse and J. A. Hobson the history of the preceding twenty years was one of ignominy and shame, and each vented his sorrowful wrath in a memorable book. The shadows are deep, both in *Democracy and Reaction* (1904) and Hobson's *Imperialism* (1902). Between 1884 and 1900 England had acquired $3\frac{3}{4}$ million square miles of new territory, with a population of over 50 million souls; and in not one area had there been any extension of self-government. To secure and maintain such an accession of territory the expenditure on our fighting services had been trebled and its ratio to

the total national expenditure had risen from one-third to
one-half. The blockhouses and the Peace Preservation
Ordinance represented milestones on the march of the new
Imperialism which professed to bring liberty and the *pax
Britannica*. The contrast between the profession and the
practice of Imperialists was brought out in page after page
of sustained irony by both these writers. Had not the
assumption of the White Man's Burden in the Cape, asked
Hobhouse, coincided with a remarkable increase in the death-
rate of the mine workers on the Rand, native and imported ?
So both men wrote to prick the bubble of imperialistic
illusion for, as they saw things, the story which should have
been the romance of King Solomon's Mines had strangely
turned into the reality which was Messrs. Werner, Beit
and Co.'s mines.

But it was not merely the political results of democracy
which disappointed reflecting humanitarians : the social
problems confronting democracy were no less a cause for
pessimism ; the recognition, as Dicey put it, of " social
evils unsuspected by the philosophical radicals ". In the
summer of 1903 there was published, after 18 years' work,
the last volume of Charles Booth's *Life and Labour of the
People of London*. The sombre moderation of this remarkable
examination of a cross-section of English social life was
disquieting enough. The mass of poverty in the London
of that day, the obstacles in the way of improvement, and
the tangled undergrowth of vested interests loomed far larger
now than they had done in the days of Christian socialism,
or in the subsequent days of the first settlement workers.
It showed not one problem but an infinity of problems,
and it begot a distrust of all short cuts to their solution.
Booth saw no triumphant ameliorating agencies and no
swiftly operating social panaceas. He stressed the fact
that in order to raise permanently the lower levels of human
life many efforts must converge. Success, he thought,
could be only very gradual and never perhaps complete.

Nor—beyond certain moderate suggestions put forward in this last volume—had he any general scheme to offer. His noble closing words express the need of the age for a social philosophy. " May some great soul, master of a nobler alchemy than mine, disentangle the confused issues, reconcile the apparent contradictions in aim, melt and commingle the various influences for good into one divine uniformity of effort." Nothing could illustrate more clearly than this last volume of Booth's the deliquescence of the old individualistic certainties. The dark shadow of *Life and Labour* lies heavily across the pages of every disinterested sociological writer of the period, and in that shadow there could be no easy optimism. Nor was Booth's the only important contribution to a heightened realistic sense of social problems. No less remarkable within its limits was B. S. Rowntree's *Poverty : a study of town life* (1901). This survey of the city of York underlined and generalized some of Booth's findings for London and, moreover, the basic figures of the two works coincided in a striking way. Rowntree found that out of 75,000 inhabitants, 10 per cent lived in " primary poverty " and a further 18 per cent in secondary poverty, the two groups together constituting 43 per cent of the total number of wage-earners ; and this was at a time of " unparalleled commercial prosperity ". A similar chilling realism is found in Mrs. Helen Bosanquet's *The Standard of Life* (1906). Her approach is psychological, rather than economic, and she uses the " interview method " rather than the statistical method, but even Mr. J. A. Hobson, her severest critic, never questioned the accuracy of her findings. Mrs. Bosanquet, one of the ablest exponents of the school of scientific charity, exhibited a detailed concrete knowledge of the poor and a profound empirical wisdom, however much her interpretations and remedial programme may have been distorted by the orthodoxy of her economic assumptions and by her strange philosophy of the human will : that philosophy which tended to disparage all environ-

mental changes not proceeding directly from the stimulation
of the very individual wills in need of reform. In her work
the stress is everywhere laid upon defects of character and
training, upon slackness, improvidence, ignorance, and lack
of ambition. Apart altogether from her interpretations,
the picture she paints is in its own way every whit as disquieting as the statistical analyses. Can the people she
portrays ever be turned into fit citizens of a democratic
commonwealth ? And are not both the fact of their existence
and the problem of their regeneration strange commentaries
upon the naive creed of the fathers of individualism ? Or
is the creed of Malthus to be the perennial middle-class
consolation ? And the problem of " equality of opportunity "
which each of these books raised was seemingly still further
complicated by L. G. Chiozza Money's analysis of the
distribution of the nation's wealth in *Riches and Poverty*
(1905) from which emerged the conspicuous fact that about
one-third of the nation's wealth belonged to less than one-
thirtieth of the population. The Victorian radicals had at
times appeared to think that they were battling with the
primary foes of society, but now it seemed as if yet sterner
work lay ahead.

The problem of poverty, however, was not the only one
of the new issues which precluded facile solution. No less
vivid was the pervasive sense of the irrational factors involved
in social life. In this respect the Edwardian era is something
other than a mere epilogue to the Victorian age ; it represents
a revolt against the very first assumptions of the Benthamite
creed. That creed had envisaged man as rational in the
sense that he would consciously and purposively direct
himself to the pursuit of his own happiness ; and in the light
of such an assumption the extension of the franchise seemed
to promise indefinite possibilities. But the facts had belied
the assumption. The cult of jingoism was significant,
and the recent development of a sensationalist Press since
1893 seemed ominous. The England of the anti-pacifist

riots, of Mafeking night, and of the " Khaki " election seemed
a strange commentary on the philosophy of Cobden.   The
blue prints of democracy had been drawn up according to
the specification of human rationality ;   yet how could a
democratic state adequately charge itself with its own
destinies if there was a fundamental inconsequentiality at
the heart of social affairs ?   Democracy, said Bryce in the
work already quoted, implies an act of faith in " the natural
average man ", but now the average man was revealing
the preponderance of irrationality in his make-up.   That,
Bryce went on to explain, was the main reason for the
contemporary disappointment with democracy : it assumes
too high a level of intelligence and integrity in the ordinary
citizen.   Likewise H. G. Wells, after a period of intense
preoccupation with the structure and organization of his
New Republic (though by no means ignoring the problems
of education) came after 1908—conspicuously in his brilliant
series of novels 1908-1912—to stress " the human limitation ".
" I have long since ceased to trouble about the economics
of human society," he makes Stratton say in *The Passionate
Friends* ;   " ours are not economic but psychological difficulties."   That remark may justly be said to summarize
Hobhouse's *Democracy and Reaction* written five years before.
It was, too, the central theme of Hobson's *Psychology of
Jingoism* (1901).   But it was left to Graham Wallas in 1908
to revolutionize social psychology by his sober analysis of
the mental processes of " the natural average man " in the
light of the latest scientific findings.

There is one passage in Hobhouse's book which catches
especially well this particular mood of the reign, and which
says with particular effectiveness what more than a score of
other writers were implying in a different idiom :—

We have ourselves coined a new abstraction : " the man-in-
the-street " . . . is now the typical representative of public
opinion, and the man-in-the-street means the man who is
hurrying from his home to his office, or to his place of amuse-

ment . . . the man who has not time to think and will not
take the trouble to do so if he has the time. He is the faithful
reflection of the popular sheet and the shouting newsboy. . . .
To this new public opinion of the streets and the tramcars it
is useless to appeal in terms of reason ; it has not time to put
the two ends of an argument together ; it has hardly patience
to receive a single idea, much less to hold two in the mind and
compare them. Equally futile is it to come before this tribunal
with any plea for those higher considerations which men recognize
in their quieter moods. . . . He knows already all about any
appeal you can make to the better side of him, and he has long
ago chopped it up in his mill of small talk and catch phrases and
reduced it to such a meaningless patter that the words which
must be used have acquired trivial and lowering associations.
(op. cit. 70–2.)

Nor is this problem of political irrationality limited to
the " submerged tenth ". The problem arises just as
acutely—perhaps, indeed, in a more insidious form—in
suburbia. Nearly all the more academic political speculations of the reign recur to this theme. " Suburban villadom
is a political and social portent the meaning of which has
never yet been analysed. . . . Politically it is a greater burden
on the nation than the slum." So wrote Hobhouse ; and
C. F. G. Masterman vividly developed the subject in *The
Condition of England* (1909). The indictment of suburbia
in all these criticisms was the same : the absence of healthy
corporate life ; the dead weight of its respectability ; its
divorce from definite public duties (" a class relatively new
in this country ") ; its insulation from contact with poverty
or from any special obligation to any class of dependents ;
and the limitation of its political interests to the simple
formula of keeping down the rates. Even Mr. Kipling,
whose admiration for " men of the blood " seemed to be
measured in terms of their distance from Southampton,
had little to say for " the poor little street bred people that
vapour and fume and brag " ; and the standing sneer about
" the muddied oafs and flannelled fools " only reduces to
a formula a vivid passage of C. F. G. Masterman's

concerning suburbia's " vicarious sports and trivial amusements ".   Mr. Chesterton again constitutes, perhaps, the
sole major exception to this general denunciation of the
suburbs by Edwardian writers.   The nearer Kipling went to
the bounds of Empire, the closer did Mr. Chesterton cling
to the " rich suggestive life in Wimbledon " ; the more
plain tales from the hills that Kipling reported, the more
ornate tales of Notting Hill did Chesterton dream.

Such was the general atmosphere of disillusionment and
disappointment in political matters during the reign.   " The
larger hopes and dreams of the early Victorian times have
vanished, never, at least in the immediate future, to return " ;
thus C. F. G. Masterman ; and Dicey in his *Law and Opinion
in England* (1905) plotted the graph of the decline and fall
of the Victorian verities, and the supersession of Benthamite
individualism—that simple faith for the Forsyte blood—
by a new collectivism which he regarded with undisguised
misgiving.   Yet the change that he noted was an empirical
one, for the social philosophy that was to guide its continuance
had not yet emerged.   " Nothing is more necessary," wrote
Masterman in the *Speaker* six months after the queen had
died, " than the clear formulation of the lines along which
social reconstruction must proceed. . . . This clear definite
system is still to seek.   The theorists who could even at
this time definitely establish the foundation of some constructive system around which could gather the scattered
and discouraged forces of progress would indeed deserve
well of this generation."

II

The working policy of nineteenth century Liberalism in
England had been the essentially negative one of uprooting
privilege.   The first phase of its application entailed the
(logically, if not politically) simple process of eliminating
much of the past : an undertaking which occupied most of

English domestic politics from 1832 to 1886. Those years witnessed a comprehensive application of John Pym's saying : " Whoso taketh away the weights from the motions is as one that addeth wings." But there is an obvious limit to such a process, and the limit of a process is the testing time of a creed. Liberalism as a political creed had been forged at a time when distrust of the predominant aristocracy meant distrust of the state, and the early Liberals (as Hobhouse explained in *Democracy and Reaction*) were apt to confuse the two elements. In consequence the creed had become negative in a double sense ; both as to the immediate *end* to be achieved and as to the *function* of the state which Liberalism envisaged. It thus tended to harden into a negative dogma bounded by an act of faith—for there was always the tacit assumption that " the invisible hand " would direct beneficiently the free play of competing self-interest. But were there any positive elements in the creed which had been left undeveloped ? That was the main ideological problem agitating the minds of Liberals from the retirement of Gladstone to the 1906 election. Certainly of Gladstone himself J. A. Hobson's remarks were true, that " constructive legislation coping with pauperism, sweating, unemployment, old age destitution, or engaging the state in constructive work for the development of the productive sources of our land and labour, lay outside his conception of practical or even legitimate politics ".

Nevertheless, force of political circumstances and urgency of social problems had compelled even an individualistic age to adopt with increasing frequency collectivist measures. Dicey in 1905 analysed the tendency and shook his head over the inevitable while trying to explain it. He noted how the emotional core had vanished from the " peace and retrenchment " formula, " significant of a very profound revolution in politics itself." He pointed out how the growth of Imperialism had discredited the old *laissez-faire* colonial policy. He commented on the hesitancy of the more recent works of orthodox political economy. But he did not develop, as M. Elie Halévy has done, what is just as important as these forces, the fact namely that at the heart of Benthamite Liberalism lay an unresolved contradiction ; and it was this contradiction which the Edwardian era made plain beyond a doubt both in its domestic politics and in its political theory. The contradiction lay between the two theorems of Benthamite political philosophy ; between the psychological fact of the pursuit of happiness by the individual, and the normative principle that it was the duty of the government to secure " the greatest happiness of the greatest number ". It was the conflict between the " natural " and " artificial " identification of interests which had already been manifest in the eighteen-thirties and forties in the disputes over factory inspectors and the early administrative bureaucracies. Yet it was a problem which would not become acute until the primary Liberal programme of negation was executed. That work had been well-nigh completed by 1886, and since then the Liberals had not been in effective power. What creed should guide the new generation ? What principles should determine the degree of state activity if the greatest-happiness theorem were to be taken seriously as the social policy of a government ? The mass of new social data had revealed the futility and meaninglessness of the merely abstract idea of " liberty " when applied to that alarmingly high percentage of the community living in primary and secondary poverty. If " equality of opportunity " was to mean anything for them it must mean something more than mere absence of restraint, it must be translated from political into social and economic terms. Might that not mean an approach to a " planned society " ? That to many seemed a fearful prospect. And Bernard Shaw was meanwhile asking what " equality of opportunity " mean* if it did not signify equality of opportunity from birth. Liberals were thus divided in their own ranks. The situation was, so to speak, symbolized by the *Tribune* episode in L. T. Hobhouse's career; for the political editor of that journal in his *Democracy and Reaction* had expounded his view that " public-spirited Liberalism and a rational Collectivism " might eventually be found to coincide, whereas, the founder and proprietor of the paper in a formal declaration of principles submitted to Hobhouse declared for " a rigid adherence to the *laissez-faire* Individualism of the old Manchester School, qualified by taxation of land values ".[1]

But Liberal thought was not only divided against itself; it was also attacked from without by those who asserted that the whole of its principles belonged to a creed outworn; that it was based on a mechanical philosophy taken over from the eighteenth century; and that the implications of Darwinism necessitated a radical restatement of social philosophy. " Physical science is already at war with some metaphysical ideas which have taken refuge in politics," said *The Times* in 1905; " the man of science and the politician are likely to fall out often in the future. The teaching of Darwin and the conception and analogies derived from physical science as to the interaction of forces have been destructive of the stiff, self-sufficient individualism of 1830 ". The phrase " survival of the fittest " had become increasingly popular in common speech and in journalistic utterance of late years, and was somehow held to justify either Imperialism or unrestrained competition (according to the particular preference or immediate purpose of the writer). A typical example of this kind of thinking is to be found in F. W. Headley's *Darwinism and Modern Socialism* (1910). The author was convinced that our civilization is the result of competition and " natural selection ", and he believed that the principles on which our society had been built up were essential to its further progress. If they were abolished " the life of the nation would be sapped ". The history of the human race has been the history of effort

[1] See J. A. Hobson and M. Ginsberg: *L. T. Hobhouse*, p. 44.

and of struggle, and collectivism which paralyses initiative is the philosophy of failure. So the " struggle for existence " is a stern but kindly taskmaster, coercing us into vigour and happiness. Our only political duty would be so to reform the existing system as to enable competitive individualism to function more freely. In spite of its jargon, however, there is really nothing " biological " whatever about such theories. They merely represent a Darwinian gloss put upon the crude philosophy of the 1834 Poor Law.

Far more important was the line of thought in that little book so frequently quoted, *National Life from the Standpoint of Science* (1901) in which Professor Karl Pearson provided Imperialism with a " scientific " creed. Reacting with violence against the dualism of Huxley and Wallace which separated the ethical progress of the human race from the general cosmic progress and which endowed man with capacities and laws of action different in kind from those which obtain in the rest of the animal kingdom, Professor Pearson passed to the equally dogmatic assertion that the laws of the lower forms of physical struggle and selection are sufficient for all purposes of sociology. He admitted that national or racial efficiency necessitated suspension of the internecine struggle (to some extent) within the racial or national group, but as between groups the crude struggle must be maintained. " History shows me one way and one way only, in which a high state of civilization has been produced, namely, the struggle of race with race, and the survival of the physically and mentally fitter race " (p. 109). In this way is the vigorous race " kept up to a high pitch of external efficiency by contest ". This, says Karl Pearson, is " the natural history view of mankind " (p. 44). The answer to arguments such as Headley's and Pearson's would somehow have to be included in any new philosophy of social progress, and if fell to the lot of L. T. Hobhouse to retell " the natural history view of mankind ".

The first work of the reign which attempted to face the

essential problems of political theory sketched above was
Mr. Herbert Samuel's *Liberalism : an attempt to state the
Principles and Proposals of Contemporary Liberalism in
England* (1902). Mr. Samuel is there found definitely
developing the greatest-happiness principle with a fairly
shrewd awareness of what its implications may eventually
be. It is the duty of the state, he wrote, " to secure to all its
members, and all others whom it can influence, the fullest
possible opportunity to lead the best life " ; and Mr. Asquith,
in an introduction of weighty significance which may almost
be said to strike the keynote of English domestic politics
for the coming century, endorsed the new principle. He
argued that liberty no longer adequately represents or
differentiates the purposes and methods of Liberalism.
" With the growth of experience a more matured opinion
has come to recognize that liberty (in a political sense)
is not only a negative but also a positive conception. Freedom
cannot be predicated in its true meaning either of a man or
a society merely because they are no longer under the compulsion of restraints which have the sanction of positive law.
To be really free they must be able to make the best use of
faculty, opportunity, energy, life " (p. 10). Such liberty
was to be obtained by employment to the full of the power
of the state, and the intention of Mr. Samuel's book was to
analyse the immediate programme of state action required
by these principles. *The Times* complained that it was
difficult to mark off such principles from avowed Socialism.
If this is to be the guiding philosophy of the new Liberalism,
it prophesied, Liberals will be logically forced into a position
whence they cannot recede, and whence they " may be driven
into alliance with Socialistic movements of an alarming
kind ". Mr. Samuel's conclusions, nevertheless, did not
receive anything like the unanimous concurrence of his
fellow Liberals. There were some, such as Mr. H. J.
Massingham, who considered the book written from Doubting
Castle inasmuch as the author appeared to be far too equivocal

in the application of his theories. They stood for a much greater degree of state intervention than he seemed willing to admit.

It was Mr. L. T. Hobhouse and Mr. J. A. Hobson more than any other two thinkers who were chiefly responsible for formulating the theory of the new Liberalism. Their influence is clearly discernible in innumerable articles and reviews of the period apart from the direct effects of their own writings. The paralytic condition of English Liberalism in the 'nineties, said the *Nation* at the end of the reign, was due to lack of constructive Liberal thinkers as much as to any social factor. In the reconstruction that followed, it added, " Hobson's writings have contributed more than any single intellectual cause." On the other hand, an American historian of English political theory has called these pre-war years the " Asquith-Hobhouse period " on the ground that it is in Hobhouse's writings that the fullest philosophical justification was given for the new phase of collectivist legislation, and this judgment the historian of European Liberalism has entirely endorsed.[1] What Hobhouse did for Liberal philosophy Hobson did for Liberal economics and the influence of both was pervasive.

It is given to few thinkers to pursue so consistently such a consecutive line of thought as constituted Hobhouse's life work. His first trilogy reinterpreting the theory of evolution [2] laid the foundations upon which his sociological trilogy [3] was based ; and although the latter did not appear until after the War yet the underlying ideas are to be found in all Hobhouse's pre-War journalism, and the ground plan of the entire system is clearly indicated in *Democracy and Reaction* (1904). That book is one of the great essays in

[1] *Guido de Ruggiero : History of European Liberalism*, p. 155.

[2] *Mind in Evolution* (1901), *Morals in Evolution* (1906), *Development and Purpose* (1913).

[3] *The Rational Good* (1921), *Elements of Social Justice* (1921), *Social Development* (1924).

the history of English Liberalism and has been made the subject of one of Lord Morley's delightful studies.[1] It is a résumé of the current emotional and intellectual trend, and it judges that trend in no mere partisan spirit but in terms of first principles which will long give the book significance to future historians of English public opinion. In it are to be found the essential ideas of the author's social philosophy and his political deductions from them. There is his basic assumption that public affairs must be interpreted from the standpoint of moral and social evolution. There is found the gist of his reply to Huxley's exposition (in *Evolution and Ethics*) of the inherent contradiction in the evolutionary process between the intentions of man and the intention of nature : a false antithesis which Hobhouse avoided by that conception of the evolution and expansion of human purpose which he subsequently elaborated in *Morals in Evolution*. He was thus enabled to redefine the plan of reason in social life, not in terms of an absolute Godwinian faculty but in terms of correlation and adjustment. From such theorems he drew his political deductions : that the theory of evolution does not justify quietism or *laissez-faire :* that the ideas of " liberty " and " rights " are relative and expanding principles ; and that, therefore, there is ample justification for interpreting democracy in social and economic terms as well as in terms of the ballot box.

In Hobhouse's view " a wave of reaction has spread over the civilized world and invaded one department after another of thought and action " during the previous twenty years. Politically, he, like Dicey, saw the reaction as a movement away from a homogeneous Cobdenite Liberalism. But this was only the expression of " a far-reaching change in the temper of the time which is by no means peculiar to our own country or to the sphere of politics ". The deeper reaction was one against humanitarianism involving the triumph of the philosophy of *Realpolitik*. At bottom it was seen

[1] *Collected Works :* Vol. XV, pp. 91–119.

to be an ethical change, an altered attitude, in part produced by, but in part producing, a pseudo-philosophy of struggle taken over uncritically from biology. Against such a philosophy Hobhouse threw the full force of his moral intensity. It seemed to him both to condone the native aggressiveness of human nature and to induce a spirit of social fatalism. Such an attitude was the very antithesis of his own, and he strove in all his writings to destroy its foundations : pragmatically, by showing its consequences, and theoretically by revealing the weakness of its assumptions and the strength of his alternative view of " orthogenic evolution ". Nor was it only in biological philosophy that Hobhouse detected the spirit of fatalism. Since " the Rhine has flowed into the Thames " Oxford idealism had " swelled the current of retrogression ". The neo-Hegelian effort to see the partial expression of a spiritual principle in every institution and belief, said Hobhouse, inevitably leads to a sapping of moral sincerity since it blurs the contrast between right and wrong and tends to " throw a gloss over stupidity and prejudice, caste and tradition ".

But there were social forces at work creating the milieu in which such ideas could flourish. To some extent the " reaction " was due to the very success with which Liberalism had done its work. A class suffering under social and political disabilities as did the middle class at the opening of the nineteenth century would obviously be more alive to the existence of injustice elsewhere. But in Edwardian England this class was no longer outside the charmed circle of privilege. Consequently in the latter part of the century there had been a powerful movement involving an enormous transfer of material interests from the reforming to the conservative ranks. In other words, a new spirit of complacency had arisen, a vast extension of suburban self-satisfaction, yielding only to the allurements of Imperialism. Hence the general metamorphosis of old Liberals into new Conservatives from 1884 onwards. And the spirit of complacency, both

Masterman and Hobhouse believed, was further accentuated by the new sensationalist Press, the extensive growth of mass interest in sport, and the dilution of the sense of personal responsibility in the vast electorates created by franchise reform.

Hobhouse was not primarily concerned with schemes of reform. His main aim was to induce a change of outlook. To some extent he believed the defects of democracy are the price we pay for liberty. But they are largely aggravated by the prevailing social and political ideas, and these can be altered by the dissemination of a new political faith. In the main, Hobhouse's hope for the immediate future seemed to rest on a belief in the rhythmic action and reaction in social life which would result in the passing of this moral depression automatically. When the clouds had lifted and the false rationalizations of fatalism had been dispelled, he believed that a convergence of Liberalism and Socialism would ensue. Those two ideas " are not conflicting but complementary " if the greatest-happiness principle be adequately analysed and applied ; and it was this for which he was pleading. Yet his whole position was antagonistic to the " philosophy of the expert " (as he called it), whether the expert be the man-on-the-spot of Imperialist apologetics or the remodelled civil servant of Fabian hopes. He stood first and last for individualism, albeit the " new individualism " which would render equality of opportunity a concrete fact instead of leaving it an empty political formula. That meant he would prefer the trial-and-error bunglings of democracy to the most efficient bureaucracy.

Apart from this book, Hobhouse's work gave a great impetus to the revival of interest in sociology. The study of sociology in this country had languished after the completion of Spencer's task. From about 1880 onwards there had been little effort towards the development of the new study. Various factors contributed to this, but perhaps the most important was the very popularity of Spencer's own work. The theory of evolution as interpreted by him seemed to imply that the will of man could not modify the working of immutable physical laws. Consequently the *laissez-faire* attitude which such an interpretation engendered had a retroactive effect upon the development of the study itself. It tended to thwart the growth of a constructive sociology since anything more than an historical survey of past development would be valueless. Two factors especially contributed to the growth of a new attitude. On the one hand was the gradual abandonment of any such fatalistic interpretation of evolution, and the restatement of the theory in terms of purposiveness ; on the other was the work in eugenics of Francis Galton and Karl Pearson which appeared to offer an obvious field for definite research. The entire collapse of the *laissez-faire* system, in addition, induced an intellectual temper congenial to the revival of a genuinely sociological interest. The foundation of the Sociological Society in 1903 was an expression of such a revival. It resulted in the production of an annual series of *Sociological Papers* until the establishment of the *Sociological Review* in 1908 with Hobhouse as editor, and thus provided a forum for the discussion of a large number of converging investigations. Meanwhile, the same spirit of reconsideration which was permeating the wider field of social theory was penetrating no less significantly the particular domain of economics.

III

Classical political economy, like the classical theory of political Liberalism, had begun as a protest, in this case, against vestigial Mercantilism. Consequently, here also the tendency had been to state it in negative rather than positive terms. Moreover (in accordance with the eighteenth-century philosophy on which it was based) the justification of *laissez-faire* had been sought in the attempt to discover and lay bare fixed and immutable laws underlying economic behaviour, on the analogy of the laws of the physical sciences. The idea of a constructive modification of the economic

system was thus essentially alien to a system conceived
in terms of impersonal forces automatically tending towards
a state of equilibrium. For the first three-quarters of the
nineteenth century such conceptions had dominated most
English economic thought, for the doctrine which had begun
—as in the case of Adam Smith—as a protest against the
existing economic system had in its turn become an orthodoxy.
Moreover, the *corpus* of doctrine that resulted had been
translated into practical precepts for the guidance of law-
givers, precepts which always derived their cogency of
command from the fact that they embodied fixed " laws "
which could be contravened only at the peril of the community
with resultant decrease in the production of goods. But
even this code of certainties seemed to disintegrate in the
latter part of the century. During the 'seventies and 'eighties
several trends of theoretical and practical forces cast doubt
upon the clear-cut assertions and negations of economic
certainty. Even the acknowledged leaders of economic
thought were not unanimous, for Mill had dropped the
wages fund theory, and Jevons had turned the simplicities
of the old theory of value inside out. More productive of
doubt even than lack of unanimity, however, were the
disturbing apologetics of such writers as Cairns who stressed
what we should now call the " fictional " nature of the
constructions of economics. Such a line of argument cast
a cold doubt upon the precepts formerly proclaimed so
unhesitatingly in the generation of McCulloch and Senior.
Yet subtler disrupting forces were at work. The theory of
evolution and the increasing emphasis on biology provoked
scepticism regarding a system of natural laws begotten of
a rationalist metaphysic and an analogy from mechanics.
And the various attacks of the Victorian ethical prophets
had somewhat discredited the " economic man ". But perhaps
chief of all the factors undermining the old certitudes was
the increasing possibility of making something like a pragmatic
criticism.   Historical research was teaching the relativity

of economic and political institutions and hence of the
" laws " which governed them ; the successful application
of collectivism during the century belied the confidently
ominous predictions that invariably preceded them ; the
increasing concentration of economic power and the growth
of trade unions destroyed the first principles of individualistic
assumption ; above all, foreign experiments—particularly
Germany's protective and social reform policy—not only
cast doubt upon liberal economics but threatened the very
supremacy of England which those economics had
rationalized.

For all these reasons, classical economics, like classical
political theory, seemed to be disintegrating in the last twenty-
five years, or so, of the nineteenth century. Marshall largely
rehabilitated its reputation in 1890 and his influence is still
very much with us ; but even he could not restore it to the
unequivocal position it had previously enjoyed, nor was his
vast erudition conducive to dogmatic precepts of the old
kind. After 1880, a recent economist has remarked,
economics tended to become an " academic diversion chiefly
concerned with the subtle elaboration of consciously hypothetical systems of theory " ; a diversion, furthermore,
conducted in terms of the old assumptions of competitive
individualism at the very time when collectivist " exceptions "
to such individualism were increasing. It would be possible
to make quite an extensive anthology of regret from the
columns of the *Times* and the *Times Literary Supplement*
regarding the lost reputation and lost certitudes of Edwardian
economists. It is a continuous theme. The *Supplement*
complains, for instance, in a review of Dicey's *Law and
Public Opinion* that the author has " not taken sufficient
note of the altered position, the diminished authority, of
political economy. Collectivism has flourished from no
cause more than the disintegration—some would say the
discredit—of the body of classical economic doctrines ".
Elsewhere the situation was more fully stated. Of six books

on political economy under discussion it said : " in all of them we miss the confidence once characteristic of the literature of the subject in well-known solutions of old problems. Contemptuous treatment of objections to the reasoning of the classical economists is rare. Conclusions are not so sharp and pointed as they once were. What was dismissed as " friction " or sentiment or accident is spoken of with respect, and as an element well worth considering. The classical divisions of the subject are no longer rigidly observed. Each writer is a law unto himself. A sounder psychology, a larger knowledge of human nature and history is evident. . . The reign of authority in political economy, one would say from these books,[1] is over."

Thus, as has sometimes been pointed out, a strange cleavage was produced between academic economist and practical reformer. The former pushed his analysis of " long run tendencies " and of " the normal case " to ever greater degrees of refinement, while the social reformer—finding little guidance from such analyses—tended to ignore economics altogether. It was the work of Hobson to try to resolve this antithesis for Edwardian England, and his starting point—like that of Hobhouse and Graham Wallas— was the desire to account for the disappointing results of democracy. He was prompted, he has written, by " a failure to find either in the orthodox English treatment of Mill and Marshall or in the radical doctrines of Marx, Henry George, etc. . . . any intellectually satis- factory account of the inequality and economic oppression which I saw everywhere around me ".[2] His *Economics of Distribution* (1900) began the work which *The Social Problem* (1901), *The Industrial System*, (1909) and *The Crisis of Liberalism* (1909) continued. It is impossible in an essay such as this to do anything like justice to the acuteness

[1] Including works by S. J. Chapman, P. Ashley, A. W. Flux, and W. Cunningham.

[2] Letter cited in P. T. Homan : *Contemporary Economic Thought*, p. 293.

of Hobson's criticism, or to the extensive influence of his writing. One can but note how the major tendencies of his prolific work fitted into the general pattern of the intellectual movements of the reign.

Hobson's writings are as practical in intention as those of Adam Smith. He pleads for the creation of a science of human welfare which shall provide the guiding principles of an " art of social progress ". Such a science must be in the midst of society " in such a way that leaders of public opinion may be deeply and systematically informed by it, so that sound information and sound modes of thinking may by many channels percolate into the general mind ". Only with the possession of such a science can a community really direct its own life by conscious planning and by the elimination of waste. Hobson, therefore, wants to see general agreement upon a standard of social utility so as to direct production and distribution towards a rational end in order to produce the maximum of surplusage for the enjoyment of the community. " The history of progress is the record of a gradual diminution of waste." So his own writings are dedicated to the task of presenting the facts of social life synoptically, the better to be able to suggest lines of social progress. Since " the same facts are ethical and economic " there can be no divorce between the two aspects ; they must both be fused in the principle of social utility. Hobson's formulation of the problem confronting economists puts the matter in a nutshell and reveals the almost complete antithesis between his own approach and that of the classical school :

Given a number of human beings with a certain development of physical and mental faculties and of social institutions, in command of given natural resources, how can they best utilize those powers for the attainment of the most complete satisfaction ?

This is the beginning of a " pragmatic revolt " in economics. Not the search for underlying laws, which are

all the while " there " and have to be " discovered ", was
Hobson's aim, but a constructive modification of theory and
practice alike in order to provide a " science and art of social
progress ". It was natural, therefore, that the bulk of his
earlier work should have been directed to the analysis of
the existing distribution of wealth, to revealing the glaring
economic evils which call for remedy, and to showing how
these evils mainly arise out of the struggle over the " surplus "
which the social system automatically produces.

In *The Industrial System*, perhaps his most influential
work, Hobson gave a comprehensive picture of the whole
productive system and developed in greater detail his basic
theses. He explained how industry creates a product larger
than is needed for the mere cost of maintenance of the system,
how this surplus is taken by the owners of the factors of
production in accordance with the economic " pull " each
can exercise, and how it thence passes in fragments to the
owners of scarce factors of production. " This unproductive
surplus is the principle source not merely of waste but of
economic malady." The connection between surplus and
malady was convincingly drawn and it was shown that the
surplus represents a failure of the competitive system to
compete. Hence, the surplus is the only taxable body.
It should be resumed and redistributed by the state. Clearly
Hobson's voice is the voice of the new collectivism about
which Dicey appeared to be so apprehensive. Few other
writers have so stressed the organic interdependence of
all economic processes, or so luminously set forth the
dependence of economic values upon the more comprehensive
interests of mankind. In *The Crisis of Liberalism* Hobson
made detailed and specific applications of his theory to
current problems and wrote an ampler comment on Green's
text that the function of the state is to supply the condition
of freedom and that true freedom lies in the expression of
the " social personality ". Once again the contrast between
laissez-faire and the " new Liberalism " was fully brought

out, and the economic implication of " equality of opportunity " concretely developed. Poverty, the sweating system,
old-age destitution, are evils of the existing maldistribution
of the surplus which equalizing of opportunity must seek
to abolish. The facing of these " new issues of democracy "
is the immediate task of Liberalism. Unless English Liberalism
grasps this last chance to express its traditional principles
in these positive forms, said Hobson, " it is doomed to the
same sort of impotence as has already befallen Liberalism
in most of the continental countries."

Almost simultaneously with the appearance of Hobson's
study was published a 400-page volume of Mr. Winston
Churchill's speeches under the title *Liberalism and the
Social Problem*. In that book this cardinal *motif* of the decade
is again clearly revealed—the attempt to restate Liberalism
in positive terms, and it is surprising to see to-day how clearly
the ideas therein expressed were converging upon those of
Hobson's book. A distinguished American scholar and
critic characterized the two books thus : " Mr. Hobson
has set out on the road to Socialism and does not seem to
care whether he arrives or not. Mr. Churchill follows at a
little distance, protesting all the while that he is going in
the other direction." A single quotation will suffice to show
both the similarity of outlook between the two books and
the line of thought being pursued by a distinguished member
of the Cabinet :

The whole tendency of civilization is toward the multiplication
of the collective functions of society. The ever growing complications of civilization create for us new services which have to be
undertaken by the state and create for us an expansion of existing
services. There is a growing feeling, which I entirely share, against
allowing those services which are in the nature of monopolies
to pass into private hands. There is a pretty steady determination
. . . to intercept all future unearned increment which may arise
from the increase in the speculative value of land. There will
be an ever widening area of municipal enterprise. I go further,
I should like to see the State embark on various novel and
adventurous experiments . . . I am of opinion that the state

R

should increasingly assume the position of the reserve employer
of labour. I am very sorry we have not got the railways of the
country in our hands . . . and we are all agreed, everyone in
this hall who belongs to the progressive party, that the state
must increasingly and earnestly concern itself with the care of
the sick and the aged and above all of the children. I look
forward to the universal establishment of minimum standards of
life and labour." (Churchill : *Liberalism and the Social Problem*,
p. 80.)

No quotation could illustrate more vividly the change that
had come over Liberalism since the days of Cobden, or the
contrast that existed between the " legitimate politics "
of Gladstone and those of Mr. Asquith.

Even philosophical idealism could be made to fit into
the newer doctrine of collectivism, in spite of L. T.
Hobhouse's criticism. Indeed, Dr. G. P. Gooch had already
taken him to task for his comments on neo-Hegelianism on
the ground that exponents of that particular philosophy
had been as conspicuous as others in the causes of social
reform and anti-Imperialism which Hobhouse espoused.
Professor (afterwards Sir Henry) Jones illustrated their
argument in his *Working Faith of the Social Reformer* (1909).
Starting from the position of Bosanquet that the nature of
the individual is through and through social, and that " there
is no element of his individuality which he does not owe
to the social world within and upon which alone his rational
nature can be sustained " (p. 278), he went on to show that
the converse of this was true also. If the individual is
essentially social, society also is real only in the individuals
composing it ; so whatever thwarts individual development
undermines the foundations of society. Thus the conclusion
is drawn that " the welfare of society depends on providing
for the individual the means for the most vigorous growth
of an independent personality—means which include, amongst
other things, full rights of private property and full scope
for private enterprise ". These " rights ", however, are
socially determined and recognized and in no sense preclude

increasing socialization of economic services. " Owing to the higher organization and the enlarged functions of the modern state, the individual is a much more powerful agent than the member of a crude community." In other words, owing to the system of institutions which the state comprises and sustains, " he can conceive and carry out purposes utterly beyond the reaches of the latter . . . The modern state is a rich treasury of resources upon which he can draw and its organization constitutes a most powerful machinery on which he can lay his hands. It supplies him with the means of a larger life, and extends and deepens the significance of his individuality " (p. 144). So Jones comes to a position which, although (one may say) almost inevitable for an idealist in a changing world, was in practice very like that of Hobhouse in the last chapter of *Democracy and Reaction* : that " individualism and Socialism are one-sided representa-tions of a fuller truth ". Only the moral consequences for the individual determine the limits of state action. This was not meant to imply that state interference was always desirable. It was rather meant as a protest against fixing the limits of state control by an *a priori* individualism of the old type. Almost exactly the same position was adopted by Professor J. H. Muirhead in *The Service of the State* (1908), which developed even more cogently along these lines the teaching of T. H. Green. Its ambiguity for practical application certainly represented the bewildered hesitancy of many Liberals. And the *Times* asked : " Does it leave any part of human sentiment safe from the State's intrusion ? What measures does it not justify ? "

IV

The chief contribution of Edwardian England to social theory—at any rate in the sense of making a sharp cleavage with past trains of thought—is to be found in the develop-

ment of a genuine social psychology. Comment has been
made earlier upon the prevailing sense of the inadequacy
of certain psychological assumptions derived ultimately
from the philosophical Radicals, and upon a growing empirical
awareness of the problem of the irrational element in social
life. Just as political individualism and economic orthodoxy
revealed in the late nineteenth century their need for
drastic revision and reconsiderations, so did the intellectualistic association psychology—which had been intimately
related to philosophical radicalism—fall into disrepute at
about the same time. The rapid development of biology
and physiology affected psychology even more obviously
than the other traditions so that the need for restatement
became patent. In some respects James Ward stands in
the same relation to traditional psychology as Marshall
does to traditional economics, and, like Marshall, Ward
enjoyed (in England at least) an almost unanimous academic
approval. The parallel may be carried further, for just as
Hobson and the reformers expressed a revolt against Marshall
and neo-classicism from purely practical intentions, so did
Graham Wallas and William MacDougall in certain respects
represent a revolt against Ward for equally practical purposes,
and both movements are related to the spread of the
" pragmatic revolt " in contemporary philosophy.

Before 1908, the relation of psychology to social theory
was a fortuitous one. Hitherto no attempt had been made to
render psychology of use to the social sciences. Each had
pursued its own path unrelated to the other. Scientific
psychology was primarily concerned with the problems of
intellectual capacities, of habit, and of the physiological
accompaniments of mental activity. The problem of motivation was left (at least since the days of Dugald Stewart)
practically untouched. The various social theorists and
economists had meanwhile improvised their own psychologies
with sundry unfortunate results. But there was little that
academic psychology could have offered them, even had they

sought it out, for their primary interests centred on those problems of the motivation of human conduct which psychology had ignored. Bagehot had sensed something of the nature of the problem in *Physics and Politics* (1869) ; he had been aware of the complexity of psychological factors involved in such problems as the nature of political obligation as well as of the unconscious and non-rational processes involved in social thinking and belief, social decisions and habit. He had, moreover, stressed the fact that the reasoning capacity appropriate to the " age of discussion " was super-imposed upon surging psychic energies derived from a remote human past. But he had not developed the theme, and nobody else did so until the Edwardian epoch. An occasional study had appeared (particularly under the influence of Tarde) attempting to analyse the factors involved in the formation of public opinion. Of these, one of the most penetrating is Hobson's *Psychology of Jingoism* (1901) which attempted to do in a small way for the Boer War what Walter Lippman's *Public Opinion* and *The Phantom Public* have done in our own day. Even that, however, was rather in the nature of an acute observer's analysis of the conditions generating " sensationalism " than a contribution to a science of social psychology.

The study of human motivation grew out of the development of comparative psychology and the study of " instincts ". The work of Charles Darwin, G. J. Romanes, Lloyd Morgan, and E. L. Thorndike had resulted in the accumulation of a large body of knowledge on the subject of instinctive and animal behaviour and had profoundly modified the old psychological conceptions. Hobhouse, in his *Mind in Evolution* (1902) added to this the fruits of his own research, and first attempted to present a picture of the linear sequence of mental evolution. It could not then be long before the implications of this new learning for social studies began to be drawn. It is particularly interesting, therefore, to find Professor James Sully hovering on the verge of those implications in a review of Hobhouse's book. His comments represent what Graham Wallas used to call " the threshold of illumination " of a new idea :

> One good result illustrated alike in the reasonings of Mr. Thorndike and Mr. Hobhouse which the desire to probe the nature of animal intelligence has brought about is a certain disillusionment with respect to the nature of much of our own mental activity. Human psychology has suffered sadly from the circumstance that logicians, coming before psychologists, set the fashion of speaking of all mental processes of a particular kind as conforming to the logically perfect type of the kind. Thus we are supposed to think ordinarily in the set formal way in which the logician finds it convenient for his special purposes to conceive of the process. Similarly we are supposed in every action . . . to go through the formal procedure of deliberately choosing ends and means . . . It might be well now to try recognizing that much of what we do even when we learn new things is below the level of reasoning out, and may accomplish itself without the intervention of a single recognizable idea.

It was precisely this investigation of those processes and forces " below the level of reasoning " that William MacDougall and Graham Wallas undertook, and both of these writers adopted as their starting point the " certain disillusionment " occasioned by rationalistic assumptions.

Looking back from the nineteen-thirties we can see that two new principles were necessary to fertilize the principles of academic psychology. The first of these was the conception of mental energy derived from an interpretation of mind as dynamic and functional, and consequently leading to a precise formulation of the notion of instinct. It had been increasingly apparent as the older associationism had been subjected to criticism, that no grouping of " ideas " could ever have compelling force, any more than the various capacities of mind could be brought into play without some need or urge requiring expression or fulfilment. And the second principle was associated with this : the conception of inner stress and conflict which would lead to the individual being thought of not in terms of successive urges but as the resultant of conflicting trends within the total psyche. The formulation and application of these two principles would involve a reorientation of the social sciences. It would mean the substitution of a dynamic for a static conception of human nature ; the view of man as an instinct-driven animal instead of man as an automatic machine of rational calculation. In place of the economic man of Ricardo's teaching and the political man of James Mill's, it would put the human being in the whole of his complicated texture. This revolution in outlook was brought about mainly as the result of two books which appeared, within a few weeks of each other, in 1908 : MacDougall's *Social Psychology* and Graham Wallas's *Human Nature in Politics*. Each stressed both the principles mentioned above, but the emphasis of MacDougall was rather on the first and that of Graham Wallas on the second.

MacDougall's book is a comprehensive effort to provide a non-introspective and scientific explanation of human motivation. It is at one and the same time a protest against the ready-made psychologies of all social theorists from Bentham onwards, and a revolt against the tendency of academic psychology towards a one-sided intellectualism. The doctrine that instincts are the original springs of human activity is fully and vigorously expounded ; the emotional and conational accompaniments of the eleven listed instincts are discussed, and an explanation is given of the way in which the primitive instincts undergo modification through learning and experience so that they become integrated into the complex attitudes and sentiments determining adult conduct. It is thus shown that social behaviour is not based upon either rational calculation or upon any hypothetical " social instinct " (such as eighteenth century thinkers had sought in their effort to refute Hobbes), but is mainly determined by the complex interplay of sentiments.

The influence of MacDougall's book has been very great. It is doubtful if any single book on psychology has sold in

England as extensively as *Social Psychology*. It was received
at the time with remarkable enthusiasm and the application
of its principles to education, ethics, and sociology both in
England and America provoked wide discussion. But
MacDougall himself did not make any application of his own
teaching to social theory until after the War. The absence
of such application in *Social Psychology* gave rise to Professor
Ernest Barker's oft-quoted criticism that MacDougall had
provided " a full account of the genesis of instincts that
act *in* society " without showing " how they issue *into*
society ". It was Graham Wallas who first saw the consequences for political philosophy of the newer anti-
intellectualistic psychology, yet curiously enough his own
book had appeared some two months before MacDougall's
and was thus an entirely independent expression of the
same movement of thought. The logical relationship between
the two books is all the more striking since almost literally
Graham Wallas began where MacDougall ended. *Social
Psychology* had ended thus :

> Enough has perhaps been said to convince the reader that
> the life of societies is not merely the sum of the activities of
> individuals moved by enlightened self-interest, or by intellectual
> desire for pleasure and aversion from pain ; and to show him
> that the springs of all the complex activities that make up the
> life of societies must be sought in the instincts and in the other
> primary tendencies that are common to all men, and are deeply
> rooted in the remote ancestry of the race. (p. 351.)

and Graham Wallas's first chapter opens with a final and
devastating analysis of the psychology of utilitarianism and
a survey of " impulse and instinct in politics ".

Human Nature in Politics was the most important book
directly relating to political theory which appeared in the
reign, and marked the beginning of a new phase of social
studies. Graham Wallas's own political experiences had
given him a pungent sense of reality in the political world
which he felt was entirely lacking in the texts of political

theory. His aim was to interpret these realities in the light of recent psychology and thus to shift the whole emphasis of political investigation from a consideration of the form and structure of government to a study of political motivation. He was as perturbed as the other thinkers of his generation at the way in which the irruption of irrational forces into political life had falsified early prognostications regarding democracy. Particularly was he disturbed by the failure of compulsory education to provide intelligent voters, and by the ease with which voting could be manipulated by innumerable varieties of public and private interests. Yet his whole personality revolted against cynical resignation. His book, therefore, was directed towards asking whether the destiny of democracy must necessarily be determined by the interested exploitation of the irrational electorate and what kinds of modification in organization would be necessary to avert such a calamity. His was in no sense a merely academic treatise for he deprecated any severing of theory and practice and definitely wanted to put the latest developments of psychology at the service of practical politics. Like Hobhouse, he not only had full realization of what the acceptance of the evolutionary principle involves for social life, but he also believed that social progress is assured only in so far as we consciously aim at improving our skill in the manipulation of the cruder legacy of nature. " Ours are not economic but psychological difficulties."

Human Nature in Politics presents with a wealth of concrete illustration from the author's experience a lucid analysis of the chief motives of human social activity : instinct, sentiment and habit. Long before the conception of the " unconscious mind " was popular current coin, Graham Wallas had stressed the nature of the unconscious forces determining human life, making full use of the work not only of William James but of both Ribot (*Psychology of the Emotions*) and Bergson. His central thesis was that human nature changes far more slowly than does the human environment, and thus that man's present psychic equipment (except as controlled by the social environment and guided by language) is essentially similar to a barbarian's. In the light of such an attitude he criticized various texts of democracy. He showed the worthless nature of their excessive generalizations and excessive assumptions of ratiocination, and pointed out how even the most recent had ignored the newer science of human nature. He then analysed the processes of political reasoning, showing how the unconscious forces of personality are evoked and stimulated by both verbal and visual symbolism, and how they are canalized into habitual responses through the use of various political entities such as the party system. The principal purpose of the existing political art was shown to consist of the *empirical* exploitation of this whole complex tendency to reach opinions non-rationally through " unconscious inference fixed by habit ". What Graham Wallas pleads for is *scientific* utilization of these same processes in the interest of the whole community for he believes that reason is a flickering light which may yet blow out. Even though the rationalistic philosophy of the early democrats may be shown to be erroneous, the purpose of democracy is not necessarily wrong. It was the stressing of this fact which led reviewers of the book when it first appeared to accuse the author of a paradox, for Graham Wallas abjured any simple anti-intellectualistic conclusions in his teaching. But his viewpoint represents only that paradox with which the development of psychopathology has long since made so familiar, the fact namely that awareness of an unconscious process is itself an essential stage in the acquisition of control over the process. Graham Wallas (in this particular book) found hope and made concrete suggestions in three directions. First, he sought what may almost be called a political therapy by the diffusion of the new findings of psychology. The extension of such knowledge, he thought, would itself be a prophylactic against deliberate exploitation. Secondly, he advocated a greater extension of the quantitative method of investigation in politics to secure the elimination of that refraction of fact by personal prejudice which always occurs when a problem is not quantified. Thirdly, he suggested certain institutional reforms in order to secure the maximum of rational activity and the minimum of irrational disturbance. The intense practicality of the book is apparent in every page, for Graham Wallas saw in a continued failure adequately to manipulate the unconscious forces of life not only the possible collapse of democratic institutions, but also the danger of an international conflagration through racial and imperial jealousies.

A richly suggestive comparison might be made between the speculative methods of James Mill, Lord Bryce, and Graham Wallas. It would reveal the way in which the democratic philosophy of the early radicals had progressively approximated to a realistic position in proportion as it both modified and was modified by social development. *Human Nature in Politics* has had a vast influence on the thought of others, and has given an impetus to a new method of investigation which others on both sides of the Atlantic (particularly Walter Lippmann) have utilized.

It was in the same year (1908) that the first of Dr. William Trotter's two studies on the herd instinct appeared in the *Sociological Review*. Subsequently they were published (1915 and 1919) under the title *Instincts of the Herd in Peace and War*. Graham Wallas commended them in his preface, and they certainly constitute another striking manifestation of that general spirit of psychological realism in revolt against the older rationalism. They were really a development of Bagehot's thesis in *Physics and Politics* concerning the compulsive power of the group over the individual. But Trotter portrayed the fact with more meticulous analysis and a fuller realization of its practical consequences. Moreover, he represented a reaction against that almost unbroken tradition in social theory which assumed that the gregarious impulses had been the cause of unqualified benefit to mankind. He showed, on the contrary, that the herd instinct had wrought vast evil in the past and might yet produce disastrous consequences in the future unless it were controlled by an adequate technique. The herd instinct has certainly given the group homogeneity, but in doing so it has become the tap root of all intolerance and all conservatism. The herd abhors variations, and much of the cruelty shown in history is explicable in terms of this principle. Moreover, the herd instinct comes to be the determining factor over a large area of man's mental life since the innate desire for group approval leaves him exposed to group suggestion. It thus determines the vast bulk of his opinions—the more powerfully because the process is unconscious ; hence it comes to be a reactionary force of great potency. This unconscious compulsion, moreover, leads to an elaborate process of rationalization which itself absorbs much of man's mental energies and invades most of his disciplines of knowledge. " The process of rationalization " writes Trotter, " which has just been illustrated by some of its simpler varieties is best seen on the largest scales and in the most elaborate form in the pseudo-sciences of political economy and ethics. Both of these are occupied in deriving from eternal principles justification for masses of non-rational belief which are assumed to be permanent because they exist. Hence the notorious acrobatic feats of both in the face of any considerable variation in herd belief " (op. cit. p. 246). Similarly the instinct determines much of man's emotional life through its operation under such guises as a " sense of duty ", " conscience ", and the like. In the very pervasiveness of the instinct lies the danger, for if the bulk of man's opinions and sentiments are unconsciously determined he will remain forever at the mercy of blind forces.

Trotter's conclusion thus comes to be like that of Graham

Wallas, viz. that adequate self-knowledge will alone enable these forces to be controlled. But he is pessimistic as to such a possibility. He sees two grave dangers menacing contemporary civilization : one lies in the entrusting of the political control of a dynamic society to the sort of person who has " a decided preference for herd tradition " over all other sources of conduct. " It is this survival, so to say, of the waggoner upon the footplate of the express engine which has made the modern history of nations a series of hair-breadth escapes." The other menace comes from that increasingly large class of people who have been unable to resolve the acute mental conflict besetting everybody from adolescence onwards between the herd instinct and the other primary impulses, and who consequently remain in a state of unstable maladjustment preyed upon by the growing volume of stimuli in an increasingly complex civilization. Such a situation is ominous for the future stability of the community, and " it needs but little imagination to see that the probabilities are very great that after all man will prove but one more of nature's failures."

Speculations such as these of the psychologists are a sufficient reply (if one be needed) to that steady stream of publications by Prince Kropotkin which appeared regularly in these years. It needs a stony heart to criticize Kropotkin. In lucid language, with transparent simplicity and gentleness, and with an impregnable faith in human nature he reiterated his doctrine of anarchistic Communism. He represented a return in outlook to Hutcheson and to the Adam Smith of *Moral Sentiments* in his revival of the view that moral disposition (as he says in *Modern Science and Anarchism* (1908)) " have developed in man from the feeling of pity, through his ability to put himself in another's place". Such dispositions are generated through experience and inheritance, " and subsequently perfected by further observation of social life." It was a doctrine born of gild, commune, and small workshop, and not of factories, and the " great wen ". His political conclusions are, therefore, at least logical. He felt the difficulty of organizing these benevolent atoms of society into any system inasmuch as the social impulses were not adapted to the vast mechanism of modern economic life. Hence (as with Godwin) after the Day of Emancipation there must be a limitation of the size of groups to the smallest possible. In *Fields, Factories, and Workshops* he criticized the idea of the geographical division of labour, and claimed that with adequate utilization of science every small locality could be made self-sufficing. In *The Conquest of Bread* (1907) he traced the working out along anarchistic lines of the " social revolution ". According to the dissolving view there presented when man becomes aware of the universality of the benevolent instincts the present organization will dissolve into communistic groups in which everyone will take his place voluntarily, with no government and no powers of coercion. It will be mainly a process of " springing up " and of " shaking down ". Groups of volunteers, public kitchens, the spirit of devotion, all will " spring up ", and after a possible phase of confusion " people will shake down amicably " into a condition of " wealth and ease for all ". The emphasis throughout is upon the instinct for co-operation he vividly pictured in *Mutual Aid* (1902)— that work which so suggestively inverted the struggle-for-survival thesis. The assumption is that when the impulses now repressed by external conditions are allowed free play, the domination of the creative and sympathetic forces will ensure the " free and creative activity of the people ". Exactly the same attitude, but stated in a different idiom, is to be found in Auberon Herbert's *The Voluntaryist Creed* (1908) which reproduced with a disciple's ardent devotion, the anarchic individualism of Spencer's *Social Statics*. In that strange essay we catch the last faint strains of eighteenth century millennial rationalism echoing into the twentieth.

V

That very vital impulse of the age which revealed itself in the effort to restate Liberalism in increasingly collectivist terms also showed itself in a considerable extension of Socialist propaganda. Yet to a generation which has become accustomed to the more astringent critical realism of G. D. H. Cole and H. J. Laski the thinking of the Edwardian Socialists seems on the whole ineffective and jejune. State Socialism was still their guiding principle, for the idea of " the discredited state " did not begin to be developed until after the 1910 elections. The Fabians were still content to point to existing collectivism—municipal and other—and to say : " we mean a gradual and continuous extension of this." But the difference between such an attitude and that, for instance, of Hobson's writings was one only of degree, and not of fundamental principles. Nor do the writings of Mr. Ramsay MacDonald seem to-day the significant variations they apparently seemed to contemporaries. In *Socialism and Society* (1905) he first expounded his views of society as a spiritual organism and claimed to find in that conception a better basis than Marxism provided for a developing policy of social evolution ; and in *Socialism and Government* (1909) he used that principle to justify the final authority of the state on the ground that the state represents the general will : " the organization of a community for making its common will effective by political methods." Such a view led to no qualitatively different conclusions from those of the " new Liberals ". In both cases the emphasis was on the gradualness of the transition from individualism to collectivism ; in both cases stress was laid on the uselessness of a mere political liberty. The idea of " hindering hindrance " to personal development could be made (as the *Times* said in its review of Muirhead's book) to justify anything. The difference between Socialists of the Mac-Donald school and Liberals of the newer school lay in a temporary—perhaps merely an opportunist—difference in the explanation of " hindrances ". Both wished to avoid " the dead hand of Bureaucracy ". And was there more than a difference of degree in MacDonald's statement of his " fundamental conception " and that contained in the quotation from Churchill cited above ?

> The fundamental conception of Socialism is that, in work in which persons co-operate, there should be organization, and that, when circumstances exist which allow a person or a class to take undue advantage of another person or class, these circumstances should be the subject of the control of all collectively in the interests of all individually."

MacDonald's Socialism, said a *Literary Supplement* reviewer in 1909, " is not that of other Socialists who are in prior possession of the field," the more so as he had clearly stated that Socialism " will not suppress but strengthen individual initiative and individual effort ; and so far from preventing property in those things which personality requires for its nourishment it will in reality make it possible for the first time for every service giver to own them ". MacDonald's criticisms of those " influences inside the Socialist movement which are making for anarchism rather than for Socialism " seemed all the more reassuring.

But if it was difficult to classify Ramsay MacDonald with " those in prior possession of the field " it was quite impossible to do so with H. G. Wells. " If I disavow the Socialism of condescension " he wrote in *First and Last Things* (1908), " so also do I disown the Socialism of revolt. If Socialism is only a conflict with poverty, Socialism is nothing. But I hold that Socialism is, and must be, a battle against human stupidity and egotism and disorder, a battle fought through all the forests and jungles of the soul of man ", and in spite of temporary fluctuations (such as the Fabian Society episode) that has been his fundamental viewpoint from the writing of *Anticipations* down to the last edition of the *Open Conspiracy*. To no single writer does our generation of the last

thirty years owe a greater debt than to H. G. Wells. No man
has more nobly poured out his burning indignation at
contemporary folly ; none has more passionately denounced
the attitude of complacency and fatalism, nor so strenuously
pleaded for the vision of a planned society. No writer more
than Wells has had a vivid sense of the possibilities which
science has put into the hands of man nor so poignantly
felt the dream within the grasp. He remains the great prophet
of his age, if prophecy mean not the inspired revelation of
a disconnected future but the forecast through subtle insight
of possible achievement ; a prophet withal in whom is more
than a little of the *saeva indignatio* that burnt in Swift. Yet
he hovers, so to speak, above the battle like one of the spirits
in *The Dynasts*. He is a determining force, but not, in
the technical sense, a political theorist. He stands for the
dream of the morrow but not for the plan of to-day.

In three remarkable books he set forth his constructive
social criticism and in a fourth he approached a specific
programme : *Anticipations* (1901) (which passed through
eight editions in one year), *Mankind in the Making* (1903,)
A Modern Utopia (1905), and *New Worlds for Old* (1908).
The first is in many ways the most remarkable, and the
surprising accuracy of so many of its forecasts has long since
become a recurrent journalistic theme. It contains the germs
of all his later ideas, it develops the two guiding principles
of his fuller philosophy : the view of the future as the
resultant of our creative endeavour in the present, and the
urgency, therefore, of the need to control our social and
economic life by a synthetic plan. He saw man as hitherto
" walking in the sleep of individualized illusion ", but now
beginning to perceive " a collective synthetic purpose to
increase Power and realize Beauty ". He stated vigorously
the contemporary disappointment with Victorian democracy.
" I know of no case for the elective democratic government
of modern states that cannot be knocked to pieces in five
minutes." And he outlined the theory which has since

become popular under his later title of the *Open Conspiracy*. Throughout the world power will gradually fall into the hands of the scientifically trained experts—engineers, doctors, investigators, and similar professional specialists. The three other classes—the shareholders, middlemen, and the propertyless poor—will gradually slip into a position of dependence upon the specialists who will eventually build up the world state " inspired by the belief in a common theory of social order ". Existing democratic states will pass away in the process, suffering the retribution of their own futilities—the futilities of inefficiency, of party, of patriotism, and of international discord. The dislocation of world warfare may hasten the process of the emergence of the élite ; but even if that disaster is avoided, increasingly technical developments will gradually throw more and more power into the hands of experts. The technocrat will imperceptibly supersede the average man. In a sense the whole movement is inevitable for it is " the essential process arising out of the growth of science and mechanism, and more particularly out of the still developing new facilities of locomotion and communication which science has afforded ". This is the dream of the New Republic that has haunted Wells's mind for over thirty years ; it is the dream which— each after his own fashion—Stratton, and Remington, Clissold, and the Broxteds all have dreamed ; it is the dream that those encountered who tumbled into the fourth dimension on the Windsor Road.

In *Mankind in the Making* (1903) Wells made another approach to the same problem. " Viewing the whole social and political world as aspects of one universal evolving scheme," it endeavoured to place all social and political activities in a defined relation to that and to supply some guiding principles for those " who would wish to leave the world better than they find it ". It began as a treatise on education written around the motto : " Our success or failure with that unending stream of babies is the measure of our civilization." It turned into an exploratory discussion of ways and means of improving the quality of citizens to hasten the coming of the World State ; and it ended with a moving appeal to the young to enlist in the cause of the New Republic. In the *Modern Utopia* (1905) the possible results of implementing these schemes was pictured, and the New Republic shown in operation. It was received with almost unanimous acclamation, and will doubtless live as long as anything of the Edwardian era endures.

Whether all those whose writings we have thus briefly glanced at are to be considered as members of the Open Conspiracy only the historian in the New Republic will be able to tell. But in any case, Wells himself has written their apology in *Thought in the Modern State* :—

> For all that, according to our lights, we who write are trying to save our world, in a lack of better saviours, to change this mental tumult into an order of understanding and intention in which great things may grow.[1]

C. H. Driver.

[1] *Collected Works* : IV, p. 355.

INDEX